Superpower Struggles

Also by John Redwood

CONTROLLING PUBLIC INDUSTRIES (*with John Hatch*)
GOING FOR BROKE
OUR CURRENCY, OUR COUNTRY
POPULAR CAPITALISM
PUBLIC ENTERPRISE IN CRISIS
REASON, RIDICULE AND RELIGION
THE DEATH OF BRITAIN? The UK's Constitutional Crisis
THE GLOBAL MARKETPLACE
JUST SAY NO
STARS AND STRIFE The Coming Conflicts between the USA and the European Union
SINGING THE BLUES

Superpower Struggles

Mighty America, Faltering Europe, Rising Asia

John Redwood

First published 2005 by
PALGRAVE MACMILLAN
Houndmills, Basingstoke, Hampshire RG21 6XS and
175 Fifth Avenue, New York, N.Y. 10010
Companies and representatives throughout the world

PALGRAVE MACMILLAN is the global academic imprint of the Palgrave Macmillan division of St Martin's Press LLC and of Palgrave Macmillan Ltd.
Macmillan® is a registered trademark in the United States, United Kingdom and other countries. Palgrave is a registered trademark in the European Union and other countries.

ISBN-13: 978–1–4039–9077–8 hardback
ISBN-10: 1–4039–9077–8 hardback
ISBN-13: 978–1–4039–9078–5 paperback
ISBN-10: 1–4039–9078–6 paperback

This book is printed on paper suitable for recycling and made from fully managed and sustained forest sources.

A catalogue record for this book is available from the British Library.

A catalogue record for this book is available from the Library of Congress

10   9   8   7   6   5   4   3   2   1
14   13   12   11   10   09   08   07   06   05

Printed and bound in Great Britain by
Antony Rowe Ltd, Chippenham and Eastbourne

For Nikki

Contents

Preface

What makes a country a great power?

A great power has views on how the rest of the world should be organised. It influences the rest of the world by example, by economic action, by diplomacy and ultimately by force. To qualify as a great power a country has to combine most or all of the following features: an active foreign policy, spheres of influence, a strong military capacity, some international following for its ideas and economic system.

Everyone agrees today that the United States of America is the world's only superpower. There is less agreement about who the other big powers are and how much influence they enjoy.

The US meets everyone's idea of a what a great power should do. Friends and foes alike accept that the US has the most powerful arsenal in the world, backed up by the largest economy. The US can tax its own success sufficiently to sustain its military supremacy. Its large companies span the globe with their ideas, personnel and investments. American technology dominates in many crucial areas.

The US has friends, allies and client states in all continents. She has an active foreign policy, expressing views on how every nook and cranny of the globe should work. The American language is the world's most commonly used second language. English is also the first language of the rich and powerful Anglosphere countries, including Britain and Canada, fellow members of the G8 grouping with the US, and Australia, a continent of a country.

There have been two important challenges to US supremacy since her comprehensive military victory in Europe and Asia with the allies in the Second World War.

The first was the long and bitter struggle with the communist bloc nations led by the Soviet Union. There were times when the Soviets appeared to be winning. They were the first to send a man into space, and they built a formidable stockpile of intercontinental ballistic missiles. The communist ideology spread rapidly across the face of the globe, capturing mighty China, much of South East Asia, the whole of Eastern Europe and various territories in South America and Africa. The US military defeat in Vietnam marked an end to the US strategy of confronting communism with force and was a low point in the twentieth-century history of the superpower.

The collapse of the Soviet system in Eastern Europe in the last decade of the twentieth century was a triumph for the power of Western ideas rather than arms. The communist system failed to deliver the economic success they needed to sustain their military expenditure. It failed to deliver a reasonable standard of living to those living under its control. It failed to innovate and change, to keep up with the explosion of new technology in the US. Communism was destroyed in Europe, and changed dramatically in China, as popular protest combined with new leaders to insist on copying the best of the Western economic way.

The second challenge to the US was an economic one. The surge in successful business development in Japan after the defeat in the Second World War led some to question US supremacy in the fields of economic growth and technology. By 1989 fashionable pundits were forecasting that Japan would eclipse her larger rival and mentor, the US. Japan seemed to be far ahead in consumer electronics. She had built a strong position in automobiles, and was reaching out into chemicals, transportation and other areas.

The ink was scarcely dry on the forecasts of Japanese economic supremacy before the Japanese economy went into a dreadful decade of collapsing property prices, stock market decline and banking crisis. Japan did not broaden out her trading success to dominate in services where she dominated in consumer electronics. She did not use her new found wealth to build a large military machine, constrained by history from any such adventure. The Japanese language was not easy to export, so she worked away in English in the markets of the world. She never managed to catch up with US leadership in university research and education. Few today think that Japan, with under half the US population, can catch the US in terms of economic size and clout. There is no suggestion that Japan wishes to become a great military power, seeking to enforce her will on others through an active foreign policy backed up by force.

In 2001 I wrote a book for the new millennium entitled *Stars and Strife* (Basingstoke: Palgrave Macmillan). In it I looked at whether the European Union would emerge as a strong rival of the United States, becoming a major power in its own right. I took seriously the statements of many continental politicians that that was their intention. I concluded that European integration was going to accelerate. Politicians would fashion single foreign, commercial and other policies, and the EU would speak more often with one voice. The emerging United States of Europe would be anti-American:

The book warns the US of the coming conflicts between the EU and the US. When the EU is in charge of affairs on the continent, there are already substantial rows across the Atlantic ... Now that the EU is seeking to move into foreign policy and defence we can anticipate a similar deterioration in the relationship in these crucial areas. The European project is born out of a strong anti Americanism. It will be driven ahead and sustained by the desire to challenge US supremacy in all walks of government life. (p. 4)

I pointed out that agriculture and trade were under EU control and had spawned many rows. It seemed inevitable that as the EU moved into foreign policy that would highlight differences of view that would result in major disputes between the EU and the US. I recognised that one such flare point would be the Middle East, including Iraq and Iran. This new book takes the story forward, showing how the war against Iraq has created new rifts in the transatlantic relationship, and illustrating just how wide ranging the powers of the new European Union will be if the Constitution it has drafted, or some similar document, is now adopted. Meanwhile the old disputes on how to respond to global warming, how to treat genetically modified foods, how to subsidise or support civil aircraft manufacture and many similar issues continue to divide the EU from the US.

I worked on the assumption that the EU would not be willing to spend the vast sums of money needed to catch up with US military supremacy. I thought instead that the gap between the US and the rest in the military field would widen:

For the foreseeable future, it is highly likely that US military dominance will survive. Indeed, such is the speed of the digital revolution in the US, and such are the relative levels of defence spending, that we may witness a further increase in the lead as US technological and defence spending outstrips those of any other country or group of countries. (p. 74)

This remains true today. Germany and France are trying to build their own spy in the sky system to rival the US, but they are so far behind in surveillance and in smart weaponry that no serious analyst sees the EU becoming a major military rival of the US. NATO remains the main defensive alliance of the West, although it is now under considerable disruptive pressure from the EU as the EU tries to develop its own independent forces. The EU may have enough power to damage the defence alliance with the US that is in place, but will not have US-style power to project beyond its own continent.

I also recognised in 2001 that the US had many enemies and opponents around the world. I worried that they might not play by the rules of Western warfare as they expressed their anger and hatred of the superpower:

> However, the giant also has a vulnerable side. We are going to live in a world where more and more countries have access to basic nuclear technology and where many countries follow in the path of Iraq by developing the capability to engage in chemical and biological warfare. Chemical, biological and nuclear warfare is difficult to counter for a democracy which does not wish to place the lives of its civilian population in jeopardy ... The world has noticed that US democracy is particularly open, that its people are understandably reluctant to sacrifice any part of their luxurious lifestyle ... The biggest threat to US power in the short term is the actions of dedicated groups of terrorists, guerrilla bands and those who are prepared to use weapons that the west has banned, to blackmail and terrorise others. This is why the US has been particularly keen to launch missile or bomb attacks on any recalcitrant tyrant who looks as if he is close to making useable quantities of biological or chemical weapons, or who may be developing a nuclear capability of his own. (pp. 74–5)

When I wrote those words I did think terrorist attacks on the mainland of the United States were likely. Nothing prepared me for the horror of the first big attacks when the planes flew into prominent US buildings. This book looks at the world beyond 9/11 and the early phases of President Bush's 'War on Terror'. It shows how the strength of the superpower response to 9/11 has led to more disagreements with EU allies and to more tensions with delinquent regimes. The US has tackled two relatively easy cases, Afghanistan and Iraq. How will it proceed in the cases of Iran and North Korea? How will US policy towards Russia and China change, two countries with substantial military capacity with different perspectives on the world to that from Washington?

Superpower Struggles concludes that no new superpower will emerge in the first two decades of this century to rival the US. Russia still has the rockets, but her economy is so weak she has no chance of matching the US again. Indeed, the bigger danger is that Russia will fall into the wrong hands, becoming a source of criminal gangs and illegal trading. Russians may be involved in arming those that would harm the US, and in subverting Western economies by helping the drug trade, the slave trade in people and the organised criminal rackets that recognise no borders. The EU will tread the boards of the world's diplomatic stage, but will lack resolve and military resources to back up their postures. Japan's economy may come back into better health, but she will remain a regional power, not a global one, living ever more in China's shadow.

In *Stars and Strife* I mentioned the long-term possibility that US supremacy would eventually be challenged by one of the more populous countries of the world. In Asia, India and China both have many times the number of people in the US. When either of them reach average incomes one third the level of the US they will have larger economies. Whilst both are making good progress, in this book I conclude that China is the most likely country to emerge as a rival to the US. Her growth rates have been impressive in recent years. She is rapidly advancing in many areas of manufacturing by welcoming in foreign capital, management and ideas. In due course China will develop a military technology of her own, as she does have ambitions to influence the rest of the world. For the next decade or more China will be more influenced than influencing, as she hoovers up available technology from the West and goes along with more Western ways of doing things. In due course she will have her own ideas of how the world should be run.

In *Stars and Strife* I also wrote about the choices facing the United Kingdom. I argued that Britain had to decide how much European integration she could accept, how far she wished to go alone, and how far she wanted to be the US's best friend. I stated:

> The UK, since 1973, has been gradually losing its innocence about the nature and intentions of our European partners. A succession of decisions and treaties has now persuaded many that the European project is intent upon taking over the individual nations of Europe and welding them into a United States of Europe. Federal such a state may be. Devolved, some of the power may turn out to be. Nonetheless the clear outlines of a superstate are there for all to see ... (p. 7)

Those words were contentious then. Today they look more and more realistic, in the light of the draft Constitution laying out the many powers of the new EU. In recent months the EU has established its own Armaments Agency. It has sent its High Representative, soon to be the Foreign Minister, to intervene in the Middle East, to set out the EU's position on the tsunami disaster, and to offer an opinion on the Ukrainian elections. EU countries are wanting to do arms deals with

China, and cosying up to Russia in an effort to counterbalance the weight of the US. The UK has learnt that even before the Constitution is in force it has lost control over important features of its immigration and borders policy. In so many areas if the Opposition wants to offer an alternative policy it has to say it will need the permission of Brussels before it can do what it wishes.

In *Superpower Struggles* I show just how radical a document the EU Constitution is. I argue that the UK should not accept it, but use the opportunity created by the Constitutional question to renegotiate the relationship. The EU economies are performing badly on the continent. Forecast declines of around one fifth in the working age population of the EU 15 will combine with low growth to make the EU more and more marginal to the world economy over the next fifty years. On the EU's own figures the EU's share of world output will slump from 18% to 10% over the half century. This is likely to prove optimistic. Why should the UK lock herself more firmly into this declining part of the world, when the English language and transatlantic friendships gives us a strong position in the US, and common language and the Commonwealth links us with rising India? The Anglosphere countries are the current winners in the world economic stakes. Why turn our backs on them when they have found a successful formula?

The book begins by examining the impact of the 'War on Terror' on the US. It analyses EU moves to strengthen central control and project the EU's voice abroad before turning to China, the emerging giant. It looks at the options facing the UK, discussing the American cultural and economic influence, the type of renegotiation the UK could hope to undertake with the EU and why the US should still value the special relationship with the UK.

The US economic and cultural model will remain a beacon for many in the years ahead. People worldwide aspire to the life of Hollywood and to the freedoms of US democracy. There will continue to be opposition from rogue states, theocracies and terrorist groups, but for the time being the general move is to go the US way. The EU will not stop this tidal wave. It will merely damage itself if it resists it too strongly.

Note

The Preface reviews the main conclusions and predictions in Redwood, *Stars and Strife* (Basingstoke: Palgrave Macmillan, 2001).

1
Iraq

America – the wounded superpower

The world changed on 11 September 2001. The American colossus was badly damaged. The media rushed pictures of the billowing inferno in the Twin Towers of the World Trade Center in Manhattan and the destruction at the Pentagon in Washington around the world. The stark images of death and destruction were played and replayed endlessly, so that the whole world could see the humbling of its only superpower. People speculated on what the fourth plane would have hit if its brave passengers had not brought it down, away from people and other great buildings. The White House was still intact.

The Pentagon had a great gash in its side. The World Trade Center, the foremost symbol of US capitalism, was a pile of smouldering rubble. Americans felt personally vulnerable and collectively exposed in a very new way. They no longer lived on an island citadel safe within their shores. They were as vulnerable to terrorist attack as the rest of the world.

The immediate reaction in the aftermath of the terrorist attacks in the United States was simple. Americans asked 'Why?' Inward looking America had been cut off from the mounting anger in other parts of the world about US policy and the American way of life. Most US military planning had been based on the comfortable assumption that all America had to do was to stay years ahead in technology and firepower, to be able to beat any conventional force in the world. It came as a huge shock to the American establishment to realise that the new enemy would not play by the traditional rules of war; to see that they would attack the US on her home soil by underhand means. There would be no pitched battle, there would be no opposing army in the field that America could engage and destroy as easily as she crushed the hordes of

1

Iraqis in Kuwait. The hyperpower giant of the world had aroused hostility in dangerous foes. The opposition intended to retaliate by stealth, with terrorism, unconventional warfare, with new kinds of weapons of mass destruction.

The second reaction in the United States was revenge. What was the point, Americans asked themselves, in having the world's most formidable arsenal if they could not use it to secure a world in their image? Surely, they reasoned, it must now be possible to deploy the mighty military machine to rout out and hunt down those who wished America ill, those who intended to pursue terrorist campaigns against the US. So was born the President's 'War on Terror'. In the early days most Americans agreed with the President. The Democrats either willingly egged the President on or were cowed into submission by the strength of public feeling. It was time for the commander-in-chief to show leadership. It was time for American forces to advance in those parts of the world which were not secure for democracy and American capitalism. It was essential that the full force of American military might was deployed to throw out evil regimes and hunt down the terrorists they harboured.

It did not turn out to be as easy as some thought to redirect and channel the massive energies of American technology to the task in hand, of finding and dealing with individual terror suspects and their backers. As the new century dawned, American military hegemony had never been greater. Over the preceding two decades a growing gap had developed between what the US military could achieve in conventional warfare and what anybody else could manage. The US had seen off the mighty military challenge of the Soviet Union and its satellites by the end of the 1980s. The communist system had broken under the strain of trying to match American technology and firepower, and had shown that its third world economy was no longer buoyant enough to support the growing cost and technological sophistication of modern rockets. In the 1990s the superpower had advanced even more rapidly as the Soviet bloc fell apart, and as the Europeans looked inwards and found other ways of spending public money.

The US came to realise that the key to military supremacy in the modern world was to harness computers and communications. New systems gave American commanders a unique ability to oversee any real or potential battlefield. For the first time in military history, the dominant superpower could find out where any enemy or unfriendly nation had stationed tanks, guns, planes and other military hardware. The US 'spies in the sky', its satellites orbiting the earth, could give precise global positions for any significant forces that might be massing. In the near perfect conditions of the Gulf War to free Kuwait at the beginning of the 1990s, America's mastery of the skies and its high resolution visual spying could, in the clear and sunny conditions that prevailed, pinpoint anything on the battlefield that it wished to destroy or avoid.

Today the US can do that in far more hostile conditions, using infrared and audio as well as normal visual spectrum detection, to see where no commanders before have been able to see. They can see weapons hidden under trees, concealed by mist, war paint, rain or buildings. They can work out what is there and where it is moving.

The Americans complemented their rapid development in surveillance technology with fast development of precision weapons technology. The American military worked to their ideal of being able to see many thousands of miles away what the threat was at any particular location. Then they learnt how to deliver from an equally remote location a missile, a drone, a high-flying aircraft or some other attacking device, to release exactly the right amount of precision munitions to destroy the target.

It is not surprising that countries are very reluctant to stand up and fight the United States of America. It must be a painful and unnerving experience to know that they can see you and you cannot see them. Your planes can be blown out of the skies before you've any idea of where the attackers might be. Your tanks and men can be destroyed on the ground by commanders pressing a button many hundreds or thousands of miles away. If you seek to shelter in individual buildings the precision concrete-busting bombs can be delivered to an individual street address once the Americans know where you are.

These techniques of all-seeing intelligence allied to huge firepower may be brilliant for preventing conventional warfare, or allowing Americans to win any conventional war that they choose to enter. They are not, however, the techniques that can easily win the so-called 'War on Terror'. It is true that intelligence is vital for tackling a terrorist menace but it is a messier, more difficult kind of intelligence than the spy in the sky can provide. American technology can, with reasonable accuracy, pinpoint substantial concentrations of military hardware and troops. It is much more difficult locating individual terrorists and their homemade bomb equipment, or identifying individual hijackers before they go about their task of waylaying an aeroplane.

Gaining an inside knowledge of terrorists and their operation requires thousands of hours of surveillance of phone lines, bank accounts and movements of people. It requires eavesdropping on many private conversations. The authorities need to build up a picture of how a terrorist cell operates, who is part of it, and when it might next strike. The CIA had begun to piece together some of the biographies and details of those who struck the Twin Towers and the Pentagon but the information did not firm up sufficiently for American security forces to intercept and prevent the terrorist outrage.

The reorganisation of American intelligence services in the wake of the 9/11 tragedy will undoubtedly lead to a growing concentration on the many individual types of surveillance and information needed to build up a full picture of hostile terrorist networks and their likely course of action.

Nor does the possession of greatly superior surveillance and weaponry to anyone else in the world guarantee success in peacemaking and peacekeeping activities. The Americans in both Afghanistan and Iraq successfully won conventional wars and toppled regimes. They are discovering that it is a far more patient and difficult task to reconstruct a civil society and police a lawless country once the war is won. Here the British forces have considerable experience from their long-term work in Northern Ireland, trying to keep the peace between two warring communities, communities that have been all too ready in the past to resort to terrorist activities on both sides in pursuit of their political ends.

A great power needs great wealth and a strong political will. The Romans, the Dutch, the French, the British, were all fabulously rich by the standards of the day during their periods of global power. They harnessed their riches to project their power and usually pursued a strong foreign policy to defend their wealth and their interests. In the cases of the United Kingdom and the Netherlands, wealth depended on trade with many parts of the world, so both countries projected naval power to patrol and maintain the crucial trade routes and to keep open the arteries of commerce. The Dutch and the British tended only to settle territory which supported their trade, and were especially keen to maintain a global network of ports through their naval activities. The French sought territorial expansion on the continent, fearing their neighbours. They sought to impose a continental, mercantilist system on most of Western Europe. To do this the French supported huge armies, training and equipping them to the best modern standards.

In each of these four cases, political will and wealth allied together to create a self-perpetuating driving force for imperial success which lasted for many decades. In none of these four cases did the dominant power of the day get as far ahead technologically, compared with potential competitors, as the US has done in the last fifteen years. The British Navy at the height of British imperial power had similar guns based on the same technology to those fitted in French and Spanish ships. British naval success was based on superior tactics, better accuracy in the use of the guns, and more frequent firing.

French military ascendancy on the continent under Napoleon was not based upon using different weapons from the armies that stood against him. The French had similar swords, cannon and small arms to the rest of Western Europe. What made the French so formidable on the battlefield was a combination of strong drill, good tactics and concentration of forces.

Even the Romans, whose engineering and metalworking skills were second to none in the world of their day, did not always have a huge technical lead over the armies they confronted and usually defeated. It was again concentration of firepower, the use of Rome's riches to pay for a well-equipped and large army, and Roman military techniques that were triumphant against the better armed and organised opponents.

The American superpower is the first superpower the world has known to be able to see an enemy that cannot see it; to be able to send weapons to precise places thousands of miles away from the commander. It is the first superpower to be able to destroy enemy forces, often without engaging any troops of its own anywhere near the scene of the battle. Its technical superiority is enormous. It is now an American boast that it is becoming extremely difficult for other members of the North Atlantic Treaty Organisation (NATO) to make a useful contribution to an American-led mission, because other members of NATO are not up with America's computer surveillance and communications technology. If a potential ally cannot see what the Americans see, cannot communicate with the American forces from remote locations, and cannot be part of the American, computer-led plan of the battle, it is difficult for the ally to help.

The war in Afghanistan was short and decisive. The rule of the Taliban was toppled. World opinion could understand the reasons for American intervention, given the Taliban's role in nurturing and helping terrorists that could and did threaten the United States. The US President's decision to topple the regime of Saddam Hussein in Iraq was more contentious from the moment he first raised it in global debate. It split the United Kingdom away from the rest of the European Union, with the UK prepared to back the President whilst the rest of the Union, led by France and Germany, was hostile to the proposal.

The Anglo-British view was straightforward. The United Nations had passed many resolutions demanding compliance from Saddam Hussein. The UN knew that Saddam Hussein had possessed weapons of mass destruction, including most unpleasant chemical weapons which he had used against his own citizens in the Kurdish part of Iraq. There was a worry on the part of the Anglo-American authorities that Saddam Hussein's weapons programme was well-advanced, and that he would soon be in a position to deliver chemical and nuclear weapons over longer distances.

Armed with the UN resolution condemning Saddam Hussein and demanding compliance again from him, the Anglo-Saxon coalition claimed it had enough support to go and topple the man before he did something more damaging. They pointed to his track record as a butcher and a dictator, a man who had invaded Kuwait illegally and who used terrible methods to repress the Kurds. Others in the UN were not persuaded, wanting to give negotiation and weapons inspection a better chance. They were unsure of the moral and legal case for war.

The decision to go ahead intensified feelings on the continent of Europe that the EU needed its own distinctive, common foreign policy, backed up by its own military forces. Bush's war acted as a recruiting sergeant on the continent of Europe, and in some parts of the UK, for the proposition that the EU needed to provide a counterweight to the Americans. The EU felt it should resist US foreign policy initiatives when these entailed invading Iraq or launching other wars in the Middle East without EU approval.

These feelings were greatly intensified by the aftermath of the successful campaign to topple the Iraqi regime. After months of searching, the American and British authorities had to admit that they had found no weapons of mass destruction in place in Iraq after all. They did not know where the old stockpile of chemical weapons had gone, and could find no positive new evidence on the ground that Saddam Hussein's WMD programme had taken major steps forward in the later 1990s and at the beginning of this century. This was a blow to the allies' case and intensified the criticisms and unhappiness of all those countries in the United Nations who had been uneasy about the Anglo-American action in the first place.

Thoughtful Americans recognise that there are problems with the so-called 'War on Terror'. There are limits to the number of unpleasant, dictatorial regimes around the world that America can and should remove by military force. It is difficult establishing the evidence of which of these regimes does most to harbour terrorism. Who knows which in the future might do most to destabilise the democratic West? Even American military might has to recognise some limits to the number of countries it can defeat in battle, police and occupy at any given time. It is not the

American intention to become the new imperial master of the twenty-first century, with its armies and navies holding down large swathes of global territory. The Americans do see themselves as crusaders for democracy and the rule of law. They usually wish to get out once they have toppled the evil regime and worked with the new civilian power to stabilise the political situation.

Nor is it possible for a free and open society, like the United Kingdom or the United States, to completely protect itself against random and wicked terrorist attack. On both sides of the Atlantic, after the events of 9/11, there has been an intensification of security activity. There are people who seem to think that if enough bags are checked, if enough people have to walk through metal detectors, if enough police ring crucial buildings, if enough concrete blocks are put down on roadways close to the centres of power, then the Western establishment can sleep easy in its beds at night. This is a myopic misconception of the worst kind. For whilst every one of those moves can damage the quality of life and limit freedoms in the countries imposing these new restrictions and security activities, there is no way that such security can offer complete safety to those it is seeking to protect.

The new type of world terrorist is a suicide bomber with no fear for his or her own life. They can do a lot of damage with relatively small munitions, or they can fashion everyday items into weapons. A plane full of fuel, a lorry packed with fertiliser and homemade detonators, a van with a homemade missile launcher in the back, poison in the water supply, gases or microbes in air conditioning systems, are all ways that the new terrorist can use to wreak carnage. It is simply not possible in a free and open society to check every person, every van, and every aeroplane in sufficient detail to be absolutely sure that no one person is about to commit an act of terror.

We have seen the impracticality of more physical security solving the problem in the UK. Two of the most heavily protected buildings, Buckingham Palace and the Houses of Parliament, have been entered illegally by demonstrators despite the massive security in place.

So what then is the best way of fighting terrorism? There has to be a twin track approach. Firstly, powerful governments in the world have to use their best endeavours to tackle the underlying political problems that act as recruiting sergeants for terrorists. The British government has regularly but unsuccessfully tried to engage the American regime more fully in the Arab-Israeli process. It is the problem of Palestine above all else which fuels Arab terrorism against the West. The West has to learn to live alongside a more powerful and more united Islam, and come to understand that Islamic countries too will want their strong armies, their nuclear weapons and their place in the world.

The second strand is remodelled intelligence systems, geared to listening to and watching the terrorist networks wherever they may be. The only sure way of preventing terrorist attack is to know in advance who they are and what they might do. We need to target the few thousand terrorists worldwide, rather than the millions of innocent people who get caught up in the clumsy and wide-ranging security operations that the West now operates to tackle the terrorist problem.

The tensions and rifts in EU–US relations which had started before the end of the last century have been magnified and accelerated by the events in Iraq. All those in the EU who were hesitant or opposed to the conflict in the first place feel vindicated by the absence of weapons of mass destruction, and by the continuing worldwide hostility to American military success in the Gulf. The draft European Union Constitution greatly strengthens and speeds the progress to a common foreign policy. It will be developed and explained by a single European Minister of Foreign Affairs, and backed up by an embryo military organisation seeking re-armament and harmonised weaponry amongst the European countries.

It may be a completely unrealistic goal for the Europeans to set themselves to be a serious military rival to the United States. There is absolutely no evidence that the European peoples wish to pay substantially higher taxes to re-arm on a sufficient scale, and no evidence that European military technology is about to make a decisive leap forward to catch up with American success. However, the growing enthusiasm for a distinctive European way of seeing the world and doing things on the world's stage is obvious. This can but increase the tensions between the US, the world's only superpower, and the member states of the EU.

The UK's position in trying to straddle the Atlantic and the Channel at one and the same time is becoming more and more problematic. The Britain that claims to be America's best ally and frank friend finds herself under a government recommending a European Constitution which points in entirely the opposite direction. Mr Blair, the British Prime Minister, is hoping people will not notice that he is doing the splits as America drifts further from the continent of Europe, and as Britain is put under pressure on both sides of the Atlantic to be a good European or to be a good NATO ally.

The decisive victory of President Bush in the November 2004 presidential election showed just how far American opinion had moved away from European opinion over the intervening three years. Europeans were willing the American people to vote for Kerry. They did so not because most of them believed that Kerry was good, or even because many of them were natural born Democrats. They did so because Kerry was not Bush. They did so because Kerry flip-flopped over his support for the war and started raising doubts about it. They did so because Kerry spoke to the Europeans in more sensitive tones than they felt George Bush did. Europeans wanted to believe Kerry when he said he would make America work with her allies and listen to world opinion. They chose to turn a deaf ear to Kerry when he said he backed the war, and to Kerry when he said the 'War on Terror' would have to continue. They forgave the pictures of Kerry out duck shooting, in a desperate bid to reassure the gun lobby, and ignored Kerry's military salute when he famously reported for duty at the Democratic convention.

For all their enthusiasm and all their willing Kerry on, they could not make one jot of difference to the view of the American people, who voted convincingly in favour of George Bush having a second term. Europeans sought to explain this away. They complained that the people who turned out to vote for Bush were extremists or born-again Christians of a kind liberal Europeans reviled. They disliked Bush's success in campaigning against civil partnerships. They drew attention to the way he spoke for a rough, tough middle America that Europeans did not like, and comforted themselves in the belief that there were many civilised eastern and western seaboard Americans who really understood the European point of view and felt as they did.

Analysis of the American ballot gives the lie to much of this comfortable, liberal rhetoric. Bush got a good swing to him in liberal New York, as well as cementing his hold on the Midwest. Bush didn't just do well amongst evangelical Christians but he did well amongst whole swathes of middle America and saw his vote increase among many of the major categories of voter.

President Bush's support rose and Kerry's was insufficient because Americans do believe that America was badly damaged by 9/11, and they do believe that American power must be used to right wrongs, to settle scores and to try to create a more democratic and civilised world. Americans regard the EU as effete and unrealistic. The American administration line is that if Europe wishes to be taken seriously, it must make a serious military contribution to the 'War on Terror'. If the EU is not prepared to stand shoulder to shoulder alongside the American marines and paratroopers, if the EU is not prepared to spend enough on having the military hardware and technology to make it a serious force in the world, then why should the US take it seriously?

The Europeans, used to the graft of diplomacy and negotiation in the Middle East and Far East, see the Americans as rough and clumsy. The EU wishes to apply a brake to the American military machine. It wishes to send signals to the rest of the world that Europeans don't think as Americans do. It wishes to do deals with the regimes that support terrorists, and sometimes even with the terrorist movements themselves. To the European mind this is commonsense, it is getting along in a world of very different views and opinions. It is necessary when the Europeans do not have access to the power and technology of the Americans.

It does not look as if this growing gulf in viewpoint, military capability and aim for the world can be easily bridged. It is very likely that in the immediate years ahead, the gulf between the United States and the European Union is going to get bigger. The main question overhanging the next few years is how far will the European Union go in its drive to centralise its own power, and to project its power beyond the shores of the North Sea and the Eastern Atlantic? It is to this question we must now turn.

Notes

The war in Iraq can be followed in any reputable newspaper. Gough (2003) has some useful historical comparisons for the process of 'regime change'.

Gertz (2004) reviews the evidence for French, German and Russian arms sales to Iraq in recent years and the US response.

2
The Emergence of a New Nation: The United States of Europe

The United States of Europe is going through a painful birth. The emergence of a new, large, potentially powerful nation is going to send shock waves around the world. The attempt to bring the divergent peoples of Europe together under one government is causing strains in Europe. The reverberations will be felt far beyond the shores of the continent.

An integrated Europe acting more and more as a single state will hasten the coming conflicts between the EU and the US. Tensions for the United Kingdom, a reluctant partner in the wider European project, have often been written about. They are a continuous feature of our relationship with the continent. The rows with the United States of America are only just beginning.

The European way is a very different one from the Anglo-Saxon. In the English-speaking world there is a love of liberty, private property, free speech and limited government. In the European galaxy, there is a strong belief in bureaucratic solutions, in powerful central government from behind closed doors, management consensus and banning difficult or extreme views. The EU legislates around the Council of Ministers' table in secret. Only unelected officials, the Commissioners, can propose new laws. Extreme views are banned and thought crimes are taken very seriously.

Europeans find Anglo-American democracy too individualistic for their taste, too free form and too swashbuckling for good order. Anglo-Americans think European government is too constrained, too regulated, too secretive, to be called truly democratic.

The UK is still attempting to bridge the enormous and growing gap between the US on the one hand and the urge of the continental European powers to unite on the other. A small minority of people in Britain believe that the UK should plunge in to become one of twenty-five states of Euroland, to take our place as a group of important regions in the United States of Europe. A larger minority believe that the UK should withdraw immediately and completely from the EU and should go her own way, relying more heavily on the defence alliance with America, and using the protection of the World Trade Organisation to trade freely with the whole of the world. Some believe we should join the United States of America and other like-minded countries in a wider and more powerful North American Free Trade Agreement (NAFTA).

Many people in the debate today wish to present Britain with an ultimatum. Those who favour the European project claim integration is inevitable, whilst spending most of their time in the UK denying that the true objective of the EU is political union. They want us to get on with becoming a series of regions in the new Europe, whilst claiming we will retain our independence in such an arrangement! Some Euro-sceptics want us to leave the EU as soon as possible, without thinking carefully about what would replace it and how we could then go forward. In practice, under pressure, such people do concede that there has to be a negotiation to end the relationship. Others in the mainstream prefer the idea of a negotiation now to sort out our relationship, and to confess to our fellow Europeans that we have absolutely no intention of joining a political union with them.

Britain has a very different history from the continental countries. Britain is at peace with its past in a way that many continental countries could never be. Whilst there have been attempts by some British historians to make us feel guilty about the work of our ancestors in China or India, by highlighting some of murkier events of the colonial and great power past, by and large British people are happy that their country has fought on the side of right and liberty in many wars, and has often been victorious. We do not have to live down the shame that many French people feel regarding the events of 1940–44. Defeat and collaboration split French communities and led to huge ill will. We do not have to live in the aftermath of the Second World War, with the collective guilt that Germany feels about the Holocaust and the aggressive tyranny which that country offered the European world in the 1940s. We do not wake up every morning like Italians to wonder who might be in government today and which government ministers might be charged with corruption tomorrow.

This means that British people, rightly or wrongly, are not so willing to see their current democracy and government system snuffed out in the name of European unity. In the last couple of years a serious mood of disillusion with government in general, and EU government in particular, has also broken out amongst the British electorate. Far from persuading them to volunteer to transfer more power from an unpopular British system to the European one, it has redoubled their Euro-scepticism. Many people intuitively sense that the growing alienation of the electorate from the government owes something to the growing remoteness of decision taking in Brussels. They dislike the lack of accountability of those taking the decisions, the growing weight of regulation, the burden of new laws and additional taxes that result from having an EU level of administration and legislation on top of all the rest.

The tidal wave of opinion against more government in the UK makes it extremely difficult for the European Union. The European project proceeds by creating more government as a deliberate act of policy. The EU often decides to regulate or legislate in areas where regulations or laws are thin on the ground in the member states, for the very reason that there is less government opposition to the EU doing this than in areas where the member states have already occupied the field. As the European Union project rolls on, they become more ambitious and they annex areas of government activity that are already well farmed by member states. The general antipathy towards too many politicians, too many officials, too many rules and too much tax, is now being expressed generally against the European Union, as well as against domestic political parties.

The US and the UK have kept a special relationship over the years, working especially closely through the United Nations and through NATO since the 1939–45 world war. Whilst there are some in America who think the UN and other world bodies are becoming too intrusive, limiting the freedom of action for a democratic country like the US, in practice the UN and other such global bodies leave much more scope for free action to individual countries than the EU. If a country does not wish to join in a common military action by the UN it does not have to do so. Security Council members, like the US and the UK, have an independent veto over action. The draft European Union Constitution is designed to hasten the day when the EU has a common foreign policy position on all the major matters of the world, backed up by credible military strength, through the formation of battle groups and common armaments procurement. The wish by the EU to establish a common army, navy and air force, in addition to NATO, is a threat to the balance of power which has seen us through the post-1945 world so far.

The United Kingdom is going the US way more than the European way when it comes to tastes, lifestyle and ways of doing business. The internet is a US creation, which is dominated by English-language communication and commercial activity. Europe is struggling to catch up. It is a dot.com world and ideas, services and orders for goods can fly halfway around the world at the touch of a button. The large US corporations are dominant. The UK is an important second force in this world of global commerce, with London the host to one of the world's big three financial markets, and home for more multinational corporations than the other large European countries. Some see the European project as an attempt to create a Napoleonic, continental system designed to keep the US out. Others realise this is a hopeless task in an age of dematerialised business, where software, computing and media are such important forces for commerce and change.

Europeans see the forthcoming battle as lying between the United States and the European Union. They seek to build EU commercial champions, like Airbus, to take on mighty US corporations. They designed the euro to rival and outclass the dollar, and see a bipolar world where the EU sits down at the top table with the US to settle the future. The EU is completely unprepared for the rise of China, now sucking a large number of jobs and industrial activities out of the European continent, attracted by Chinese enterprise, low costs, and dynamism. Where the EU is in charge of affairs on the continent, there are already substantial rows across the Atlantic.

EU agricultural policy entails endless disputes between the EU and America over levels of subsidy, husbandry techniques and safety of products. These have led to a series of trade disputes and bans on each other's products. The EU is in control of trade policy for the European countries. The EU as a deliberate act of policy escalates trade disputes with America, seeking to establish its own position as an important player in trade negotiations and in the day-to-day management of relations. Now the EU is seeking, through its Constitution, to move more strongly into foreign policy and defence, we can anticipate a similar deterioration in the relationship in these crucial areas. We've had a taste of it in the European attitude towards American Middle Eastern policy in general, and the American decision to go to war in Iraq in particular. The European project is born out of a strong anti-Americanism. It will be driven ahead and sustained by the desire to challenge US supremacy in all walks of government life.

US policy makers should study the European Union Constitution carefully. It should make them hesitant about welcoming the idea of dialling one number for Europe. Far from making Washington's task easier, it will mean that on so many issues the US finds an argumentative voice on the line. A special alliance with the UK and other like-minded countries around the world is the better option for the US, allied to flexible diplomacy in coalition building around particular causes and purposes. If the UK became fully absorbed in to the EU, the separate voice for freedom and free enterprise on the eastern side of the Atlantic will be silenced. Even a superpower as strong as the United States of America needs moral and political allies that can come out and back it when world opinion is otherwise hostile. The US appreciated this very much when the Labour Prime Minister, Tony Blair, gave it full backing for the Iraqi enterprise, at a time when few others thought it a good idea. It would be a great pity if, having freed the world of so much communist tyranny by winning the battle of ideas, the Anglo-Americans now let the Europeans reassert collective vices, high taxes and over-regulation, damaging world trade and prosperity in the process.

Building a stronger NAFTA, leaving the members free to make their own decisions in a democratic way, strengthening the forces of global enterprise, makes sense for the US and the UK. It makes no sense for Britain, and little sense for America, for the UK to plunge itself into the full intricacies of economic, monetary and political union. The European Union Constitution has generated a huge debate in Western Europe about how quickly and how far the member states should proceed in creating a United States of Europe. Few can read the European Union Constitution and fail to understand that its architects are serious about creating an important power called Europe, which wishes to exert its weight and influence well outside its own boundaries.

The European Constitution

The European Union Constitution makes it clear at the outset that it is creating a political union. It will establish a federal state. The draftsmen tell us that the EU will proudly fly the '12 stars flag'. This will be accompanied by the strands of Beethoven's Anthem 'Ode to Joy' and will be reflected in the 'Unity and Diversity' motto designed to sum up the spirit of the new state. The state will have its own Europe Day on 9 May, its own currency – the euro, its own President, its own Parliament, its own Supreme Court, its own Court of Auditors, its own executive government called The Commission, its own Foreign Minister, and much else besides.

Only in the UK do senior politicians attempt to say that this is not the creation of a new state. The Belgian Prime Minister welcomed the Constitution on the basis that it is 'the capstone of a federal state'. The official European Union view is that this is a constitution for a union of states, an ever closer union, allowing them to project EU power at home and abroad. As President Chirac of France put it, 'Europe today has more than ever the need and necessity to reinforce its unity: that is the goal of the Constitution.'

The Constitution sets out its own purposes near the beginning of the lengthy document. It states 'The Union shall offer its citizens an area of freedom, security and justice without internal frontiers, and an internal market. It should combat social exclusion and discrimination. It shall promote economic, social and territorial cohesion and solidarity among member states.' It goes on to say 'The member states shall facilitate the achievement of the Union's tasks and refrain from any measure which could jeopardise the attainment of the Union's objectives', and caps it all by stating 'The Constitution and law adopted by the Union's institutions in exercising competences conferred on it, shall have primacy over the law of the member states.'

It is difficult to read these clauses and to agree with the British government that this is a constitution for a club rather as a cricket club has a constitution, not the constitution of a state. I know of no cricket club constitution which lays down the primacy of the cricket club's laws over the laws of the state in which it is established. It is true that some grand cricket clubs run to a flag, could have their own song, and might sport a motto. It is true that they might even make bylaws or rules to govern the members who chose to join. No cricket club creates citizens, asserts the primacy of its law, has its own supreme court or parliament, its own bank holiday, and the right to issue its own monopoly currency. Only the British government amongst all the member states governments continues with the absurd argument that this Constitution is a tidying up exercise, a few rules to govern friendship and cooperation amongst a series of sovereign nation states.

The Constitution demolishes that argument in its early paragraphs, through its strong assertion of the primacy of Union actions and law making, the appeal to the citizenship of Europe, and the establishment of wide-ranging purposes similar to those of independent nation states.

The British government states that the Constitution 'brings together the main existing treaties in one, simplified treaty'. There's nothing simplified about the Constitution which is a lengthy and complex document. Nor is it a just a tidying up exercise, laying down minimum rules in the way that the British government seeks to imagine. The Constitution drives forward European Union powers, especially in home affairs, justice and foreign policy. The Euro-sceptics in Britain are united with the federalists on the continent in believing that this is a constitution for a new state, and that it goes a long way to completing the powers necessary for the EU to behave like other states on the world stage.

In particular, the Constitution seeks to break the log jam over common foreign policy that has sometimes disrupted the EU's activities outside its own borders. The Constitution is energetic and straightforward on this matter. It states 'The European Union shall conduct a common foreign and security policy.' It goes on to say 'The common foreign and security policy shall be put into effect by the Union Minister of Foreign Affairs and by the member states.' In case there is any misunderstanding, the Constitution buttresses this comment by saying the member states 'shall support the common foreign and security policy actively and unreservedly in a spirit of loyalty and mutual solidarity'.

The British government states that this represents no change from the current position. They do not want us to believe that this will represent a strong new presence for the EU on the world stage. They ignore the fact that under this Constitution common foreign and security policy becomes central to the EU's structure, rather than being entirely inter-governmental and outside the formal structure of the Union. They are correct that crucial decisions on foreign policy remain matters for unanimity, giving any country a theoretical right to veto. What they ignore is the history of the EU in such matters, where the pressure can become quite relentless on any member state, or small group of member states, who think they can hold up the Union's common view by threatening use of the veto. No state likes to feel isolated or under pressure or out of line. The Constitution makes it clear that member states have to support anything once agreed, and have to make a strong contribution to creating a common line on everything, including agreeing to things they do not want to agree to.

Even more importantly in my view, is the statement in the Constitution that member states 'shall refrain from any action which is contrary to the interests of the Union or likely to impair its effectiveness as a cohesive force in international relations'. There is no argument about this and no right of veto on that proposition. If properly enforced, this would prevent a member state from saying anything on the world stage that could be anti the EU's view of the world.

If, for example, the Falkland Islands had been invaded after Britain had joined such a constitution and a Union, we might have been prevented from taking action to reclaim it. Several European countries, led by Spain, were not happy with the British decision to invade the islands to recover them. If we had already signed up to a general policy of peace and trade development with Latin America – eminently likely under EU auspices – the Union could then have claimed that a British invasion of the Falkland Islands disrupted the agreed policy of amicable diplomacy and commercial activities.

The EU view of the common foreign and security policy is that it will lead to a foreign policy expressing an opinion on the crucial questions of the day. It will be backed up by an EU diplomatic service, and led and implemented by the European Foreign Affairs Minister. The intention is to increase qualified majority voting in the area over time, understanding the sensitivities at the beginning over preserving the veto. Euro-sceptics go a little further: they say that the European Foreign Affairs Minister as the Chairman of the Foreign Affairs Council can set the agenda taking us much closer to being a single state with a single foreign policy. Euro-sceptics point out that the Treaty also includes the provision that the United Kingdom will have to put forward the EU view at the Security Council of the United Nations, rather than her own if they differ.

Again, in order to make sure the UK complies with this, the Treaty expressly sets out that the European Foreign Affairs Minister can attend any Security Council meeting he or she wishes to join, and speak on behalf of the UK and France. The British Prime Minister constantly points out correctly that the EU does not gain a seat on the Security Council of the United Nations, and that under the rule of the United Nations it will be still France and the UK who are the two permanent representatives at the Security Council from the European Union. What he ignores is the very important provisions in the Treaty that seek to circumvent the UN rules by imposing EU rules on how we use the seat. It could be summed up by saying that Britain keeps her seat on the UN but loses her voice. It is difficult to see that having a seat without a voice amounts to very much, other than short-circuiting the need to change the UN's Constitution, replacing the UK and French representatives with the EU one. America is becoming rather wary of this, as it is strongly of the view that the European Union should not end up with an effective chair in the Security Council for the Union as well as two chairs for France and Britain.

The UK government's view is that the preservation of unanimity on the main issues will leave the UK as free to do as it wishes as it has been to date. In the carefully worded prose of the government's explanatory leaflet, 'Member state countries would retain ultimate responsibility for their own foreign policy.' This is in strong contrast to the view of, for example, the Prime Minister of Spain who has said on the public record 'Europe must believe that it can be in 20 years the most important world power.'

The European Foreign Affairs Minister is a very important new departure for the European Union. Up until this point Commissioners have been unelected. British eyes tend to view them as senior officials whilst most continental Europeans see them as important European politicians. They lead the government of the EU in private at Commission meetings, and Commissioners play important roles in support of the Council of Ministers meetings in their specific subjects. Commissioners draw up the agenda for the individual Council of Ministers meetings, their team of officials draft the regulations and laws, and they administer any EU funds and programmes. The Chairman of each individual Ministerial Council is the subject minister from the country holding the Presidency of the Union for the time being.

The new European Minister of Foreign Affairs cuts through all this. He or she will have all the usual powers of a Commissioner, dealing with the foreign affairs portfolio within the Commission meetings, constructing the agenda of the Foreign Affairs Council, and using his or her staff to draft all the relevant documents. In addition, the Foreign Affairs Minister will chair the Foreign Affairs Council of Ministers, and will be the high representative of the European Union at home and abroad on all matters to do with foreign policy.

The Constitution charges the Foreign Affairs Minister with constructing a comprehensive Foreign Affairs agenda and pushing it through the Foreign Affairs Council. There's no doubt about it that one of the two areas where the EU wishes to make the strongest advances in its power, by means of the Constitution, is the common foreign and defence policy.

There has also been much debate in Britain about whether the Constitution takes forward the cause of the EU having its own army. The British government has always been adamant that there will be no European army and there will be no occasions when British troops will be sent into battle on the say-so of the EU. It is particularly important to study the prose of the draft Constitution carefully, as recruiting, directing and using military force is one of the most distinctive capabilities of a state.

The Constitution says 'The common security and defence policy shall include progressive framing of a common Union defence policy. This will lead to a common defence.' The use of the words 'shall' and 'will' is interesting. There is no doubt in the minds of the Constitution drafters that there will be a common Union defence policy. They do accept it's going to take time to create a comprehensive and successful common defence but that is the intention of the sentence.

The document goes on to direct 'Member states shall make civilian and military capabilities available to the Union for the implementation of the common security and defence policy.' Moreover, 'Member states shall undertake progressively to improve their military capabilities. The European Armaments, Research and Military Capabilities Agency shall be established to help in this task.' Again, there is no doubt about the intentions behind this part of the Constitution. Member states are told that they have to improve their military capability, and they are told that there will be a European Armaments Agency. Indeed, this agency has already been established without the Constitution being endorsed by parliaments and peoples in the member states.

Finally, the Constitution says 'Member states can join a scheme of permanent structured co-operation in military matters.' Here the words are different to allow for accelerated common military activity by those member states who wish to do so, and have the military forces to make it worthwhile.

In summary, the general European Union view is that the Constitution will speed the development of a Euro corps, common armaments, a bigger armaments industry in the EU, and European-led military missions around the world. The EU has already created a series of battle groups and is actively considering where it wishes to deploy EU troops outside its continental area. The Euro-sceptic view would agree with this and add the phrase 'a common defence' means what it says. Euro-sceptics think there is a danger that the European Union will rupture the US alliance, cutting the UK off from US intelligence and security information, and making member states more dependent on EU forces. Re-armament by the Europeans would be expensive and would be insufficient to match American technology but will be undertaken, nonetheless, with a view to creating a more independent European Union.

Once again, it is only the UK government view that thinks very little of significance is happening in this constitutional document, and in the parallel developments in the Union itself. The government says that the UK's defence will remain based on NATO and the US alliance. It states that the UK will veto EU initiatives it does not like, and reaffirms 'British troops could not be sent anywhere without the agreement of the British Government.' This particular statement is stronger than the government statement on our room for manoeuvre in the field of foreign policy. It is true that under the Constitution there is no device to make British troops do things that the British government doesn't wish them to do. But there is a considerable amount of moral and political pressure for the UK to pool more of its military might, and to be a willing participant in the EU military missions.

The UK is a leading collaborator in the Eurofighter project. The project has been bedevilled by difficulties in drawing up a common specification, given the varied needs of European air forces. It has experienced considerable cost overruns and project management complications as it is a large scale, technically advanced project taking place in several different countries, with agreements brokered in different languages. The European side believes that they have produced a working, flying plane that will be better than anything else on offer in the world, apart from the much larger, more powerful and stealthier F22 American warplane. The EU has accepted that it cannot match American technology but believes that in the competitive world air force market there will be takers for the Eurofighter, as it should be superior to anything countries like Russia can offer.

The EU has very different views on where and when to use military force from the United States of America. Many people in Western Europe fondly believe that the European Union is a more peace-loving place than the United States, and will be a restraining influence on America whenever she wishes to use military might to halt dictators, root out terrorists, or introduce democratic regimes. The evidence of the European Union since it developed some limited military capability points in the very opposite direction. The EU was very keen to use military might in the former Yugoslavia, although it did so before it had all the necessary capabilities and had to seek American help and support. The French are very active in using their military forces in parts of Africa where they still have some influence, yet see no irony in then opposing the United States of America using military force in the Middle East, where France has often supported or benefited from corrupt and dictatorial regimes.

The emerging European Union as a world power will want to project its military power overseas, and is actively considering how to procure the necessary equipment to do so. The main constraint on EU policy is not any moral belief that it is wrong to intervene with forces in other people's countries but the lack of effective force to do it.

The truth in life is that the US has a monopoly on all of the up-to-date weapon systems. Never has a superpower had such a phenomenal technological lead as the US enjoys today compared with all other military powers around the world. The EU knows this and resents it but lacks the cash and the taxable capacity to spend enough to make up the shortfall.

The second big area where the EU intends to strengthen its powers and controls through the Constitution, is the area of asylum, immigration and crime. The Constitution declares 'The Union shall constitute an area of freedom, security and justice.' It becomes very specific, pointing out that 'Measures concerning passports, identity cards, residents' permits or any other such document and measures concerning social security or social protection may be laid down by European law or framework law.' Whilst this is carefully phrased using the word 'may' rather than 'shall', the intention again is very clear. The EU wishes to control who enters the Union and on what terms. This is made apparent by the use of the word 'shall' in the following text: 'It (the EU) shall ensure the absence of internal border controls for persons and shall frame a common policy on asylum, immigration and external border control, based on solidarity between member states, which is fair towards third country nationals.'

Until recently in the British debate, both major parties in government have argued that the control of borders, the issuing of passports, decisions on visas, and matters relating to the criminal law, are all central to being a nation state, and are decisions which should be taken by the British government in Parliament not by the EU. As a result of British pressure, these areas were always kept outside the full EU structure. They were treated as an inter-governmental pillar under the Treaty. This meant they were decided by unanimous decisions between the member states, without the intervention of the Commission and European Court. In addition, the Conservative government kept the UK out of the Schengen Agreement on common borders and frontiers, and this practice continued during the early years of the Labour government. More recently the Labour government has switched and said that it is happy to see the EU taking a lead role in many of these matters, as it now believes these are Europe-wide problems rather than specifically British ones.

As a result, the EU view is now that the UK has more or less signed up to an EU common border scheme. They believe the UK will come to accept EU decisions over who enters the country, who receives visas, and in due course will accept EU border controls and border police. The Euro-sceptics take a similar view, seeing that the European Union Constitution completes the takeover of asylum and immigration policies begun in the Treaties of Nice and Amsterdam, signed by the Labour government. Euro-sceptics think it will not take long using the opt-in system, which the British government has developed for UK policy, to be taken over by European policy.

The British government argues that 'Britain would retain its existing flexibility'. They say this because the British government has reserved the right to say yes or no to any particular proposal coming forward from the EU under the common asylum and borders policy. It is true that if Britain vetoes a particular proposal then, for the time being, Britain retains some flexibility to have its own policy in the area affected by the veto. It is also true that the British government now seems to welcome a large number of these common initiatives. Every time Britain consents to one of these proposals from the EU, it then loses all future right to flexibility or a different policy in the UK. It is a one-way ratchet which could be deployed quite rapidly to secure control by the EU over our migration policy. As the Dutch Prime Minister has commented, reflecting the general Euro-enthusiast view, 'There is one reality as far as immigration and asylum is concerned.'

Similarly, the EU has made a huge advance in the area of legal and criminal justice systems. The Constitution declares 'The Union shall develop judicial co-operation in civil matters having cross-border implications, based on the principle of mutual recognition of judgements.' In addition, 'Judicial co-operation in criminal matters in the Union shall be based on the principle of mutual recognition of judgements and judicial decisions.' This is exactly how the powers of the European Economic Community were built up in the area of the single market, first using mutual recognition to encourage greater freedom of movement of goods and some services, then leading on to legislative activity and EU control. The Constitution shows that they have the same in mind for the criminal and civil justice systems. It states:

> European laws or framework laws shall establish measures to establish rules and procedures to ensure the recognition throughout the Union of all forms of judgements and judicial decisions; prevent and settle conflicts of jurisdictions between states; encourage the training of judiciary and staff; facilitate co-operation between judicial authorities of the member states in relation to proceedings in criminal matters having cross-border dimensions.

The use of the word 'shall' is instructive, especially as in this area qualified majority voting is to be adopted instead of unanimity.

Not content with these proposals, the Constitution goes on: 'European framework laws may establish minimum rules concerning the definition of criminal offences and sanctions in the areas of particularly serious crime with a cross-border dimension.' To complete the EU move into this field, we read 'In order to combat crimes affecting the financial interests of the Union, the European law of the Council may establish a European Public Prosecutor's Office from Eurojust.'

The significant introduction of qualified majority voting into these very sensitive areas is perhaps the single, most important advance in EU power in this particular Constitution. Whilst the foray into criminal and civil law is going to take time, and commences with mutual recognition rather than a huge legislative programme, the outlines are already there for a more substantial legislative endeavour, and the Constitution invites the member states to sign up to the need for such a substantial programme. There will be an increasing number of areas where the EU decides on what is a crime and how it will be punished. There will be more harmonisation of the judicial process and more cross-border policing. The UK government says that the English Common Law is safe in their hands and that cooperation is limited to a minority of cross-border areas. They will find, as time passes, this is no longer true. The EU is destined to become more and more powerful in the legal field. Lawyers and judges who think this is untrue should examine the history of the single market, and see how the idea of freer trade between member states through mutual recognition soon led on to a substantial legislative programme. It ended with the assertion of complete control over important areas and substantial control over all the rest in a matter of a few years.

The EU is still in the process of completing a single economy. The Treaty reminds us that the EU has exclusive competence (or power) over 'Customs union; the establishing of the competition rules necessary for the functioning of the internal market; monetary policy, for the member states whose currency is the euro; common commercial policy.' These are wide-ranging powers where member states no longer have any ability to settle their own futures. The Constitution continues: 'The internal market shall comprise an area without internal frontiers in which the free movement of persons, services, goods and capital is ensured in accordance with the Constitution.'

The drafters of the Constitution failed to achieve the important advance they wanted in the area of general economic policy, more common taxation. They were left saying 'No member state shall impose, directly or indirectly, on the products of other member states any internal taxation of any kind in excess of that imposed directly or indirectly on similar domestic products.' Furthermore 'A European law or framework law of the Council shall establish measures for harmonisation of legislation concerning turnover taxes, common excise duties and other forms of indirect taxation', but all of this is still subject to unanimity. To reassert power in this area, the Constitution reminds member states that they 'shall conduct their economic policies in order to contribute to the Union's objectives ... member states shall regard their economic policies as a matter of common concern and shall co-ordinate them within the Council'.

In the view of the federalists, the combination of EU budget rules, the single market and the euro, are creating one economy in Euroland. They believe the straggler states will join in due course. They do not think the Eastern states that have recently joined the Union are yet ready but, once they have brought their economies closer to those of the West, they will be expected to join. In the case of the United Kingdom, Sweden and Denmark, many federalists still believe it is a matter of time, as they have not understood the breadth and depth of hostility to the currency in Britain. Many federalists are irritated at the lack of progress on common taxation but remain keen to create VAT as the first truly federal tax, and to harmonise many more of the features of corporate tax.

The UK government points out that a member state outside the euro does retain substantial discretion over taxation and its spending plans. They remain wedded to the idea that the UK will join in the euro later 'when the conditions are right'. There is no sign of the UK being better equipped in their view to join the euro today, than seven years ago when they first came to power saying it was their intention. Euro-sceptics are quite sure that the UK will never join the euro. The polling is so consistent with such a very large margin for the no camp over the yes vote, that no serious analyst believes any British government could win a referendum in favour of the euro. All now recognise that the leading opposition party in the country is against the euro in principle anyway.

Euro-sceptics understand that the UK will, therefore, stay outside the poorly performing Euroland economy but will still suffer from too many EU regulations, taxes and the common policies, which it is forced to import under existing and prospective provisions. The growing irritation on the continent with the lack of progress of the Euroland economy has led Wim Kok, the former Belgian Prime Minister, to say in a report commissioned by the EU that the European Union needs to name, shame and fame member states, depending on their success with economic policy. The Union is seeking to shift the blame from itself to the member states for the poor performance in growth, technological development and jobs.

The European Union is at last becoming aware of the problems it has with creating a dynamic and enterprising EU economy. The very foundation of a superpower is a large, dynamic and strong economy. The European Union would love to have mighty corporations in the numbers and with the success rates of the United States of America. It would love to have the long reach of American investment and trade around the world, and it would love to have the high living standards that many Americans enjoy. Instead, the Euroland economy has grown much more slowly than the US, both before and after the introduction of the euro. Efficiency, productivity and technology continue to lag very badly.

On 10 November 2004, the Council of the European Union issued a long confessional document entitled *The European Competitiveness Report 2004*. The structure and ordering of the report was symptomatic of the EU problem. It opens by stating:

> Both because of its size and its involvement in economic life, the public sector exerts an important influence on economic performance.

The first three chapters of the report review the impact of the public sector on productivity growth, the role of public sector funding in research and development and the performance of the health sector, a key component of the public sector. Chapter four looks at the European automotive sector given the huge importance of this to the ailing German economy, and chapter five looks at the impact of China on Europe and the world.

Any US competitiveness study would devote most of its effort to examining the private sector in the United States of America, and how competitive markets could be strengthened. It is a typically European fixation that most of the Competitiveness Report looks at the public sector, reflecting the reality that the public sector is still relatively very large in the EU compared to the freer world of the Americas and Asia. European politicians are still preoccupied by doing things by public sector means. What is unusual about this report is that, far from praising the superior public sector methods and regarding it as a great advantage for the EU that it has such a large public sector and so much state involvement, it is extremely critical of the impact EU government and regulation has upon the EU economy.

The report states:

> Available studies suggest there is scope for further improvement in public sector efficiency in the EU, and that the current public sector output could be achieved at a significantly smaller cost. There is also some evidence suggesting that smaller governments are more efficient, pointing to the existence of declining marginal products of public spending beyond a given size of government.

This is revolutionary material for the European Union, brought up on a doctrine that the EU is superior to the US because it has a larger, more caring state sector, and because politicians are actively involved in influencing business, regulating industry and ensuring transfers of income and wealth. The report goes on to say that 'Empirical research suggests that privatisation is usually associated with increased efficiency, profitability and capital investment spending.'

When I used to argue that case in the 1980s in the United Kingdom, a bevy of UK and continental authorities and politicians argued that this was completely wrong, and that it would take us in the US direction which they loathed. There was never any interest when I suggested a privatisation directive for the EU as a whole, and great reluctance to accept the need to introduce competition into crucial areas like energy and transport, where the public sector tended to dominate. After continuing the traditional free enterprise argument, the Competitiveness Report comes to the remarkable conclusion 'The EU, in particular in comparison to the US, is seen to place a relatively heavy regulatory burden on enterprises. It has been suggested that an increase in competition in product and in labour markets to US levels could raise euro area gross domestic product by even as much as 12%.'

The EU is saying that British people could be 12% better off if they were not burdened with the huge number of regulations and the anti-competitive practices that we currently see in the European Union. To put figures on it, it means that British people would have £130 billion more of income if they could achieve US levels of competition in product and labour markets. That means that every man, woman and child in the country could be £2,000 better off, or a typical family £8,000 better off, if we did not face this governmental burden according to the EU, which is one of the main causes of it.

In recognition of the over-weaning burden of government activity on enterprise and business, the EU leaders solemnly signed up to a dramatic programme of improvement at Lisbon, as long ago as the year 2000. The Competitiveness Report some four years later shows that nothing has changed for the better, despite the leaders agreeing at that summit that there were too many regulations, that there was too little competition and choice in many European markets, and that improvements in both of these areas could improve the welfare and incomes of European people. We need to ask ourselves will the European Union Constitution make any difference to this? As far as I can see, the only difference it will make is that it will make the problem worse. The European Union Constitution, in contrast to the Competitiveness Report, does not require privatisation of nationalised industries on the continent of Europe, nor does it represent a decisive break with the regulatory and anti-competitive past. The immediate result of signing the Constitution will be a lot more

European law on top of the very large law codes many member states have already assembled for themselves.

Nor does the Constitution solve the other great European problem, the disillusion of many European people with the EU itself. Turnout in European elections is low. There is no active engagement in political debate about the EU legislative programme each year, and a sense of helplessness by many of the subject peoples within Europe over what their European government does. The idea of the Constitutional Convention was to crack just this problem. The terms of reference for those who assembled to negotiate a better future for the Union, centred around the need to reconnect EU government with the citizens. Instead most of the members of the Convention saw it is an opportunity to grab more power to the centre. They tried to model themselves on the founding fathers of the United States of America when they drew up their constitution but instead ended up with an extremely long, tedious and complex document, which advanced federal power to some extent but also continued to incorporate a series of difficult political compromises in ambiguous language in other areas.

The net result of the Constitution is a further substantial shift in power towards the federation. The number of areas where vetoes apply is reduced. The EU gains sole power for important areas and strong powers in all the others, under what is called shared competence. The EU's idea of shared competence is that the member state can only do things that the EU hasn't done, or things that do not contradict decisions the EU has taken. Collapsing the three pillars structure into the European Union itself strengthens the Union's hand in foreign affairs and home affairs which were previously inter-governmental. The decision to press on with a comprehensive foreign policy and a substantial criminal law legislative programme mark an important quickening of the pace in these areas.

The UK government asserts 'The EU Constitution would not change the central role of member countries.' Once a Foreign Affairs Minister gets into office the UK is likely to regret those words. As Mrs Ferero-Waldener, the EU Foreign Affairs Commissioner, has stated, the EU is going to be 'A dynamic global protagonist' in world affairs.

Commissioner Verheugen, the Industry Commissioner in the new Commission that took office at the end of 2004, has also stated 'Today, you have to understand that the rest of the world sees us as a continental power that does not assume its responsibilities.' This leaves the Commissioner with a view that the Union must assume its responsibilities and will need EU military forces to do so. The Prime Minister of Spain has confirmed that the European Union Constitution is 'A milestone on the road to European military and economic superpower', and the Dutch Presidency of the Union in 2004 stated 'The battle groups (13 so far with 1,500 troops each) are at the forefront of capability improvement, providing the Union with credible rapidly deployable coherent force packages.'

No one can say they have not been warned. Most continental politicians and Commissioners are entirely open about the aim – the creation of a strong European power playing an important role on the world's stage, and the means – the Constitution. Only in Britain do leading politicians on the government's side bury their head in the sand and pretend that something else is happening. In the United Kingdom, both Government and Opposition have promised a referendum on the matter of the Constitution itself. Since the Constitution was drawn up the polls have been very consistent, showing that there is something like a 3 to 1 majority against Britain joining it. Most political analysts and commentators believe there is no chance of turning British public opinion around to win a referendum on this issue, and most agree that there will be a referendum whoever wins the General Election in 2005.

This means that the EU will be faced with an interesting choice. If all the other important member states do ratify the Constitution, whether by parliamentary vote or plebiscite or both, I am sure that the EU will wish to go ahead without Britain. It will give the UK a marvellous opportunity to negotiate a different and better deal more suited to the temper and mood of the British people. We should not want to stand in the way of France and Germany, if they are able to complete their political union, and to carry a significant number of continental countries with them. Nor should we harbour the strange idea that if we join we would somehow then have remarkable influence, and that it would be in our interest to do so. Their project is different from our aspirations and their view of the world at variance with ours.

The Constitution offers us the opportunity to negotiate friendship and trade, a pattern of relationships based on our interests as well as those of the continental powers. It gives us the opportunity to help them over their problem – British reluctance to complete the political union – at the same time as allowing us to protect our interests.

The Constitution will strengthen the internal power of the EU over its members but it will not succeed in creating a mighty rival to the US. The EU will be difficult towards America and will join the argument on a whole range of issues against her. Over the next ten years there is no prospect of the EU having serious military power to rival the US.

Notes

The progress of the debate about British membership of the EEC can be charted in the *Hansard* record of parliamentary debates.

The Union of England with Wales under the Tudors is covered in Elton (1997), especially pp. 175–7; and the union with Scotland in Ashley (1965), pp. 228–31.

The policy of the Labour government on devolution is set out in Redwood (1999).

Writing is only just catching up with the breathless dot.com phenomenon. I found Davis and Meyer (1998) captured the mood well.

This chapter is taken from the published text of the Constitution (HMSO July 2004) and the British Management Data Foundation's 'European Union in Perspective'. The author ran a series of seminars at All Souls College Oxford in Michaelmas Term 2004 with Sir Jeremy Lever QC. Speakers at this series gave informed views on how to interpret the draft Constitution, including specialists in defence, foreign affairs, home affairs, immigration and borders, and economics.

Contrasting views on the evolution of the EU can be found in Leach (2004) and Gillingham (2003).

3
The Rise of China

The EU has its global pretensions, but is unlikely to emerge as a superpower with the military might it needs to be effective a long way from home. A much more effective competitor to the US, potentially a major global player, is rising in the Far East. In recent years the Chinese economy has grown at a staggering 9% per annum. It has already overtaken Italy to become the world's sixth largest economy, and will soon pass the size of France and the UK at market exchange rates. By the next decade it will be larger than Germany, in third place, poised to overtake Japan.

Whilst the EU squabbles about how to come together to challenge the US, America is having to adjust her sights to deal with a potentially far more significant rival on the other side of the world. The Chinese economy is growing rapidly in the industrial sectors to start with. China has such a huge population, that partial success economically will give her enormous influence. The EU debates a new Constitution. China invites in investors with the best technologies to revolutionise the backwards and rural Chinese economy.

China for centuries was inscrutable. Closed off from the West, governed by scholar officials following the theories of Confucious, China kept herself to herself. The trading and invading Europeans who arrived in the sixteenth century made a modest impact. The Opium Wars between 1839–42 and 1856–60 demonstrated to China Britain's might and quickened the pace of her exposure to Western ideas. In 1912 the last Chinese dynasty, the Qing, succumbed to nationalist pressure as Sun Yat-Sen carried out his nationalist revolution.

In the twentieth century the struggle between nationalists and communists ended with Mao Zedong's victory over the nationalists in 1949. They fled to Taiwan, declaring a People's Republic there. For the next half century we had two Chinas with two systems. Nationalist China on

31

the island of Taiwan flourished. It followed Western theories of capitalist development, and was alert to adopt as much Western technology as it could import. It became a very prosperous island with 22 million people and huge foreign exchange reserves. In contrast, the massively populated mainland of China remained mired in communist policy. The communist system delivered little other than famine, oppression and the chaos of the Cultural Revolution from 1966 onwards. When Mao died in 1976 China was far behind the West, experiencing political and social chaos. Most people still worked on the land in very unproductive, state-owned farms. The rest worked in basic, heavy industry for nationalised concerns.

Deng Xiaoping took over in 1976 and began economic reform. He dismantled collective farming and gradually introduced some freedom into China's ossified economy. In 1979 industry accounted for around half of officially measured national income. Compared with agriculture's 30%, the service sector was small, reflecting the poor state of development of the Chinese economy under the communists.

Between 1989 and 2002, Jiang Zemin led a collective leadership. The Communist Party is now under the general guidance of Hu Jintao. Mr Hu Jintao is General Secretary of the Communist Party and State President. Mr Jiang Zemin remains Chairman of the Central Military Commission controlling the armed forces. Wen Jiabao is the Prime Minister. The main decisions are made by the Committee of the Political Bureau of the Communist Party. China remains a one party state.

The Chinese leadership continues to drive forward economic liberalisation, whilst at the same time retaining strong political control. They have been through a round of privatisation, putting some nationalised enterprises into the hands of a rich few. They have signed up to World Trade Organisation (WTO) entry terms. On 10 October 2000, China was granted permanent, normal trade relations. This international agreement reduces the Chinese tariffs on many farm and industrial goods, and gives Western companies some access to Chinese markets.

The economic liberalisations, where they have occurred, have been remarkably successful. The Chinese economy has exploded into growth in recent years. Between 1978 and 1998 national output quadrupled. In the 1990s and well into the present century foreign investment has soared.

Over half the population still work on the land. Since the late 1970s the collective farms have been broken up, leading to huge leaps forward in agricultural production. Agriculture accounts for around a fifth of the nation's output, showing there is still plenty of scope for mechanisation and productivity improvement.

Any glance at the map of China will show that the massive areas to the west and the north are inhospitable terrain, incapable of growing anything. There is a little bit of oasis farming in Zinjang and Qinghai, and some irrigated areas in Inner Mongolia and Gansu. The overwhelming bulk of Chinese agricultural output comes from the lower lying, better favoured, eastern part of the country, and most of the agricultural output comes from just one tenth of the total land. China is the world's largest producer of rice and wheat, and a big producer of sweet potatoes, millet, barley, peanuts, corn, soya beans and potatoes. It is the world's biggest producer of cotton and tobacco, and a significant producer of oil seeds, silk, tea, hemp, sugar cane and sugar beet. The north and west manage livestock raising through nomadic, pastoral activities.

China is the world's largest producer of red meat. China is also well-favoured with many minerals. She is the world's largest coal producer. The country contains large iron ore deposits and big oilfields. Some petroleum engineers believe that there are even larger oil deposits off the coasts of China which may come to the rescue, as China is now a large oil importer, requiring huge quantities for her rapidly growing industry. China has significant reserves of tungsten, antimony, tin, magnesium, mercury, manganese, barite, salt, uranium, gold and lead. There are deposits of aluminium, vanadium, copper, fluorite, nickel, asbestos, phosphate, pyrite and sulphur.

Most of China's energy is still generated from coal. As this is high sulphur coal, it has produced a massive increase in world pollution as China's industrialisations proceed apace. There is considerable potential for more hydroelectric power which currently accounts for about 5% of the country's energy production.

China has set a very attractive corporate income tax rate of only 15% in special economic zones, and a 24% rate in the fourteen coastal open cities where much of the industrial development and foreign investment is taking place. The national rate of business tax is 33% but relatively few people pay this, as most of the investment is concentrated in the favourable areas.

A big success in building and concentrating new industry is very evident in the Shanghai region of Jiangsu and the Qangdon province adjacent to Hong Kong. Shanghai and Guangzhou are the traditional big textile centres, and many new investments have been made in the cotton growing provinces of North China and along the Yangtze River.

There was no more magnificent image of China's success in joining the first world in substantial parts of its economic development than the Chinese Grand Prix, held for the first time in 2004. It was another of

China's shop windows on the world. It showed China's new found ability to see through a major first world construction project to high standards, to complete it on time, and to offer excellent facilities to a world class sport at the leading edge of international technology. As the pictures were beamed around the world from the new Grand Prix circuit, those who were doubters about Chinese success and expertise had to think again. It was a clear statement from China that she has now arrived on the world's economic stage as a major player, and a clear indication that China intends to absorb the best of Western technology and ideas, and be there amongst the foremost of the world's economic powers. China will make an even more dramatic statement to the world when she unveils the 2008 Olympics in Beijing.

The economic data shows that the Chinese economy is now sixth largest in the world. By the end of this decade, China will be in third place. These figures are based upon the national income figures of each country at prevailing exchange rates. In practice, this grossly underestimates the scale and importance of the Chinese economy already. The Chinese currency, the renminbi, is greatly undervalued on world markets. Economists have attempted to adjust for so-called purchasing power parities, to give a better idea of the scale and importance of the Chinese economy. For the year 2002, the Chinese economy produced an output of US$1.27 trillion at market exchange rates. Economists believe that a more realistic value for this using purchasing power parities would be US$6 trillion, putting China already into second place position in the world in terms of size of the economy.

The reason China is already so colossal lies in her very large population. The Chinese population is around 1.3 billion. This is four times the size of the US population and more than three times the size of the EU population. Even at relatively low levels of income per head, this creates an economy of gargantuan proportions. The Chinese income per head at market exchange rates is a little over US$1,000 today, growing at around 7% per annum. Income per head at purchasing power parity rates is around US$4,700.

The half of the Chinese economy which is taken up by industry is especially geared to export production. Major industrial products produced in an abundance include textiles, chemicals, agricultural machinery, iron and steel, building materials, plastics, toys and electrical goods. China is following a path trail blazed by Japan in the post-war period, combining massive inward investment into her country in new industrial activities with substantial export earnings from the resulting products.

Before 1945, heavy industry was concentrated in Manchuria. It has become regionally more diversified in later years. The huge iron and steel industry is organised around major centres like Anshan. There has been a steady drift of people into the large cities to find the new industrial jobs. Several of the large cities like Shanghai, Tainjin and Guangzhou are also the country's principal ports.

China is very dependent on the investment boom which has been underway for some years. By 2003, gross fixed investment represented 42.9% of total national activity. Exports also surged, reaching 29% in the same year. The Chinese balance of payments is in substantial surplus, with a favourable current account balance in 2002 of US$35 billion. Some economists are already worried that the Chinese model of development, based on a massive amount of investing and export, is unstable or cannot be sustained. There has been an active debate over the last year, including within the Chinese government itself, over whether they can and should decelerate the rate of Chinese growth to reduce overheating. The increase in interest rates on 29 October 2004, from 5.31% to 5.58% was the first such increase in nine years, showing the caution of the Chinese authorities in making changes to their successful economic policy, and their reluctance to bring a very successful expansion to a juddering halt. They have managed to keep the rather rickety banking system going by creating substantial extra liquidity.

It is possible that Western economists are too concerned. The Japanese economy showed that it was quite possible to sustain massive industrial investment and export activity in the early years of its economic lift-off. The Japanese long period of growth in due course was sustained by the development of much more domestic demand, to supplement Japan's greater success in conquering the American and European markets with its manufactured products. China has even more scope than Japan with such a large population to create a self-sustaining and important domestic market for its industrial products. China herself is going to need much of the iron and steel, many of the agricultural machines, many of the trucks, cars and other vehicles that she will soon be making. It is a very under-mechanised country going through a very radical and rapid development.

The West's consumer electrical industries have already discovered what a significant competitor China has become. Even the EU is at last waking up to the reality of a super-competitive China in its most recent Competitiveness Report, issued from Brussels on 8 November 2004. This survey devotes a whole chapter to examining the competitive position of the European automotive industry. This industry suffered a substantial competitive attack from Japan in the years of Japanese success and supremacy towards the end of the twentieth century. The EU retaliated in its normal protectionist way by seeking to impose quotas on Japanese exports, and forcing Japanese producers to set up plants within the European Union itself to overcome the worst of the obstacles. The Competitiveness Report concludes:

> Success in the future is clearly not guaranteed. Japanese manufacturers are equally strong in investing in automotive innovations and US producers are taking advantage, ... the competitiveness of the automotive industry and of the European economy depends on a coherent and cost-effective regulatory framework ... there is still progress to be made as concerns reducing regulatory complexity and designing regulations serves to meet their goals whilst taking into account possible conflicts between regulations, their cumulative impact and their external aspect.

This rather garbled prose shows that the EU is at last aware of dangers ahead but it is still looking primarily to Japan and America to provide the main challenge to the European automotive industry. The significance of the vehicle industry to the EU in general, and to Germany in particular, has warned EU officials to beware. To date, they have not produced anything like a sensible strategy for cutting the regulatory and tax burdens sufficiently to deal with the traditional threats from America and Japan, let alone the emerging threat from China.

The competitiveness survey devotes its fifth chapter to the question of China. Whilst the draft has recognised that the rise of China offers market opportunities to Europe's countries, they are on the whole negative, preferring to concentrate on the likelihood that China's competitive pressure will do considerable damage to the EU, especially to the new member states that have recently joined. The EU recognises 'Abundant natural resources, a very high savings rate, a huge supply of low cost labour, a potentially large domestic market, as well as a sophisticated administrative system bode well for economic development.' China's high savings rate has been especially driven by the dismantling of some of the social protections afforded by the low income communist system, motivating many to save what they can out of their relatively low incomes against future ill health or old age. Close to 900 million people in China are in the age group 15 to 64, rising to an estimated 1 billion of working age by the year 2015. The mass exodus of unskilled labour from the rural areas to the cities has kept wages low, allowing rapid expansion of Chinese industrial production.

The EU recognises that China is seeking to match the West in technology and innovation, and is busily trying to obtain as much technology as possible. China is not going to be content with remaining a backward, low wage, labour intensive producer of anything.

The EU in its study identifies four problems for China, in a way which implies the Union hopes that things might go wrong for the emerging giant. The first is the unhealthy relationship between a weak banking sector and state-owned enterprises. The banks are directed by politicians to finance projects that may not yield a good return. As long as state enterprises get favourable finance, they in turn are not motivated to invest the money as wisely as they should. Goldman Sachs has estimated the cost of baling out the Chinese banking sector at around 40% of national income. A great deal more privatisation needs to be undertaken to bring more enterprises under the discipline of the market.

The second problem the EU perceives is an irreconcilable gap between labour supply and demand. The Chinese authorities have recognised the need for more private initiative to mop up the large numbers of people who will be displaced by more efficient methods of working in former state enterprises and in the agricultural sector. This perception lies behind the policy of promoting so much inward investment. The EU thinks there could be serious social unrest. It may misunderstand the Chinese mind and the new found flexibility of the Chinese economy, despite the prevalence of political interference and state enterprises in some sectors.

The EU dislikes the degree of regional disparity in China. In 2002 the level of per capita income in the richest province was more than ten times that in the poorest one. The poorer western regions have suffered a brain drain and have sent their savings east to find the better returns. Such large disparities are quite normal in fast growing economies in their development phase but they frighten the European Union mind, who would wish to address regional disparities in a way that was unlikely to work. Western Europe has been cursed with many decades of regional policy but has very little success to show for it all.

The fourth problem the EU revels in, in its analysis of China, is corruption. It states:

China's policy of creating national champions by means of selective support measures and an accommodating, regulatory policy as well as institution building, recalls memories of unsustainable industrial polices in Korea and South East Asia, which eventually led to the dramatic events of the Asian crisis in 1997 to 1998. China's national champions policy co-exists with a highly underdeveloped competitive system. The allocation of resources and resulting industrial structures are to a considerable extent not the outcome of market processes but rather of political fiat. This has inevitably led to corruption.

The EU does not believe strongly that these four problems will be insuperable or would derail the Chinese economic locomotive. If they did believe that, I doubt if they would have devoted a chapter or even a few pages to China in their Competitiveness Report. The EU perceives that there are already skilled labour bottlenecks in China, reflecting the success of the growth strategy. There are now stories in the Western media of the new found power of the skilled Chinese worker or the English-speaking Chinese employee in the labour market. China's success can be seen in her share of world trade in her leading export areas. She accounts for 55% of world trade through her exports of textile products, 76% of leather and leather products, 23% of office machinery and computers, 32% of radio, television and communication equipment, and 13% of electrical machinery. There is a strong correlation between the success in world trade in these areas and the amount of foreign investment and private enterprise activity in the sectors concerned. Foreign enterprises account for 73% of the output in electronic and telecommunication equipment, 62% of office machinery, 53% of leather and sports goods, and 42% of garments and plastic products. China has played the inward investment game extremely well, regularly attracting about a quarter of the total of such investment going to developing countries.

Every year over the last decade the biggest European inward investor into China has been the United Kingdom. In 1994 the UK invested just under US$700 million in China, compared with US$450 million for France and Germany combined. By 1997 the UK's investment had hit US$1,850 million, compared with France and Germany's US$1,500 million. Since 1999, Germany and France have increased theirs more substantially. In 2002, for example, the UK invested just under US$900 million in China, Germany a little over US$900 million, and France US$575 million.

The EU is a little panic-stricken by China's success in challenging in high technology areas. The EU notes that America is the 'predominant actor in computers and the internet, and is leading in IT software development'. Japan took over the lead in consumer electronics from Europe during the early 1970s but has relocated much of its assembly operations throughout South East Asia. In the future, not only assembly but also upstream production of hi-tech components is likely to expand rapidly in China. Indeed, the EU itself acknowledges 'China is becoming *the* hub of electronics manufacturing in the developing world and is a key step in the value chain of many electronic products.'

The Chinese textile industry is one of the largest in the world. The WTO liberalisation coming in progressively over the first decade of the twenty-first century will see a big impact in the textile area, traditionally one of the most protected of all industries. All import quotas on textiles into the EU were removed on 1 January 2005, enabling China to increase her market share. In the first round of liberalisation which followed Chinese succession to the WTO, EU imports of the products liberalised surged by 46% in value and 192% in volume from China, against a background of prices halving.

In contrast to the very successful electrical, electronics and textile industries, China is making slower progress in engineering, chemicals and pharmaceuticals. In these areas it has been less willing to liberalise and to open up the markets to foreign inward investment and new technology. China is beginning to revise her ideas in these areas, understanding the success of the foreign investment and technology model in the areas she now dominates in world trade. The EU is right to be concerned that it may only be a matter of a few years before the Chinese economy is a serious international competitor in automotive and other engineering products.

The EU's advice to the companies and governments in its member states is quite simple. They should continue to innovate and keep their best technology at home. They should take advantage of the cheaper products that China can produce, based on a plentiful supply of relatively cheap labour, but should be hesitant about sharing with China secrets of first world technology-driven economic success. In practice, the governments and companies of the EU are joining a rush to share their technology with China, so they do not lose out on the growth of the world's second biggest market in ten or twenty years' time.

The UK Treasury has attempted its own analysis of the impact of China and the other Asian stars on the global economy over the next ten years. The Treasury recognises that there will be a huge shift of global economic activity towards the rising Asian economies. The Treasury understands that technology will be the driver of economic advance, with an increasing amount of international specialisation and global competition. The Treasury itself recognises that China, now the world's sixth largest economy, by 2015 will be the world's third largest economy, putting Chinese output at around US$5 trillion by 2015 at market exchange rates. The Treasury reckons that the G7 countries – the

US, Japan, Germany, the UK, France, Italy and Canada – which accounted for half of world output in 1980 and around 43% in 2004, will decline to a little more than a third by 2015. Over this same period, China will have surged from 3% of world output to 19% of world output. The UK Treasury agrees with the EU that China will be particularly significant in the textile industry. They quote the World Bank estimating the Chinese share of global garment production will increase by between 20% and 50% by 2010. By 2015, emerging economies in developing countries could well account for approaching 40% of global exports of manufactures.

The British government anticipates China and India doing increasingly well out of foreign inward investment. In 1990, China received 1.7% of all global inward investment. This had risen to 10% by 2003. China is also likely to play an increasing role in both innovation and service provision across frontiers. China educates over 2 million graduates annually compared with 250,000 in the United Kingdom. The Chinese level is likely to increase still further. Developing and emerging countries shares in manufactured exports have grown substantially over the last two decades. This has been particularly marked in hi-tech products where local skills have been combined with inward investment, to allow the developing country to catch up.

China is already exerting a growing influence on world commodity markets and prices. In 2004 the surge in the oil price took place against a background of a big increase in Chinese demand to meet her industrial requirements. China is the world's largest user of steel, copper and iron ore. In 2003 China consumed 232 million metric tonnes of steel compared to 101 million by the United States, out of a global total of 864 million. China is now the world's largest market for mobile phones, with some 250 million handsets, illustrating the enormous capacity of the domestic Chinese market to make demands on world resources. In 2001–03, China contributed more to global growth each year than the whole of the G7 countries combined, when measured in purchasing power parity terms. China now consumes 17% of the world's wheat compared with 5.5% for the US; 31% of the world's cotton compared with 5.8% for the US; 19.8% of the world's copper compared with 14.9% for the US; and 26.5% of the world's steel compared with 11.9% for the US. The world steel shortage at the beginning of 2004 was driven by the phenomenal success of the Chinese in raising their industrial output.

The structure of China's secondary industries has changed fundamentally since the 1980s. Until 1978 output was dominated by large, state-owned concerns. Since then private entrepreneurs, as well as foreign investors, have made the running along with collective enterprises organised by local governments. The state-owned enterprises, controlled by economic ministries in Beijing, represented only 16% of industrial output by 2002. Out of China's US$327 billion of exports in 2002, 12.7% were apparel and clothing, 11.1% computers, 9.8% electrical equipment, and 9.8% telecoms products.

All this goes to demonstrate that the Chinese economy is large, growing rapidly and will one day become the dominant economy of the world. The United States of America has a phenomenal lead and it will take many years for the Chinese economy to overtake the American at market exchange rates. However, everyone recognises that the Chinese currency is currently very undervalued and the American one very overvalued compared with the Chinese. Part of the adjustment in the figures will take place at some point or other by currency realignment. Most of the change will take place as a result of further sustained, phenomenal Chinese growth, lifting China from the poverty wages and poverty conditions of the 1970s to a more acceptable standard of living, by the second and third decades of the twenty-first century.

It is a sobering thought that Chinese people only have to become one quarter as rich as Americans for the Chinese economy to equal the size of the American one. If we can look forward to the day when Chinese people are half as well off as Americans, China will have an economy twice the size of that of the United States. Why does this matter?

It matters because the origins of a country's power in the world lie in a strong and large economy. If you ally to the very numerous Chinese population better living standards and more modern technology, China will be a huge force to reckon with in the world. It is difficult to forecast how the US will react, and how long it will take before the US recognises that the true challenger to her supremacy in the world is not the European Union and its somewhat laughable attempts to square up to the United States of America, but China.

The relationship with China is already causing dispute between the United States and the European Union. France and Germany are quite keen to resume arms sales to China, which had been discontinued in 1989 following the brutal Chinese government repression of their own citizens in Tiananmen Square. The US is resolute in wanting to prevent China gaining access to advanced Western technology in weaponry. France, and to a lesser extent Germany, see a great commercial opportunity. They believe that they would curry an enormous amount of commercial favour with China by relaxing the arms embargo, as well as triggering substantial export orders for the French armaments industry following relaxation. The US is very suspicious of the idea of arming China and points to the continuing poor record of the Chinese government on human rights issues.

Above all, the United States has a very different relationship with Taiwan than the member countries of the European Union. America regards Taiwan, or nationalist China, as a kind of US protectorate. The success of the US-style capitalism in Taiwan, and the strong commercial links between the two countries, has reinforced America's sense that she should protect and encourage Taiwan as an alternative to the communist-style, authoritarian regime on the mainland. Throughout the bitter years of the Cold War, it was the US Navy and the threat of US missile support which kept China from invading Taiwan and reuniting the country under one communist rule.

The UK took a different line from the US when it came to the question of Hong Kong. Although it was only the New Territories adjacent to Hong Kong on the mainland that were leased from China, the UK decided to negotiate to give up the whole of Hong Kong, including the freehold island, when the Chinese put on pressure to regain control over their outlying regions. In a most extraordinary act of generosity, they also gave all the large foreign exchange reserves which had been accumulated by the Colony and built a new airport for the new owners. Similarly, the Portuguese gave back Macau, which had been a successful Portuguese trading post opposite Hong Kong, to the south of China, adjacent to Qangdon Province.

The Americans instead dug in and supported Taiwan's wish to remain fully independent. Taiwan, with her 22 million people, lies around 150 miles offshore from south-east China, gazing across at the mainland beyond the Taiwan Strait. There have been regular occasions when the Chinese have appeared to threaten the island and when the American Navy's presence has made it equally clear that the US would come to the aid of her ally and friend in the region.

This different approach toward the reunification of China is very significant. The British government gave the Chinese development machine a major fillip. It was both tangible in the form of the huge sums of money passed as a dowry when the Colony was returned, and in the form of the highly advanced capitalist markets of Hong Kong, which have helped to power the Chinese economic revival. A great deal of investment money has flowed out of Hong Kong into the mainland and the neighbouring province of Qangdon has clearly benefited. What started as a hinterland serving the successful Hong Kong economy itself, is now copying the techniques and styles of Hong Kong capitalism for its own purposes.

It is as if the United States has always been aware of the distant threat of a very powerful China with a very successful economy, whilst the European countries have always been much keener to see China as a possible trading partner that they must not embarrass, upset or try and resist. It is one of the ironies of the European Union project that in the name of wishing to exert their influence and express their power in the four corners of the world they have done so, in the case of the evolution of China, by turning a blind eye to the methods and styles of the Chinese administration. They have seen an opportunity in encouraging China at the very time when America is more wary or concerned. On this occasion it is the US that has stood out in favour of putting on pressure over issues like violation of human rights in China, whilst the Europeans have turned a blind eye, believing that good commercial relations with China are far more important.

I well remember the difficulties I encountered when, as Trade and Industry Minister in Britain in the early 1990s, I wished to encourage better trading links with Taiwan. The Foreign Office launched strong objections to any idea of a visit. They said it was both massively important that the United Kingdom did not recognise Taiwan as a separate country and did nothing to inflame Chinese sensitivity on this important point. After a long battle, it was finally agreed that I could make an official visit to Taiwan on the condition that I never used any language to suggest that I recognised Taiwan as a separate nation or country. We had to ransack the dictionary and the thesaurus for more and more synonyms for 'area', 'region' and 'place', to avoid the diplomatic problems that the Foreign Office foresaw.

Bigger problems have emerged between the US and the EU over high level defence technology. As we have seen, the supremacy of the United States of America as the world's only superpower is based upon its superior generation of command, control, communications, computing and intelligence technologies, which give it comprehensive surveillance of the world's fighting forces, and the ability to see a battlefield in a way that no other commander or superpower has done before. The US is naturally very careful about who has access to the intelligence it can generate, and who can use the technology it has pioneered.

The US has established a Global Positioning System. This is a series of satellites in orbit around the earth which can be used from any location on the ground to give a precise location to the observer. The system can also be used to pinpoint places at a distance from the observer anywhere around the globe. The US has made the Global Positioning System free to users around the world. It is now the way most people navigate their boats and ships, and has been adapted for commercial use to produce vehicle routing systems. All the time people use the American system the Americans retain ultimate power to monitor the flows of information over the system, to intercept or to jam if they believe the system is being used inappropriately.

The US is well advanced on a new breed of military robots. It is developing more drones, remote controlled vehicles, precision weapons, and smart bombs which can be sent to any postal address anywhere in the world picked up by the Global Positioning System satellites. The US intends to be able to see any concentration of firepower, army equipment or weaponry anywhere on the planet, and to be able to remove it by sending a large enough bomb or missile from a remote location, without any of its ground troops having to be involved in the explosion.

The EU has rejected the idea that it should continue to rely upon America's Global Positioning System. Instead it is planning to spend more than €3 billion on a rival satellite network called Galileo.

France, on behalf of the EU, has already hawked this project to China and has secured a Chinese minority stake in the investment. This has sounded alarm bells in Washington. The last thing the United States military wishes to see is China participating fully in a European satellite positioning system which could very easily become a military intelligence system. They still believe China may have evil intentions towards Taiwan, and the last thing they want is European collaboration offering China the kind of technology she needs to start to match America.

The United Kingdom, trying to straddle the Atlantic with a foot in both the EU and the US camps, is finding its footholds increasingly insecure. There is a danger that the US will now lock the UK out of its more interesting technology, given the UK's involvement with the EU Galileo project. Brussels is keen to encourage rival expenditure on the drones and smart weapons that are required to back up the positioning and spy system now under development. The US has already made it clear that if the Chinese involvement in Galileo leads to inappropriate military uses, the US will not hesitate to blow the system out of the sky. The US Congress is not prepared to grant Britain a waiver to the general rejection of sharing advanced military technology with the EU. This is likely to force the UK more rapidly into the arms of the Europeans. The US remembers that French defence firms armed Saddam Hussein before the Gulf War, and watches with concern as President Chirac courts Beijing. China is an ally of North Korea and no friend of Taiwan.

At risk as well is the longstanding sharing of intelligence between the United Kingdom and the United States. It was a good two-way street in the Second World War when Britain took inventions to the United States of America, and in return benefited from American technical and military assistance on a big scale. Throughout the Cold War the two countries shared a great deal, as they sought to ward off the communist threat from the Soviet Union. Today there is a similar need for shared intelligence to combat terrorism and dangerous authoritarian regimes in rogue states. At this very moment the relationship is jeopardised by the EU's passion to do deals with China to annoy the US and for its own commercial interest, at the same time as building a separate and different weapons industry on the Continent to that which has sustained the Anglo-American alliance for the last sixty years.

Coming rows between the EU and the US are going to be intense over the development of China. Barring major political and social accidents in China, we are going to see a quickening pace of Chinese development now she has passed certain thresholds in lead industries. What China has been able to do already in textiles, computer hardware and electrical products, she will also be able to do in vehicles, engineered products and basic chemicals. The more China opens her market up to foreign investment and foreign technology the bigger and richer she will become. Just as we are living through the years of American supremacy on a huge scale, where the lead has never been greater, we can see already the outlines of the emerging giant which will one day challenge that very American supremacy. In the meantime how to react to the emerging giant will cause growing strains in the relationships between the European Union, the United Kingdom and the United States of America. France will lead the EU in the normal French policy of encouraging the anti-American position, and in doing deals with the communist and former communist states. The US will be more cautious and, as a result, will increasingly go it alone.

Critics will say that China will be held back by the poor state of her banking industry. They argue that she cannot sustain her growth. They anticipate political troubles ahead. Even if these gloomy predictions come true, the sheer size of China's population ensures that she will emerge as a substantial force in the world economy over the next few decades. It will happen more quickly without the setbacks some forecast, more slowly if the critics are right. Now that China's gates have been opened to Western ideas and capital there will be important changes that the West needs to understand.

One day China will turn her new found economic power into military power as well. For the time being her success will be heavily concentrated in industrial products and product markets, and her main impact on the West will be felt in the rising price of commodities as Chinese demand surges. Unlike Japan, she will not remain neutral and lightly armed. As her economic success develops so too will her military and political might.

Note

The chapter draws on the UK Treasury's recent study of global economic opportunities and challenges facing the UK, and on the EU November 2004 Competitiveness Report.

4
Britain and Britishness at the Crossroads

European big government versus Anglo-Saxon democracy

For the United Kingdom there are two great different visions on offer. Some want a protectionist, highly governed Europe which looks after those in work but is no good at getting the unemployed back to work. They want higher taxes because they believe governments spend your money better than you do. They want more rules and regulations because they are suspicious of individual effort and the machinations of free enterprise companies. They want to shut out people, ideas and capital from other continents because they think it makes it easier to control what is going on. It is a watered down version of socialist planning which failed in the 1960s and 1970s. It has been recycled in a European and 'caring' guise. Instead of the government owning everything, it seeks to run it by proxy through more laws and more taxes.

Others want a free, open dynamic world where ideas and capital move easily. We want the new technology to be used to strengthen democracy, not to strengthen government. We want trade to be free, not protected; taxes to be lower, not higher; more attention to be placed on pricing people into jobs, not on excluding them. We believe the UK should be part of the English-speaking NAFTA alliance, a close friend of the United States. We still have other battles to win if democracy and freedom are to triumph in the wider world.

For many years British governments have argued that Europe is coming their way. By this they meant that they believe a mid-Atlantic Britain can pull the continentals more in the direction of open and free markets American style. It becomes increasingly difficult to believe this when each year sees another 2,500 regulations coming out of the Brussels legislative factory, and each year sees the economic gap between the US and the EU getting larger in America's favour. The EU itself is becoming aware of the difficulties it faces. Wim Kok's inquiry into European competitiveness discovered that Europe was falling further and further behind, largely because it had a very bad public sector.

The EU is desperately trying to grapple with its fundamental paradox. The very thing that makes Europe different from the US is bigger government. Europeans have been very proud of this over many years, believing that bigger government embodies their values of greater fairness and social solidarity compared with America's accent on personal initiative, private sector enterprise and higher living standards. Indeed, for years Europeans argued that there was nothing incompatible between bigger government and higher living standards, only to discover that year after year markets have proved the opposite.

The crisis of British identity

There is a crisis of British identity. Those of us born into a settled land thirty or more years ago are shocked that the bedevilling question at the turn of the twenty-first century is 'Can Britain survive the next couple of decades?' In the 1970s, a minority campaign flourished for Scottish and Irish home rule. In 1972 we joined a Common Market with countries on the continent of Europe which developed rapidly into something more than a free trade area. Today, petty nationalisms and European federalism are uniting to destroy confidence in the United Kingdom and its values. Obtuse constitutional debate since 1972 over how we should be governed attracted little interest as politicians argued how to remodel their own jobs and their own lives. Now the impact of some of their decisions is being felt more widely, as British people slowly wake up to the loss of the freedoms embedded in the old constitution. At exactly the same time as politicians are plunging Britain into a crisis of identity, seeking regional governments, seeking to create regional identities in an England very reluctant to adopt them, and offering the people of Wales and Scotland more powers of government in their own capitals, people themselves are asking the question 'What does it mean to be British?' Diverse Britain is in danger of breaking up under the pressures now being exerted upon it.

A nation, like an individual, lives in the present. The present is a strange amalgam of ideas, feelings, half-remembered thoughts from the past, experiences of the present moment, and aspirations for the future.

We must explore the legacy of the past before casting our mind forward to what might emerge from the pressure cauldron into which Britain and the British are being plunged. We are in a constitutional crisis today. It is now that we have to take our first steps towards solving it. Leaving it for too long will make it more difficult or impossible to sort out.

The impact of the European Union on the UK

Membership of the European Union commenced when we joined the Common Market in 1973. At the time we were told by most politicians that we were not sacrificing our sovereignty. All we were doing was joining up to a better, smarter kind of trade arrangement which would increase our prosperity and safeguard our jobs. This idea was given further support when a successful cross-party referendum campaign in 1975 persuaded people that Britain's rightful place was in the Common Market with our European partners. The propaganda of the day assured people we would keep our Parliament, our Queen, our law courts, our army, our navy, our currency, our right to independent decision in every field that mattered. We would only need to compromise with our partners on industrial and commercial affairs, and even here we would retain a veto. People felt this was a price worth paying for the benefits they were promised of greater trade and more prosperity. People could see the advantages of expanding trade with our nearest neighbours on the continent, and were prepared to accept the need for some common rules for the conduct of business.

The European Union that has displaced the Common Market has journeyed a very long way from the days when it was still possible for British politicians to claim it was nothing more nor less than a trading club. They knew it was called the European Economic Community, if one wished to be formal, but they preferred the term Common Market. From those early days in the 1970s, most British politicians either did not read or scrupulously ignored the statements in the founding Treaty of Rome in favour of much greater union. It was possible to see in that early treaty the outlines of a European super-state in the making. Most politicians and most electors chose to turn a blind eye to these statements.

Since 1973 the UK has gradually been losing its innocence about the nature and intentions of our European partners. A succession of decisions and treaties has now persuaded many that the European project is intent upon taking over the individual nations of Europe and welding them into the United States of Europe. Even the reassurances that it will be a federal state ring increasingly hollow when people read of the strong central powers envisaged in the draft Constitution.

The startling development of a United States of Europe has only become apparent to the majority of the British people in the last couple of years. It is a clear threat to the British state and British identity. Whilst national identity is not the same as government identity, the two are strongly connected. It is possible to have a sense of national identity without having a national government but there are usually tensions if a nation has reached that point. Most of the civil wars and conflicts within states take place when groups within a particular country claim their independence as a separate nation, and seek self-government. The Spanish state has found it difficult to contain the Catalan and Basque nations who assert their right to much more independent government. The Canadian state has found it difficult to handle French-speaking Canadians, many of whom feel their French identity stronger than their loyalty to the federal Canada.

British identity is strongly bound up with having a central government based on the Westminster Parliament and the Whitehall Civil Service. It is connected to the success of Britain as a governing entity over many centuries. It is entwined with Empire, with the safe passage of Empire to Commonwealth, with Britain's role in the wider world, and with the way in which Britain in the last couple of centuries has fought on the side of democracy, freedom and the self-determination of peoples.

The problem with the European project is it is trying to overwhelm or displace national government influence in crucial areas, long before it has succeeded in creating a sense of European nationhood, and long before it has persuaded many of the subject peoples of the European Union of the legitimacy of power wielded from the centre in Brussels.

Regionalism in Britain

The second present threat to British identity comes in the strengthening force of regionalism within the UK, itself part of the European project. The UK only succeeded in uniting the islands of Ireland, Wales, Scotland and England for a relatively brief period in the last 1,000 years. A successful revolt of the Catholic Southern Irish around the time of the First World War ended the union of all the peoples of this island group, removing the Republic of Ireland, the most recent addition. The union of what remained has been of much longer prominence with deeper roots. The union with Scotland began with the ascension of James VI of Scotland to the throne of England as James I in 1603, and was finally cemented in 1707 with the Union of Parliaments. The union with Wales goes back further. It was already in existence when Henry Tudor marched on London from the west in 1485. The Tudor kings and queens in the sixteenth century completed the absorption of the Welsh governing system into the English.

Despite the historical roots of the full union, there is no doubt that it is under stress. Some Ulster Unionists worry the move towards peace and compromise in Northern Ireland is the beginning of the long process, which will see Protestant Northern Ireland absorbed into Catholic Southern Ireland as part of an independent republic. It is this worry which has led to a split in the Unionist movement and created resistance from some sections of Unionist opinion to power sharing and proceeding by consensus. Limited moves towards cross-border government between the two parts of the island of Ireland worried many Unionists. They also fear the reliance on future plebiscites when the balance of Catholic and Protestant may have shifted more in favour of the Catholics.

In Wales, Welsh Nationalists can scarcely believe their luck at their success in persuading Westminster to preserve and develop the Welsh cultural heritage. They wish to cement a sense of Welsh nationhood and cultural separation. They were successful in persuading previous Conservative governments to introduce compulsory Welsh language teaching in Welsh schools, recognising that knowledge and mastery of the language was crucial to Welsh Nationalist sentiment. Those who want an independent Wales are keen on strengthening the role of the language. Those English-speakers living in the principality who want to remain part of the UK are worried about this change. More recently, Welsh Nationalists have been even more successful with the new Labour government, persuading it to introduce the Welsh Assembly to provide a focus for the Welsh political nation who elect the Assembly representatives. The Assembly is very much a second class body compared with the Scottish Parliament, having very limited powers to do anything, and Welsh Nationalism is still a minority view. However, the Welsh Nationalists do have their platform and will look forward to future generations of Welsh people knowing rather more Welsh than preceding ones.

It is in Scotland where the strongest rift in the Union has been made so far. Consistent and tough campaigning by Scottish Nationalists has now succeeded in forcing the introduction of a Scottish Parliament. The Parliament has limited tax raising powers and wide-ranging legislative powers. It has already chosen a number of areas where it is at variance with Westminster. Scottish Nationalists are very likely to use the Scottish Parliament as a continuing platform compared to the Union. They will seek to identify areas where the Scottish Parliament has no power and claim that it must be given control in the interests of justice and fairness for Edinburgh. The Nationalists will look for every opportunity to find policies hammered out in Westminster which they can portray as mean or unfair in Scotland, and seek a different answer through the Edinburgh Parliament. They will place more and more pressure on any governing party in London, especially where the governing party in London is also a governing coalition partner in the Scottish Parliament, as with the current Labour Party.

Labour's abortive attempt to introduce regional, elected government in England outside London shows that the public are wary of more attempts to split the Kingdom. The English have awoken a little from their slumbers and now regard England as an important country, whose rights should also be represented in the constitutional settlement of Westminster. The decisive vote against an elected regional Assembly in the North-East was a rallying cry for a united England. The English are fighting against the Balkanisation of their country, and fighting for it to have its due recognition at the centre, as it is the dominant part of the Union. England was always self-effacing to the point of self-neglect until Welsh and Scottish nationalisms made progress, persuading the Westminster government to establish the Welsh Assembly and the Scottish Parliament. Now the English people want, at the very least, the Westminster Parliament to only allow English MPs to vote on English issues, to try and balance up the Kingdom. Why should Scottish MPs come to Westminster and vote on health, education, local government and the environment in England, when they are not able to vote on those matters in Scotland, and when English MPs cannot even debate those issues for Scotland, let alone decide them?

In the autumn of 2004, the British Labour government decided to hold a referendum in the North-East of England on the subject of elected, regional government. The British government claimed that this was part of its home-grown devolution programme.

The electorate has always been suspicious about the idea of splitting up England. There is great resentment in England that the EU refuses to recognise England as a place on its maps but always instead recognises artificial constructions, called the North-East, the North-West, Yorkshire and Humberside, East Anglia, the West Midlands, the East Midlands, London, the South-West and the South-East. None of these areas have any sense of identity, common history or political purpose. Successive British governments themselves have been casual in drawing the regional map boundaries, creating different limits to, for example the South-East, for different administrative and governing purposes. Loyalties in England are either local or national, they are not regional.

The European Union wishes to split up England because England is too large to fit in with its plans for groups of regions with limited powers of self-regulation, all under the federal control of Brussels. Many English people deeply resent the idea that we should have to create yet another layer of government, with all the politicians and bureaucrats that go with it, in order to accommodate the European dream.

The British Labour government has constantly denied that it wishes to introduce regional, elected government into England in furtherance of the European project. They say it is a mere coincidence that they too, like Brussels, have come to the conclusion that there is a sense of regional identity in England. They think that sense of regional identity needs to be recognised through the creation of representative institutions, with limited powers to administer and regulate. The Labour government decided to test this proposition in open referendum in the one part of the country that has traditionally been dominated by Labour representatives at all levels of government. The North-East is also one of the regions furthest from London, closest to Scotland with its own independent Parliament, with a worse record on levels of income and job creation than the more prosperous South. The North-East was told that if they had an elected Assembly they could have more favoured treatment like Scotland. For Labour's purposes this seemed ideal. They set out to test the proposition that the people of the North-East felt united, and wished to express this unity in the same way as the people of Scotland by having their own elected Assembly.

Early polls indicated that the government might win. The government fielded their top team and were stunned that 78% of the people of the North-East of England rejected the idea of an elected government in the region. They did so for one very strong reason above all others. They felt passionately that they had more government than they wanted, more government than they needed, and more government than they could afford. They viewed a North-East Assembly as yet another layer of politicians and bureaucrats taking money from them for their own purposes. They anticipated a further increase in taxation in order to pay for it. The subsidiary feeling amongst some of the voters was that it was part of a European project they did not like, and they had no wish to dance to Brussels' tune.

In the North-East it is not wise to go to Sunderland and praise Newcastle or vice versa. Similarly, in the South-West it is not a good idea to go to Plymouth and say that they should be governed from Bristol, or to go to Cornwall and say they should be governed from Exeter in neighbouring Devon. Local loyalties are much stronger and deeper than any possible regional identity. The government has learned this the hard way and has now abandoned its attempts to push through elected regional government in England.

Today we find Britain and Britishness at a crossroads. Those who feel themselves to be more European in Britain share the French worry about the growing Americanisation of world commercial and cultural life. Those who fear that a European Union will damage those most precious elements of Britishness and British government would rather welcome more commercial influence from the US as a counterweight to European government. It leaves Britain with four possible avenues of development. The choice is close upon us. It will be taken wittingly or unwittingly in the few years that lie ahead.

Both main political parties have promised a referendum on whether to adopt the European Union Constitution or not. Such a referendum will be the first opportunity since 1975 for the British people to have a spirited debate on how they see their country and where it should go. They are very likely to vote 'no', forcing a review of the other options for the United Kingdom.

The four options for Britain

There are four options for Britain to choose from in the next few years. The first is to decide that our destiny does lie with our European partners and to plunge in as a willing partner in the construction of a United States of Europe. The British people would need to vote 'Yes' to the constitution and see that was part of the substantial movement of power to Brussels, leading to a common foreign and security policy, and to an ultimate severing of the US alliance. We would have to share the French view that the intention of this was to create a mighty counterweight to the power of the United States of America. We would be drawn in to measures and choices which would undoubtedly distance us from our US cousins rather more.

The second choice would be to deliberately strengthen our ties with the US as being the best way to enjoy the military protection of US forces and to gain more benefit from the undoubted commercial and technological dynamism of the US peoples. This course of action would include joining NAFTA and seeing if that could develop into a wider union of the English-speaking peoples led by America with Britain as a strong second force. This would require rejecting the European Constitution and renegotiating our position.

The third option is to see if Britain can continue to balance its position as it has tried to do in the last twenty-seven years both by being a member of the EU and by strengthening its trade and friendship links with the US and NAFTA. Some people believe it is possible to continue this delicate balancing act, saying no to the more extreme moves towards European federalism, whilst at the same time developing a better relationship with the US to enjoy defence and commercial collaboration. According to this model we would be in Europe but not run by it. We would remain part of the Common Market but we would refuse to surrender sterling as our currency, and we would have no truck with common defence arrangements. We would have a world role as the United Kingdom, but we would also have influence with our European partners through the institutions of the EU and we would have a special relationship based on common language, common interest and often good working relationships between president and prime minister with the US. This is looking increasingly unrealistic as the pressure to conform and to surrender more powers to Brussels intensifies. The Constitution poses us with the fundamental question, are we fully part of the European project or aren't we? If we vote 'No' and the others all accept, it forces us into a renegotiation.

The fourth option would be to go it alone. There is a gathering body of opinion in Britain which would like to see us pull out of the European Union altogether. Whilst some of those who would like us to pull out argue very strongly for the second option, the English-speaking union based first of all on membership of NAFTA, others believe that Britain is large enough to continue to be an independent country with representation in a number of international fora and trading with the five continents of the world. Those who advocate withdrawal from the European Union advocate negotiating a new set of arrangements so that we could continue to trade on sensible terms with our partners. They point out that companies in the EU member states export more to Britain than British companies export to the continent, so there should be plenty of leverage to get a satisfactory deal. The EU has more to lose than Britain, on this argument, as Britain is a net contributor to the Community budget and as Britain is the importer of last resort for many European countries.

These, then, are the possible courses of action for the United Kingdom. They give the lie to those in the various camps who claim that their future for the UK is the only one available. Many Euro-federalists believe there is no alternative for Britain but to plunge into a proper union with our partners. Many Atlanticists believe there is no hope for Britain unless we do the opposite. Many of us wish to renegotiate, explaining to our partners in Europe that we do not wish to be part of their centralising, federalist project. We, nonetheless, do wish to come to a conclusion about the best kind of links we should maintain over trade, the environment and other matters of common interest. I believe that any one of these futures is possible for Britain. Some of them could work with bold and sensible political leadership.

25th state of Euroland or 51st state of the Union?

It is now time for the politicians and public to debate how each of these futures would be secured and which is the more desirable. It really comes down to defining who we are and what our future should be. It is something where each one of us has to look into our own hearts, minds and memories to ask ourselves, 'How British are we, and how British do we wish to remain?' We could become the 25th state of Euroland. If we do so, we will discover that the main decisions have been taken and many features of the EU structure will not be to our liking. Our size and wealth will make us more than just one-25th partner, but we will not have the weight and influence of Germany or France. We have to accept that the United States of Europe (USE) is an idea fashioned by the Germans and the French, designed as their method of preventing future military conflict between their two countries. We may think such conflict unlikely, or preventable by NATO and other forces. They believe strongly that the structure of the Union is crucial to their futures.

We could try to become the 51st state of the American Union. Many who dislike our drift into European control often propose just such a solution. As I will show, this is more akin to what Churchill had in mind. There would be no language barrier, and less of a legal, cultural and political barrier than submerging ourselves in Europe. It would, however, represent a similar surrender of sovereignty to joining the USE, and be a substantial wrench in a new direction for our foreign policy. It was an option with which Harold Wilson toyed in the 1960s when he was the UK's Prime Minister.

The first two of these routes offers the abolition or substantial transmutation of Britain and Britishness. It is also quite clear that the fourth requires a substantial strengthening of Britishness which many would claim is now impossible. We must ask ourselves, 'What is Britishness; what are its unique characteristics? Do these unique characteristics make it worthwhile keeping? How British do each of us feel we are, and how

British are we likely to feel in the years ahead as the inevitable political, constitutional, economic and personal changes unfold?'

The British character

Britishness is often defined as a set of attitudes developed by the peoples of the United Kingdom in their imperial role. The Empire was quintessentially British. It was purposefully called the British Empire and not the English Empire. It was the plaything of the Scots, the Welsh and the Irish as well as the English. Indeed, it was often the Celtic parts of the United Kingdom that plunged disproportionately into Empire to compensate for some of the problems at home. In the hands of some modern interpretations like Norman Davies' *Europe: A History* (1996), and Andrew Marr's *The Day Britain Died* (1999), the death of Empire is sufficient reason why Britain itself should now die and should be replaced by the English, the Scots, the Welsh and the Irish assuming their more normal and rightful position in European politics.

Britain defined its relationship to Empire through a set of values. Britain exported the English language, the Christian religion, a sense of fair play, honest administration, impartial justice, commercial acumen, industrial enterprise, sporting enthusiasm and military prowess to its conquered territories. In the heyday of Empire it is true that Britain was not keen to encourage indigenous manufacture to rival the mighty manufacturing capacity of the home islands. It is true that Britain often introduced no democracy at all when ruling the subject peoples, whilst at the same time developing a red-blooded wide-franchised democracy at home. It is true that a lot of the imperial endeavour was based upon continuous military activity and there were occasions when Britain showed little fairness or tenderness when putting down rebellions or dissent among subject peoples.

It has been fashionable for some years now to write about the darker side of Empire. A group of historians have taken pride in doing Britain down, in highlighting the Black Hole of Calcutta in India, the unpleasant Opium Wars which characterised part of our relationship with China and the concentration camps in the Boer War. It has been less common in recent years to remember the enormous strengths of British imperial achievement and to judge them by the rather barbaric and unpleasant standards of the age in which they were set. Whilst other peoples' and countries' barbarisms cannot excuse any barbarism from the British imperial side, it is important to understand the background, the attitudes and the standards of the day. It is also important to weigh on the scales the undoubted pluses which British Empire brought.

Many British people still see the imperial virtues as characteristics of the British race. The Empire was an expression of Britishness in all senses, not least because the Empire itself was polyglot and Britain itself is now polyglot. The imperial process was a two-way process. Britain took its standards of impartial justice, independent administration and commercial progress to the imperial territories, and received and took back people, artefacts and many aspects of overseas culture from its territories and dominions. We imported the curry, sweet and sour dishes from Asia, tobacco and potatoes from the New World, a feast of food, words and attitudes as British people travelled and learned.

The arrival of a large number of Commonwealth immigrants into Britain in the second half of the twentieth century has brought much of the infinite variety and excitement of Empire back to the home islands. As a result, Britain is now a more tolerant, multiracial and more colourful society. Britishness is the natural identity for dwellers in the home islands wherever they or their parents may have come from.

When a new immigrant settles in London and decides he (or she) does wish to adopt a new identity that is compatible with his new home, it is always British rather than English that he chooses. You do not find settlers from Africa or Asia in Edinburgh saying they are Scottish, in London saying they are English, or in Cardiff saying they are Welsh. As they decide to make this their home and adopt a new identity, it is always the British portmanteau identity which they adopt most easily.

The use of words to define who we are is becoming very potent in this new, brittle world of changing identities. If someone now very firmly says to me that he (or she) is English rather than British, I know it probably means that he is tired of paying for the Scots, is becoming keen on the idea of an English Parliament, and is drifting towards a petty English nationalism which would like to tear the Union apart. If a Scot ferociously tells me he is Scottish and not British, I know that he has exactly the same attitudes from north of the border, seeking an independent Scotland as soon as possible, and wishing to turn his back on the old enemy to the south. The word 'British' is now the healing word, the word that tries to bring together, or keep together, divergent peoples of the United Kingdom islands. It will be a much more difficult place for settlers from Eastern Europe, from Asia, from Africa, from the Caribbean, if Britain does fragment into England, Scotland, Wales and Northern Ireland, as those smaller nations will have a more urgent, younger sense of nationhood which is more exclusive than the British idea deliberately created to encompass the world and run an empire.

The rise of nationalist sentiment in the regions of the UK

It is a sense of frustration at the political process which is leading to some fragmentation of political allegiance and loyalty. Whereas in the 1950s and 1960s the Labour and Conservative parties accounted for 85–90% of the vote, today they are lucky to gain 75% of the vote. A quarter of the electorate or more is now inclined to vote for Liberal Democrats, Welsh Nationalists, Scottish Nationalists, UKIP and other fringe parties. British politics, fractured in the past around the issue of how much government was wanted, with Conservatives offering lower taxes and less government and Labour offering a more enveloping welfare state, now wishes to split over different issues. It is the issues of national and international identity, foreign policy and our relationship with Europe which motivates a significant proportion of the electors who find that the present two-party system does not reflect their passionately held views. This lies behind the disintegration of belief in the British nation and its political expression, the Queen in Parliament.

Tony Blair tells us his Britain is a new country. He seems to think history began in May 1997, when his party swept back into power; or conceivably it began under Margaret Thatcher in the 1980s, an era Blair occasionally conjures up to frighten the children. Anyone who knows Britain better knows that it is an old country. It may have a great future, and we doubtless live in the present, but the past is all around us.

Defining a nation

Some say the past is its own country. Modernisers want to put it behind us, deny it exists, or claim that it is at best an irrelevance and at worst an obstacle to our progress. Yet the past is still our country. It is there in the landscape, in the architecture, in our memories. A country has a past, a present and a future. You can only hope to understand the present and forecast the future if you have first visited the past. You can only work out where we might be going if you know where we have come from.

We each travel daily in our own time machine. Each minute, each second, we decide whether to indulge in memory or spirit-up the future. In our very choice of language we choose a tense for our words. We will make different choices as the day wears on. Each action requires a memory of times past when we did it before.

So it is with a nation. It cannot rid itself of its past, but can in the present draw on those memories of the past which suit it most, or which are most useful to the here and now. A nation can and does change its past by altering perceptions of it. Some nations set out to destroy their ancestry by revolution, rewriting the history books in a wilful act of self-denial. The past usually comes back to haunt them. It lingers on in the landscape and individual memories. A country which tries to destroy its past is not at ease with itself. Our nation has favoured evolution, not revolution; constantly shifting and accommodating the past as each corner of the future opens up a new perspective.

There is a folk memory and a written memory in the form of history. The buildings cannot lie, the landscape changes but slowly, the church bells toll as they have for centuries, the river winds its way across the lea. Each family remembers exploits great and small, local and national, incidents of huge and of no import, and passes them down from generation to generation.

It happens to each one of us. From the moment we are conceived we have a separate history, but it is one interwoven with the history of our families, our communities, our nation. As we move from home to school so our history shifts from all family to partly local and institutional. Some are more influenced by the past than others. Some are more influenced by national events. Most dwell more in the world of family and local events. A few have a broad and deep knowledge of national history. All have some intuition of our history from their own lives, family anecdotes and half remembered school history.

No one leads an entirely contemporary life. Some people are self-consciously archaic, others self-consciously modern or futuristic. All to some extent live in the past. Everyone owns furniture and personal effects acquired over many years. From the day the new toy is delivered to the child, an ageing process starts for both artefact and owner. Most people live in homes that have collections of items representing a span of many years. In most people's minds there is a similar muddle of past, present and future. As a general rule, as people age so they live more in the past, because they have so many more memories and their response to change slows or dulls. This is not universally true. Some older people are revolutionaries, some young fogies deliberately conservative. Some middle-aged people in senior roles are more in touch with the cutting edge of change than many younger people.

The man who is the most passionate opponent of class, hierarchy and inherited privilege may also be the staunchest defender of his rural views. He wants some types of change but not others. The woman who wants promotion at work, a change of job, may be fighting to keep her family together. She is against change at home.

The 40-somethings and 50-somethings are on the whole proud of their youth. They still seem to think 1960s style is modern. They recreate the pop music, the car styles, the permissive climate of their teenage years. Their idea of modern is more archaic than anarchic, more sentimental than radical.

How history shapes a nation

So what then is the nation? Why is Britain a nation? Can Scotland and Wales be called nations again? Why is Europe not yet a nation? Can it ever be? The answer lies in the past. The past is not another country, but a defining part of present countries. Changing the past means adding the present. It means changing the perspective of a people about its past. It means adjusting the focus of a nation's glasses.

Just as individuals time-travel, so do nations. British people do not travel as part of a European nation, because we have not lived in one before. Memories of the Roman occupation are not a part of our daily experience, and we might not be that well disposed to the legions if we studied them more carefully. We have a more vibrant memory of the last few hundred years, and our strongest memory is of the last few decades. The US nation has little collective memory of events on the continent before the arrival of the Pilgrim Fathers.

Collective memories are like grains of sand. They build up on the beach of the nation. They can be buried and shifted, forgotten, or regarded from a different vantage point, but not destroyed. They are there for rediscovery. A nation has a mood, a feeling, that at times burns brightly. Are national memories as strong as family ones? Are they to be compared?

Each nation has its own symbols, ceremonies, traditions and colours. These emblems become important when there is conflict over what constitutes a nation. In 1939, Welsh and English, Scottish and Northern Irish agreed that Hitler and all he stood for was evil. They rallied to the red, white and blue of the Union flag. There was agreement that the United Kingdom had to stand for democracy and the self-determination of peoples against the force of German imperialism and racism. That conflict defined our nation's values sharply. Victory allowed us to write a chapter of European history, and ask that others saw the changes of 1945 when democracy triumphed as good in itself. We did not then create a united European nation, but took pride in how Britain had stood alone, and then with US help, for a common cause.

People can no more lay aside their past than a snail can shed its shell. Nor can a nation cast it off. A nation carries its past like a snail its house. Any nation which tries to shake off the shell is vulnerable to breakdown and attack. Revolutionary eras shake off the past only to provoke civil wars and reaction. Revolutionary change still cannot purge a country of all its history, it can only suppress and distort it. Revolutionary Russia changed all the place-names, rewrote the history books, tried to suppress the religion of the people and the culture of the Tsars, only to see its work reversed with the collapse of communism. Today, the greatest pride in Moscow is in the great buildings of the Kremlin, the home of the old ruling dynasty. At the heart of France is a hole where the monarchy and Church once stood. The Catholic Church has not been eliminated by the atheistic outlook of the Jacobins. The elected presidency has adopted some of the trappings of the old monarchy it replaced, and pursues through its monumentalism the search for a centralised secular governmental soul.

Britishness is similarly bound up with the past. In the 1940s and 1950s it was easy to define the British. Mother and father were married and stayed together. Large areas of the world were coloured red on the maps. Large-scale immigration into Britain from the New Commonwealth had not started. British people travelled proudly around the world after the war despite the poverty and drabness. People were born into a world of settled values. These were to be shattered or questioned by what happened next. The sexual revolution undermined the conventional family. The arrival of people from all over the world led to a multi-ethnic Britain.

The idea of Britishness transformed itself into the embracing identity of today. Many felt ill at ease as families were rent asunder from within, and the old nations of the UK started to bridle at the union from without.

The past is there in the landscape. The Roman occupation left straight roads like Fosse Way and Watling Street, villas and forts, grid-iron patterned towns, coins and artefacts. The French invasion of William the Conqueror in 1066 left us Battle Abbey, the White Tower of London and some of our government machinery. The attempted invasion by the Spaniards in 1588 is commemorated in the Armada train that departs daily from Plymouth, in the tourist attractions of that city and in our folklore and history. The Catholic powers' attempt to kill the king and change our religion in 1605 is remembered annually on Bonfire Night. Napoleon's failure to conquer us is there for all to see at Waterloo Station and in Trafalgar Square, celebrating the two most famous British victories of the long Napoleonic Wars. The defeat of the German invasion plans in 1940 is relived through many a war movie; there are war memorials to the dead in every town and village, and statues to the great military leaders in London.

The history of Britain in Europe

Britishness is bound up with this difficult relationship with Europe. The first millennium after the birth of Christ saw the country regularly pillaged, conquered and settled by marauders from elsewhere in Europe. Romans, Normans, Danes, Angles, Saxons – all made their mark. The second millennium saw a nation emerge, founded on liberty and a sense of justice, that fought off threats to its independence by making good use of the moat around these islands. Our defeats of France, Spain, Holland and Germany during the second millennium prevented any one power becoming dominant on the continent. After we gave up Calais we spent 500 years fighting European wars; not for conquest of territory, but to keep the balance of power. We usually allied with the smaller and weaker powers against the greater.

Those who want us to be fully engaged in Europe have usually had their way. We were regularly at war on the continent. We were again in the 1990s in the Balkans. In the twentieth century, British lives were lost in two world wars, in the Spanish and Russian civil wars and in lesser conflicts on the continent. We have twice had to remodel Europe with our US allies, through the Treaty of Versailles and at Potsdam after the Second World War.

Should Britain have been this committed? How would we have fared if we had not plunged into the First World War? What if we had intervened to stop Hitler earlier? Would there have been a Hitler at all if the UK and the US had not helped France to such a comprehensive victory in 1918? Could it be that some of our military intervention made it worse, not better?

The UK could have followed a maritime strategy of constructive disengagement from continental land battles. If we had fewer ambitions to influence the direction of events on the continent we could have defended these islands at less cost to ourselves in lives and treasure. Why do we want all this influence? Is it significant that the Liberal government which led us in the First World War through such atrocious losses was the last Liberal government? Perhaps the people never forgave them for the slaughter and the sense of futility captured in the songs and poems of that era.

The thesis that Britain had to stop hostile occupation of the Low Countries is flawed. There is limited truth in the idea that the Channel ports are a pistol loaded and pointed against England's soft southern underbelly, the Thames estuary and the Kentish coast. The idea that we could stop hostile occupation of Calais and Dunkirk by continental military intervention is not well based in historical events. After the return of Calais to France in the mid-sixteenth century the nearest Channel ports have remained in French hands, and France has often been hostile to Britain. They never succeeded in using them to launch a successful invasion. For many years in the seventeenth century the Dutch challenged Britain's supremacy at sea. They did not succeed in mounting a successful opposed invasion, although the political leaders of Britain did invite in a Dutch king and queen as a solution to an internal British crisis in 1688. The transfer of Belgium from one owner to another until its establishment as a separate country did little to damage Britain.

For Britain has been defended by three physical, mental and military barriers. The first is the Channel which has proved such a formidable barrier to invaders. Channel tides and winds helped to destroy the Armada. Napoleon never dared put his barges to sea. Hitler gave up when he failed to control the air and sea.

The second line of defence has been the Royal Navy, and more recently its air arm. Many continental imperialists thought better of it when they saw the force of Britain at sea and more recently in the air. The Royal Navy was crucial in destroying the Armada with fireships. Napoleon knew his ships could not see off the Royal Navy. Hitler failed to win the battle for air supremacy, let alone naval supremacy to allow the invasion forces to cross.

The third line of defence is the spirit of the British people. 'Britons never, never, never shall be slaves' is written in the hearts of many. Britain would fight street by street were any continental power foolish enough to invade and strong enough to get across the narrow straits.

Had we kept out of the First World War we would probably have maintained our empire for longer. Had we relied on sea and air power we could have defended ourselves and left the French and Germans to fight over the future of the continent. We were weakened by the First World War. We were late to intervene as Hitler rose to power. The effort needed to crush him by the 1940s was enormous. It led to an early collapse of our influence in many other parts of the world after 1945, and to an easier assumption by the US of first-power status. We have paid dearly for our European entanglements. It is easier to argue we have been too involved in Europe, than to argue that we have not been involved enough.

US nationalism and understated British nationalism

The British Union has been much less bombastic about itself in the last fifty years than the US. It is never easy holding together very large countries, even where there is military and imperial success, a common language, and other obvious means of keeping people together. The idea of US nationalism is sold daily to the US people. Whenever you visit someone in authority in America there is always the Stars and Stripes flag in his or her room. For all main public celebrations, red, white and blue is predominantly used in the balloons and the bunting, and even the drum majorettes would usually be dressed in patriotic colours. Every young American is taught the wonders of the Constitution, and encouraged to express loyalty to the aims of the founding fathers of the United States of America. The oath of allegiance has only just been dropped as a compulsory opener to the school day. New arrivals in America are encouraged to learn English as the way to gain a job and get on in the world. Most of the volunteers that go to the US willingly sign up to the US idea of self-help through capitalism. Indeed, that is often the reason most go there in the first place.

There is no such constant repetition of the brand of Britain in British education or in British life. The British are curiously reticent now about expressions of Britishness. The adoption of the national flag as a symbol by an extreme party in British political life has made many people nervous of using their own flag for more emollient purposes. It is a great pity that people are put off using our flag, but understandable when they feel that some of the people brandishing it are connected with hooliganism or even racism.

The understatement of British life is clear in any ministerial office. No flags are ever stood in the corners of the rooms, and British government is remarkably undemonstrative about its belief in Britishness or its wish to promote it. History teaching in schools now seems keener to undermine the achievements of Empire and of the British by offering many timely reminders of the mistakes that were made, rather than seeking to show that British achievement around the world was notable. Devolution has taken hold in many of our schools. In Welsh schools there is a passionate wish to teach the Welsh language and to give children an independent sense of Welsh identity. In Scottish schools, Scottish history and Scottish attitudes predominate where once British views were more prevalent. The English are beginning to think of retaliation with growing signs now of English nationalism in teaching south of the border, but with that same English sense of understatement and self-criticism which characterises the race.

Team sports are very important ways of organising senses of identity. In America people are desperately keen to see US teams do well around the world, and to see US athletes scoop the pool when it comes to gold medals in the Olympics and other international sporting meetings. The British have never had the same sense of Britishness through sport, despite the fact that the British are a very sporting race who have exported a large number of interesting games to the rest of the world, only to see the rest of the world play them considerably better than many British teams are able to do.

It has been accepted in British life that most of the sporting activity takes place in the old nations that predated the Union. Intense rivalry between Ireland, Scotland, Wales and England is prevalent in soccer, in rugby and in many other team sports. One of the great national games is cricket. Welsh people willingly play as part of the English team. Scottish people have usually kept their distance from the whole idea, although in the most recent world cricket competition Scotland fielded a promising looking side of its own. In rugby, most passion is given to developing the individual home teams of Scotland, Wales, England and Ireland. It is the one aberration in Irish life where Northern Irish and southern Irish come together and play under the same Irish colours. The British Lions have their day and have their successes, but they do not attract the same degree of sustained passion as the individual national teams. In soccer, many fans are left wondering what a British team would look like and where it might rank in the world. For the last thirty years separate teams of England, Scotland, Wales and Ireland have not been that successful. No one could imagine the US fielding four or five different teams from different parts of that large country. Nor could anyone now imagine the Federal Republic of Germany fielding four or five teams representing the larger federal states within their union.

If we were serious about developing and treasuring British identity we would do rather more to develop British sporting teams and to field them internationally. The presence of a British soccer team, the more sustained presence of the British Lions in the world of rugby, and the development of a British cricket team could make quite a difference to popular perceptions of where true loyalties lay. The antipathy between the old nations within the Union can be so great that many a Scot would willingly cheer for an opposing foreign team against England, especially if Scotland has itself been eliminated from the international competition.

A sign that the Union is not all dead comes from the English who would nearly always cheer the Scottish, the Welsh or the Irish team in circumstances where England has been eliminated and where one of the other home teams was going on and meeting foreign competition to try to win the trophy. It is easier for people from the dominant part of the Union to feel relaxed about the Union, but it is also important for those who wish the Union to survive that this remains so.

A sense of European identity is slow to emerge. In English schools children feel overwhelmingly British. It nails the lie of federalists that we are to plunge into a European Union for the young people who feel themselves to be more European than British. The younger generation is more enthusiastically British and less European in its sensibilities than the parental generation that preceded them. This is not surprising, as young people do not regularly travel to the continent on business to trade in the way that the middle-aged generation does. Young people in the true British tradition wrestle with foreign languages with considerable difficulty. The language barrier is probably the main impediment to a greater sense of European identity and to more exchange and conversation across the Channel.

The advent of cheaper air travel has begun to change people's travel patterns as well. In the 1970s and 1980s the package holiday market opened up travel to Spain, to Italy and to France for a large number of people who had not travelled abroad before. More recently, the advent of good-value transatlantic fares has opened up the US to many more visitors. Many British people prefer to travel the long distance across the Atlantic than the short distance across the Channel because they feel more at home in an English-speaking culture.

Summer gives government Ministers the opportunity to travel abroad to promote British exports, to work with British companies and to learn how others do things. There is always a long queue of requests for Ministers to visit the US, Canada, Australia, New Zealand and English-speaking Asia. Few want to visit Bonn or Frankfurt or Paris or Rome. On one occasion the Foreign Office sent round a memo saying that it could not accept any more visitors to the US, but it urgently required people to go to the major European capitals to give some sense of our Europeanness and some encouragement to our partners.

The reluctance of senior, well educated people in governments wishing to be more European to travel to European destinations spoke volumes about how those people see themselves in practice. Although their heads – the Prime Minister and the Foreign Office – tell them they should feel and be European, their hearts and their instincts drag them across the Atlantic. In many ways the Atlantic is a narrower divide than the Channel.

Some making footfall for the first time in the US are amazed by its differences, but many see a familiarity of outlook and approach. The shared history is everywhere to be seen. In some ways America has preserved eighteenth-century Britain rather better than Britain herself. Some roads are still called turnpikes. They still have a means of impeaching their elected monarch when we have lost the process of impeachment against the evil councillors of our government. They have preserved more of the vitality and independent spirit of the Protestant and Puritan religion than we have succeeded in doing in apathetic Britain. The very architecture of Washington is a perfect model of the European revival of classicism that came from the grand tours and the fevered study of Greco-Roman artefacts and fragments.

What, then, are we to make of ourselves as a mixed people who have spread our influence so widely around the world, and now find the world coming back to spread its influence on us? As we eat our curry and rice, or contemplate going to buy sweet and sour pork at the local Chinese restaurant, are we British, European or English? As we read our English-language newspapers about a sex scandal in the presidency, watch old US movies and enjoy US comedies imported by our television companies, are we Little Americans, or are we still Europeans? As we sit in a street café, freezing out of doors (because that is how the Italians do it), drinking a cappuccino, planning a package holiday to Spain for the summer, but speaking in English and paying in sterling, are we British or are we Europeans? Are the cappuccino and street café culture just signs that varied Britain can absorb influences from everywhere? Why should the street café and the cappuccino be more influential in defining our identity than the McDonald's or the Coke float? If we go to Disneyland in Paris, are we going because we like the US cultural achievement, or because we like Paris, or because we like both, or because we are simply muddled? Do we have to be careful in case regressing to Scottish, English and Welsh identities makes it very difficult for many new Britons who have arrived over the last forty years from various countries and climes? Could Englishness, or Welshness, be an inclusive identity, as successful as British in absorbing new peoples and creating a polyglot new culture?

The US has been a great melting pot by insisting on compulsory Americanisation. Whilst New York is still split into a dozen different districts, preserving much of the cultural origins of its people – the Italian area, the Spanish area, and so forth – the rest of the US is more united, showing the success of a policy based on one flag, one anthem, one central bank, one government, one language and one idea of nationhood. Britain has been more relaxed or more careless about its idea of nationhood. Into the cultural and educational vacuum that is sometimes being created, new nationalisms are being poured. The present British establishment does not believe in Britain and is actively encouraging, or conniving in, the destruction of Britishness by the forces of Europeanisation from without, and devolution from within. This is a time for Britain to start making some decisions. It is time for people to decide for themselves whether they value being British, and if so, whether they are going to do something to define a new Britain for the new century.

Notes

A fresh approach to Britain and the British can be found in Gidoomal et al. (2001). J.C.D. Clark (2003) raises some of the longer-term issues in the UK's relationships with the US and the EU countries. The general choices facing Britain are set out in Rosenbaum (2001), drawing eclectically from across the spectrum of views. The Union of England with Wales under the Tudors is covered in Elton (1997), especially pp. 175–7; and the union with Scotland in Ashley (1965), pp. 228–31.

The policy of the Labour government on devolution is set out in Redwood (1999).

Sampson (1965, 1982) sets out the institutional structure of the UK.

Walker (1970) gives an insider's view of the workings of government.

Bogdanor (1999) provides a Liberal view of the changes to government structure in the UK in recent years.

Jenkins (1995) attacks the centralisation of power in quangos under the Conservatives, a process which has got far worse since 1997.

The views of other commentators on the present trends in British politics and society can be read in Hitchens (1999), Heffer (1999) and Marr (2000).

The new style of European history is typified by the blockbuster work of Norman Davies (1996).

The wider themes of nationhood and ethnicity are well studied in Mortimer (1999).

5

A United States of Europe or a Union of English-Speaking Peoples: Two Rival Models for the US and Britain

Churchill's vision of Britain, Europe and the US

Winston Churchill set out his view of the development of a United Europe and the eventual union of the English-speaking peoples in two crucial speeches in 1946. The first was delivered on 5 March at Westminster College, Fulton, Missouri. In it he paid tribute to the enormous power of the United States and the way that power was used to further democratic purposes around the world. He regularly associated the UK with US aims and constantly referred to the English-speaking peoples.

Churchill set out the task for the English-speaking peoples over the years ahead. He said that together we must stand up for 'the safety and welfare, the freedom and progress, of all the homes and families of all the men and women in all the lands'. He wanted the US and Britain to stand against tyranny, war and famine. He called upon America to back his plan for United Nations forces to reinforce the new organisation to keep world order. He drew attention to the great common tradition between the US and Britain when he said:

> we must never cease to proclaim in fearless tones the great principles of freedom and the rights of man which are the joint inheritance of the English-speaking world and which through Magna Carta, the Bill of Rights, the habeas corpus, trial by jury, and the English Common

Law find their most famous expression in the American Declaration of Independence.

In a moving passage, he pledged:

> all this means that the people of any country have the right, and should have the power by constitutional action, by free unfettered elections, with secret ballot, to choose or change the character or form of government under which they dwell; that freedom of speech and thought should reign; the course of justice, independent of the Executive, unbiased by any party, should administer laws which have received the broad assent of large majorities or are consecrated by time and custom. Here are the title deeds of freedom which should lie in every cottage home, here is the message of the British and American peoples to mankind.

Churchill's aim was common citizenship between the United Kingdom and the United States. He called upon the US in this epoch-making speech of 1946 to grant a special relationship between the British Commonwealth and Empire and the United States. He said:

> for eternal association requires not only the growing friendship and mutual understanding between our two vast but kindred systems of society, but the continuance of the intimate relationship between our military advisers, leading to common study of potential dangers, similarity of weapons and manuals of instructions, and to the interchange of officers and cadets at technical college.

The US and UK should use each other's bases and provide mutual military security. He foresaw, 'eventually there may come the principle of common citizenship that we may be content to leave to destiny, whose outstretched arm many of us can already clearly see'.

In the rest of the speech Churchill revealed the threat as he saw it from communism. His memorable phrase about an iron curtain descending across the continent was so strong that it has taken people's minds away from the leading theme and main opening of the speech, urging the English-speaking peoples to a stronger union. Churchill looked forward to a world fifty years on where he would see:

> seventy or eighty millions of Britons spread about the world and united in defence of our traditions, our way of life, and of the world

causes which you and we espouse. If the population of the English-speaking Commonwealths be added to that of the United States with all that such co-operation implies in the air, on the sea, all over the globe and in science and in industry, and in moral force, there will be no quivering, precarious balance of power to offer its temptation to ambition or adventure. On the contrary, there will be an overwhelming assurance of security.

Churchill passionately believed that only the US and Britain standing strong side by side could see off the communist threat and persuade Russia not to open another war.

The parallel speech on the tragedy of Europe was delivered at Zurich University on 19 September 1946. Churchill drew a contrast between Christian faith, Christian ethics, culture, arts, philosophy and science that had come from Europe over the centuries with the 'series of frightful nationalistic quarrels originated by the Teutonic nations, which we have seen even in this twentieth century and in our own lifetime, wreck the peace and mar the prospects of all mankind'. He was stirred by the vision of famine, tyranny, migrating peoples, desolation and destruction. Churchill never wanted to see such desolation and despair again. His remedy was very simple. He wished to make all the continent of Europe or the greater part of it as free and happy as Switzerland. He decided the way to do this was 'to recreate the European family, or as much of it as we can, and provide it with a structure under which it can dwell in peace, safety and in freedom. We must build a kind of United States of Europe.'

Throughout the speech Churchill was careful to stress that the British were in a different position with their Commonwealth of Nations. He went on to say, 'The first step in the recreation of the European family must be a partnership between France and Germany. In this way only can France recover the moral leadership of Europe. There can be no revival of Europe without a spiritually great France and a spiritually great Germany.' A United States of Europe would reduce the strength of any individual European state, and give small nations an important part in its constitution. He sketched the idea of a federal United States of Europe based upon the four freedoms that President Roosevelt had set out. It would be achieved by forming a Council of Europe led by France and Germany. The speech ends in a conclusive way, 'Great Britain, the British Commonwealth of Nations, mighty America, and I trust Soviet Russia – for then indeed all would be well – must be the friends and sponsors of the new Europe and must champion its right to live and shine.'

No one reading these speeches could be in any doubt about Churchill's aim. Churchill categorically wanted a United States of Europe involving only the continental powers. He was assured that Britain, with its Commonwealth and Empire, was one of the big players and would remain so. He was passionately committed to an ever greater rapprochement between Britain and the US, seeing the growing dominance of the US stretching ahead. He was well aware that the US had the keys to the nuclear bomb technology shared between Britain, the US and Canada. He was very keen that this technology should not fall into hostile communist hands and that the breathing space granted by the technical lead should be used to create a strong English-speaking union that could police freedom and democracy around the world. Churchill sowed the seeds of an idea which still has relevance today, as the US begins to question its enthusiasm for a United Europe including the UK.

Kohl, Chirac and EU views of the future

Despite the clarity of these comments, those seeking to build a United States of Europe have constantly quoted the one phrase from Churchill which, when taken out of context, could lead people to believe that he wanted Britain to be part of this new structure. There is no better place to start in seeing this misquotation than in the works of former Chancellor Helmut Kohl, far and away the most influential of the European political leaders of the 1980s and 1990s, keen to establish a federal United States of Europe. In 1991 Chancellor Kohl delivered an important address to Edinburgh University when receiving an honorary doctorate there. Kohl set out his vision of unity in diversity for Europe. He stated, 'for many reasons, not least geographical and historical ones, we as Germans are particularly keen to see Europe become more and more integrated'. He went on to quote Churchill's phrase about a kind of United States of Europe with approval. Kohl's speech is littered with assumptions that Britain will be part of this common structure. He nowhere refers to the obvious sense of Churchill's speech that Britain would not.

Where Kohl and Churchill did agree was in seeing a United States of Europe on the continent as being some kind of guarantee that there would be no more nationalistic wars. To Kohl, 'German unity and European union were two sides of the same coin.' The Edinburgh speech pointed in two directions at the same time. The audience was assured by the German Chancellor that Germany would not become eastward-looking but would remain firmly bedded in the West. On the other hand, the speech proudly pointed out: 'Krakow is the centre of Europe and Prague and Budapest are at the heart of Europe.' Chancellor Kohl was always determined that not only were the two Germanys to reunite quickly, but Poland, Hungary and Czechoslovakia should rapidly gain admission to the EU.

Kohl also believed the EU would be developed and furthered by the strengthened powers of the European Community itself. He stated in the Edinburgh speech, 'European stability largely depends on being able to enhance the scope for action of the Community both internally and externally.' He always sought not only economic and monetary union, which he won for the continental countries in the Treaty of Maastricht, but also political union, which emerged somewhat watered down from the Treaty of Amsterdam. Kohl sought a common foreign and security policy leading on to a common defence policy. He and his advisers felt that within a decade there would be a common European army able to enforce it. He stated at Edinburgh, 'we vitally need a common European police force that would be able to operate without let or hindrance in all the Community countries'. Chancellor Kohl sought much wider powers for the European Parliament, a European currency, a single European interest rate, more common regional policies, a European criminal justice policy, common frontiers and immigration controls, a single passport, a single foreign policy – in summary, he wanted a federal super-state, including the UK. His Edinburgh speech was less reassuring to his British audience than he had perhaps hoped, although it was on reflection wise that he delivered it in Scotland rather than in a more Euro-sceptic part of the UK.

Kohl took his thinking further when he made an important speech on European union on 17 May 1992, when presenting the Konrad Adenauer prizes. This was one of his boldest statements of his enlarged vision for a united Europe. He stated:

in Maastricht we laid the cornerstone for the completion of a European Union. The process leading to this objective is irreversible. We have shown with our contribution that united Germany is actively assuming its responsibility in and for Europe.

European federalists led by Kohl were always keen to show that the thing was inevitable and irreversible. Kohl's thesis was that a united Germany greatly enlarged by the addition of the eastern *Länder* and representing a colossal part of the population and geography of central and Western Europe had to be bound in to this new European super-state. He felt that only by this process could German power and influence be harnessed for a greater good and the interests of the smaller countries around taken properly into account. His careful choice of the words 'irreversible' and 'responsibility' are part of this theme.

To Kohl, the Treaty on European Union marked the beginning of a new and decisive phase in the process of European unification, that in a few years would lead to the completion of that for which Konrad Adenauer, Jean Monnet and Robert Schuman – as well as other fathers of modern-day Europe – had laid the foundation. Kohl was always worried that momentum or progress towards an integrated Europe was going to falter. There are always countries out to get a better deal, and there was always the problem of Britain seeking to veto progress. Momentum had to be achieved and an impression of rapid progress was created through speeches and decisions. It was also important in Kohl's view to root it in some sense of an evolving past. The EU needed its heroes, its guides and its progenitors, and they had to be regularly lauded. Figurative candles were lit to their memory, rooms and buildings were named after them as the European Union created its own sense of history and subtly attempted to have the whole history of Europe rewritten as a progress towards its ultimate consummation in a European Union. Charlemagne, other Holy Roman Emperors, and even Napoleon, jostle with Monnet and Schuman in the temples of European togetherness.

Kohl asserted that at Maastricht we agreed a political as well as an economic and monetary union. This was the most contentious part of the whole Maastricht negotiations. Britain and some other countries had vigorously resisted the idea that on top of a single currency the member states had to sign up to the effective integration of everything else – the completion of the EU that Kohl had always sought. The ink was scarcely dry on the Maastricht Treaty with its much-watered-down general provisions for political union before Kohl and his advisers were briefing that the process was nonetheless irreversible and that Maastricht represented an important movement in that direction. For Germany and for Kohl, political union was the prize and monetary union merely the instrument and the sacrifice to France to bring it all about.

The European Union Constitution continues the development in exactly the way Kohl was seeking. Franco-German consensus has moved on since the 1990s. It has become impatient with the slow rate of progress, created both by the reluctant Europeans – the UK, Denmark and Sweden – and by the necessary diversion of taking in the ten new member states of the East. That is why the European Union Constitution not only carries common defence and security policy much further than Maastricht but why it also allows for accelerated cooperation between leading states like

France and Germany. The two founding powers and driving forces of the Union are keen to complete what Kohl and others began.

Foreign policy

In his Munich speech Kohl revealed exactly what political union entailed.

First of all, formulation of a common foreign policy. In the course of the next few years the Union will be speaking with a single voice on all major foreign policy matters and in particular it will be undertaking joint foreign policy action.

The idea of a common foreign policy was bitterly fought by Britain and some others. Britain was naturally worried about its special arrangements with the United States and wanted to keep British security firmly based on NATO and the US alliance. Nonetheless, the British government conceded the principle of a foreign policy spokesman and a common European line where it could be agreed by unanimity. Germany and France wished to press on, desperately seeking the common foreign policy achieved by qualified majority voting and enforced by strong personality.

European army

Kohl also believed that 'a European security and defence identity will need to be formed ... This initiative is not directed against anyone. On the contrary, our European partners are invited to take part in this project.' France and Germany were tiring of the slow progress being made by the other member states, especially Britain. As Kohl told his audience, they had gone ahead with a joint army corps, a clear indication that they wished to create a common European army, navy and air force. The rather crude comment that the initiative was not directed against anyone did little to reassure people. It was clearly not directed against Russia itself, towards whom Kohl always pursued a very friendly policy. Russia understood that it was the US and NATO rather than the common European army that it should worry about. If anything, the initiative was directed against the UK, reluctant to come alongside this very important major step towards the creation of a super-state in place of a common market.

Common criminal laws

After making some noises aimed at a reassurance that the US would still be important and the transatlantic relationship still mattered, Kohl expatiated on his third area, 'integrating the core areas of interior and justice policy'. He sought a European police force to fight drug abuse and organised crime. He was after a common asylum and immigration policy. In this crucial set of areas Kohl was well ahead of German opinion, as his speech made clear. Germans shared some of the British fears about having immigration and criminal justice matters settled internationally rather than nationally. Germany feared that it would mean even more people crossing its permeable frontiers and less strict control than the German nation might exert for itself. The idea of a European police force was broached to fight obvious transnational criminal problems, where Kohl thought he could get most support from other countries. The intention, however, clearly went much deeper, and was part of a process of trying to create a powerful European state backed by a strong police presence.

Creating an area of common security and justice has been strongly embedded in the new draft Constitution. Not even waiting for the member states and parliaments to catch up, the European Union is making rapid progress in implementing the common asylum policy and is spreading common justice by mutual recognition of decisions and judgments. The plan is developing much as the French and Germans wanted in the 1990s.

A stronger European Parliament

His fourth aim was 'to improve the ability of the European Parliament to impose democratic controls on the European Commission authorities in Brussels ... In Maastricht we undertook important steps in this direction, however, this was not enough.' Kohl allowed himself another sideswipe at the inadequacies of the Maastricht Treaty where he had failed to convince all his partners of the need for rapid and urgent progress. Britain and France were both reluctant to see a strengthened European Parliament, preferring the power to reside around the Council of Ministers' table in the hands of elected ministerial politicians answerable to some extent to their national parliaments rather than the European one.

After urging immediate discussions to broaden EC membership from the twelve to include Austria, Sweden and Finland, Kohl said that at the same time institutional strengthening had to take place in the EC. In this, Kohl spoke on the correct side of the European debate about whether a widening of the Community, and expansion in its number of members, would lead to a loosening or a strengthening of central control. Kohl was quite clear that it had to lead to a strengthening of central control as it had done at the time of previous enlargements. Events proved Kohl to be right, and those British Euro-sceptics who thought that a widening would lead to a loosening were once again thwarted. Kohl had to deal with the growing German disillusion with the idea of the abolition of the Deutschmark. He told the European peoples that a common European currency 'will open up numerous freedoms and, as such, expand horizons'. He wanted the common currency to be just as stable as the Deutschmark. He claimed credit for having put into the Maastricht Treaty a central bank modelled on the Bundesbank. This, he told his audience, would guarantee that stability.

We now know that events turned out rather differently. Over the first year of its life the European Central Bank, whilst using German structures, adopted a rather loose monetary policy which has led to a rapid devaluation of the external value of the euro. The European Bank may well have as little political influence over it as the German one and have a certain kind of independence put into its statutes. Unfortunately, it has not presided over a stable currency in the way that the Bundesbank did for many years. The conclusion to Kohl's speech summed up his general message over his lifetime at the head of European politics.

> The European unification process has been a key factor in the history of the Federal Republic of Germany. Only if we continue to pursue this course consistently will we continue to be successful in Germany, in a strong and united Europe. We remember what Konrad Adenauer said in his memoirs: 'in my view the European nation states had a past, but no future. This applied in the political, the economic, and the social sectors. No individual European country was able to guarantee its people a secure future on its own strength.'

Kohl reminded his audience of a provision in the German basic law of 1949, the eventual unification of Europe in line with Churchill's vision.

German thinking externalised the problems they had had in constructing a democratic, free and peace-loving state onto the rest of Europe. One of the most contentious parts of Kohl's thought was his statement that we needed a European Union to prevent future wars. This reflected Churchill's thinking from a very different era. Whilst it was just about understandable that Winston Churchill, in the immediate aftermath of the war, was worried not only about the communist threat but also about the remote possibility of the resurgence of German nationalism, it is more difficult to understand why democratic leaders of free Germany in the 1980s and 1990s had the same kind of fear. Kohl's critics offered two different lines of attack on his thinking. One group, myself included, pointed out that democratic peace-loving Germany of the 1980s and 1990s was not likely to go to war or to seek aggressive control over other people's territory again. He was fighting a spectre. Other critics said that there were much better guarantees against such German action in the future through NATO, US involvement in Europe, and the United Nations Charter. Most of us felt that there was never any likelihood of Germany declaring war on its neighbours in the second half of the twentieth century. This was not because Germany had joined the Common Market or the EU, but because the whole structure of German and European politics had shifted decisively against such action.

Nonetheless, German thinking became dominant in the new Europe of the post-war world. The irony is that a structure invented by Churchill to deal with the futures of the devastated and defeated powers on the continent was transformed into an instrument for European Union, and subsequently came back to haunt the United Kingdom which had been carefully kept apart from any such proposal by Churchill. Many federally inclined British thinkers often quoted Churchill without bothering to read his speeches or realising that he wanted something very different from a United States of Europe where Britain was just one province among many. Churchill, I am sure, is turning in his grave as a result of what has now happened with the reunification of Germany, the sidelining of the Commonwealth and the failure to follow through the move to union which he started in his special relationship with the US.

Kohl's legacy lives on and now shines even brighter. The present German government is a strong proponent of 'political union', the remodelling of Europe as a single federal state along German lines. President Chirac of France wishes a core of European countries to rush forward to something more like a centralised French state. Kohl's candle has become a brazier, inflaming the European skies.

The attitude of France

On 27 June 2000, Jacques Chirac, President of France, made an important speech to the German Bundestag. Chirac said that the division of Germany was a tragic parenthesis in the story of unification of Germany and the continent. He began in high-flown phrases, praising German unity and the return of the capital to Berlin. As the first foreign head of state to address the whole of Germany, he expressed delight at the huge change in France's former adversary. He chronicled how Konrad Adenauer and General de Gaulle worked together to create a Franco-German alliance, how this was strengthened by Willi Brandt and Georges Pompidou, continued by Helmut Schmidt and Valéry Giscard d'Estaing, and developed further by Helmut Kohl with François Mitterrand. Chirac sees the European Union as 'the world's leading economic and trading power'. He sees it as 'a research and innovation giant', greatly strengthened by the adoption of the euro as part of the unification process. He points out that the EU is making its voice heard well beyond its borders, and he welcomes the development of a separate EU foreign and security policy. Chirac looks forward to the arrival of Europe as 'a world power in which majority voting is the rule and which reflects the relative weights of the member states'. He is keen on developing an inner or pioneer group of states clustered around Germany and France that will take the process of political integration forward much more quickly. The immediate task he wishes to undertake is a central economic policy, a stronger defence and security policy and a common fight against crime amongst the pioneer group. Chirac wants a European constitution setting out the functions of the different levels of government, and is an enthusiast for the charter of fundamental rights. Chirac praises new alliances in aerospace, chemicals, energy, insurance and services, and looks forward to more mergers and common working between French and German business. Whilst some saw in the speech a little cooling of ardour compared with Herr Fischer's dramatic statement of the need for a United States of Europe, there is little in Chirac's words to comfort British politicians. Whilst Chirac may be more careful in how he explains his ambitions, looking behind him to the French audience as well as to the front to the German one he was addressing, the end result is the same. Chirac's idea of the united Europe is one which harnesses industrial, commercial and military power, has a single economic policy, a single currency, a single foreign policy and a combined military machine to back up that foreign policy stance. In more recent speeches, President Chirac has spoken warmly of how the European Constitution will unify Europe to a greater extent, something which he strongly favours. Like the German government, the French government is determined that the EU should speak with one voice in foreign affairs; should back up its foreign policy with a common defence force; and move rapidly to common borders and a common justice policy.

Britain at the edge of Europe but at the centre of the world

In his Fulton, Missouri, speech, and in his writings generally, Churchill always stated that Britain, with its Empire – or Commonwealth, as imperial countries gained independence – should stand alongside the US and the newly united Europe as one of the big three influences upon future world development. Churchill was even more of a visionary. He looked forward to a day when British power, even with its Commonwealth and Empire, might not be sufficient on its own to fulfil these onerous responsibilities. He was quite clear in all his writings that the solution was a union of the English-speaking peoples.

Churchill's aims for the post-war world

Churchill the historian wrote *A History of the English Speaking Peoples*. He did not write 'A History of the European Peoples', which would have been the natural thing to do had he wished Britain to be part of a united Europe. The *History of the English Speaking Peoples* shows his love and enthusiasm for Australia, New Zealand, South Africa, the Indian sub-continent, the United States and Canada, as well as the home islands. Churchill felt that the ties of kinship, language and common governmental systems were such that it would be possible to bring these countries together in one large English-speaking union.

Nowhere in his speeches and writings does Churchill look forward to the modern world where mighty Asia emerges as the dominant force on the world landscape by dint of huge population and growing economic strength. Nowhere did Churchill forecast the enormous increase in the commercial power of Japan, nor did he contemplate what would happen when over a billion Chinese began to make some sensible decisions about their economic and political development and wished to have some influence in the world. It is possible that he dimly grasped what might happen to the relative size of Britain and even the US as these events unfolded. It may just have been that he had a powerful emotional tie to all of the territories of the former Empire and then the Commonwealth, such that he hoped one day on different terms the original Empire could be put back together again as an English-speaking union. This is the more likely explanation, given the passion of his campaigns to try to keep India in the Empire and his obvious reluctance to see its dismemberment.

So how realistic, then, would Churchill's aim be? In his writings he makes it clear that it should begin by a defence alliance or merger. Indeed, something along these lines has in practice occurred in the post-war world. Britain has become dependent on America for the supply of weapons systems, technology and armaments, and there is a great deal of common procurement between the mighty US military machine and the rather smaller, but still very efficient, British one. British and US men in arms have regularly undertaken ventures together. Experiences shared and learned in the Second World War have continued through a series of engagements in the Middle East, in Asia, and now on the continent of Europe.

Churchill felt that things would then branch out from a defence and foreign policy alliance to a more wholehearted union. He thought it impossible from his vantage point in the middle of the twentieth century to forecast exactly how that would occur, but he seemed confident that the natural pressure of events would lead to some common destiny for the English-speaking peoples. Today there are people on both sides of the Atlantic who wish to see Britain join NAFTA, and who wish to develop the Anglosphere. As this book is being written, plans are advancing to create an Anglosphere Institute on both sides of the Atlantic dedicated to the propagation of Anglo-Saxon values, and to greater collaborative working between the English-speaking countries of the world.

The case of European enthusiasts

European enthusiasts are equally confident that Britain's natural destiny is to be a full part of the United States of Europe now emerging from the various European treaties. The European Union has come a long way from the early days of the Treaty of Rome and the Messina Conference. Those who favour greater European integration always regret Britain's reluctance to grasp the agenda in the 1950s. Although Britain attended the Messina Conference to set up the European Economic Community (EEC), the ministerial and Foreign Office line at the time was that a United States of Europe would never work and that Britain should not be part of it. Thus began Britain's agonies as it anguished over whether it should join, how it should join, and how far it should go in accepting the considerable degree of unification implied by successive treaties drafted at the behest of Germany and France.

Whilst it is still endlessly debated whether it would have been different or better had Britain gone to the Messina Conference with proposals of its own to shape the new Europe, there is little point now in crying over spilt milk. It is possible that had Britain offered leadership at the Messina Conference for a free-trade open Europe with less political integration and less law from Brussels, it might have had some influence. If, in the 1950s, 1960s and 1970s, Britain had stated consistently that Europe needed to be more open to the outside world and less regulated, it may have moved the position somewhat. The fact is that Britain made a decision in 1955 not to join and then subsequently regretted it. The 1960s were dogged by Britain's failure to persuade France that it should be allowed to join the newly strengthened EEC. When membership finally came in 1973, a large number of decisions had been made, treaties written, and a series of important diplomatic relationships established in the community of six which were difficult to break into. Since 1973, Britain has learnt in a painful way that the Community really is based upon a Franco-German alliance. As the years have rolled by, so the close-working cooperation between French and German government officials at all levels has been matched by the willingness of French and German leaders to meet before every EC then EU conference to sort out between them how they thought the debate and decisions should go. Britain has never succeeded in prising France and Germany apart on the big issues and has therefore been left with surprisingly little influence over the outcome of the Union's development.

Committed Euro-federalists say that a United States of Europe is not only inevitable but desirable. They see that the Parliament, Commission, Court, Bank, Court of Auditors, flag, anthem, common frontiers and all the rest are the building blocks of a new federal state. They believe that Britain's rightful and only place in the world is to be one of the important groups of regions within the new Europe. They think Britain might have a bit more influence over what comes next if it were more wholeheartedly committed, but the honest ones accept that the crucial decisions have now been taken and Britain has to make a decision whether to take it or leave it. Indeed, many committed Euro-federalists believe the choice is as stark as that. They do not believe it realistic for Britain to carry on doing what it has done over the last twenty-five years, reluctantly accepting some parts of the Union and refusing to join in on others. They believe that it will soon be impossible to dine *à la carte* in the Community and that a country will have to choose either to have the whole *table d'hôte* menu or to leave the dining room altogether.

The isolation of the UK in the EU

One of the things that strikes any travelling British person interested in these arguments when talking to the political and business elites on the continent is how little understanding and sympathy for Britain's position there is. Indeed, Euro-scepticism of any kind is often greeted with broad incomprehension, immediately followed by anger and petulance. The governing and corporate elites of Europe do not think Euro-scepticism is a respectable political view. If a British voice expresses enthusiasm for European cooperation but insists on less law, less taxation, less regulation and less interference from Brussels, there is then a reluctance to sympathise followed by a powerful counter-argument. Anyone in Britain sceptical about the pace and size of government they are trying to create is made to feel unwelcome in many of the debates and seminars on the continent, as the juggernaut of European integration careers on its way.

It has been very difficult, if not impossible, for Britain to avoid being isolated. Over so many things Britain is naturally boxed into a corner. The origins of the dispute lie in a fundamentally different approach to nationhood and sovereignty. All British governments, whether right, left or centre, do believe that most important decisions about British life should be taken by the British government and debated in the British Parliament. All British governments find it difficult to square this with a strong and deeply felt wish on the part of continental politicians for more and more decisions to be taken by a bureaucracy in Brussels and not put through their own domestic parliaments.

The European Union began as the *Club des Battus*. The defeated nations of Western Europe – including France, which had been defeated and put under German occupation for several years – decided there had to be a better way. Britain, a nation which had not been conquered or overrun for many centuries, did not share the fears and feelings of France and Germany, Italy and Belgium, Luxembourg and Denmark as they emerged from the Second World War. British politicians misread the strength of feeling and the likely developments on the continent. They and their advisers felt that the EU would make very little progress. They felt that Britain could stand aloof, with its Empire, its Commonwealth and its strong US links. They dithered as to whether they welcomed the developments or not, and they dithered as to whether we should plunge in and shape them or not.

This ambivalence towards Europe is reflected in a whole series of political decisions and reverses over the last fifty years. It is reflected in the attitudes and outlook of many British people themselves. Many of us know that we are European, in the sense that Europe is our continent and that we live cheek by jowl with our French, Belgian and Scandinavian neighbours. Many of us know well that much effort and activity in our history has been taken up with the question of Europe, trying to settle relations with our at times ambitious, aggressive and warlike neighbours. There is in the British heart a wish that Europe should live at peace. Some also believe that a united Europe might be more likely to live in peace than a disunited one.

However, we are also an island people. We take pride in our centuries-long success as an independent country. We see that all previous attempts at European Union have been doomed. We know that most previous efforts to reunite Europe were based on military aggression and repression. Whilst we can see that this latest European project is proceeding by different means and in a different style, we have apprehensions that those who are driving it are going too far, too fast. There is a great danger that they are running ahead of popular opinion on the continent.

There is a recent development in business thinking on the continent, especially amongst German industrialists which has some sympathy for the British agenda of less tax and less regulation from government at all levels. This is causing some worries for the Euro-enthusiasts who have decided the best way to accommodate this, is to tell the United Kingdom that the EU is 'now going the UK's way'. By this they mean the Lisbon Summit in 2000 adopted a general statement of aims to cut regulation and to reduce the intrusion of government in business affairs. Unfortunately, there has been no delivery. Instead the legislative machine has marched onwards, increasing the costs and burdens on business. Few have been taken in by the adoption of a little Euro-sceptic rhetoric in the Lisbon Summit conclusions, other than apparently the British government who love to claim that Europe is now going their way and so all is well. Only the British government has ostrich-like enough qualities to be able to ignore the gathering momentum of more government interference at all levels, and a tightening of the grip of the European government on the business and enterprise sector in the EU, at considerable cost to jobs and wealth.

The importance of history to a nation's destiny

If you embark on a journey it is possible to conduct it in the present and future only. At any moment you can find your position by compass and observation. You can keep yourself pointing to your future destination. But that is not the only way, and not the way we usually choose to travel. We rely heavily on our sense of the past. We know where we started from, and where we have travelled through. When we pick up a map, we do not usually reach for the compass and the coordinates, we trace where we have been and know from that our direction of travel. As we pass through villages or past well known landmarks, we make a mental note of that past event to guide us on our future way. So it is with a nation and its collective consciousness. Britain has a particular kind of parliamentary democracy. In practice we can only understand why we have this particular version if we know how it has come to be created through past events. If we want to reform or improve, it is wiser to do so from an understanding of how it came about rather than from the imposition of a new set of principles.

Teaching is largely about passing on a corpus of knowledge from the past. It would take too long, and defeat too many, to expect a child to discover the universe anew for him- or herself. We are, as they said in the seventeenth century, dwarves standing on the shoulders of the giants so that we can see further. Teachers receive the wisdom of the past and pass it on to the present.

Much of our teaching is nationalistic, in the sense that it comes from a national rather than international tradition of knowledge. Understandably, in Britain children are taught in English, and English literature is the main recommended reading. Where teaching goes beyond the national tradition, it usually does so within an English-speaking framework. US works are more easily accessible to the British teacher than Russian or Chinese, or even French and German, ones.

Until recently, history has been written and viewed primarily from a national perspective. Most history teachers in British schools will not have read a history book written in any language other than English. Their only understanding of the different ways in which French, German, Italian or Spanish historians view European history will be based on the reading of foreign works by the authors of the English accounts they read. Practically no books of French, German or Spanish history have been translated into English for common use.

The difference in interpretation can be significant. To English students, Dunkirk is a British success. An army was rescued to defend Britain, and lived to fight another day. Victory in our story was plucked from the jaws of defeat. To the French, it was the British abandoning an ally and leaving France to the fate of certain Nazi occupation. It reflected British perfidy and incompetence, abandoning the French to themselves and the continent to the Germans. To the US it was a worrying event, but not one of such significance as the electrifying raid on Pearl Harbor.

To British students, Churchill's decision to scuttle the French fleet in Marseilles – to prevent the Nazis using it – once it was obvious the French had lost was a resolute and important act. It showed that Britain had determination to resist the Germans and a strong sense of purpose. It would have been crazy to British minds to allow the Nazis to assemble an extremely powerful fleet and deploy it against Britain. To many Frenchmen it was the ultimate act of treachery, destroying the flower of the French navy after abandoning the French army in the north to the advance of the Nazis.

We see the same English-speaking-centred approach to more modern events. BBC news and current affairs programmes are dominated by events in Britain and the English-speaking world. The BBC will offer quite good coverage of a US presidential election campaign, but practically no coverage of a German or French election, which arguably now has a bigger impact on Britain than the US one given the number of decisions taken for us in Brussels by a Franco-German led administration. The BBC regularly runs news items of purely US national interest, plunging into US debates about property, race and abortion.

The BBC has been fascinated by apartheid and its abolition in South Africa and regularly presents programmes and features on South African society and politics. It has been mesmerised by the Truth and Reconciliation Commission, and has gone deeply into issues of South African economic progress or failure. I have never seen or heard a programme on the race problem in France, or the problems of poverty in Germany. The language barriers get in the way and the producers seem to lack interest. The whole way of thinking of successive generations of BBC producers is based on the English-speaking world, although the intention is usually to expose the weaknesses and failures in the English-speaking world whilst turning a blind eye or a deaf ear to any similar or worse weaknesses in the French- or German-speaking worlds. It is a kind of inverted bias, fascinated by the English-speaking world but determined to run it down wherever possible.

The new school of history is attempting to introduce a similar Eurocentric bias into their work, but it will take time for them to recruit a big enough army of historians to rewrite the whole history of these islands from a European perspective. Such a perspective would often regard Britain as either an irrelevance or an annoying nuisance on the periphery of the continent. Certainly, ever since the Henrician break from the Church of Rome in the 1530s there have been very different currents of development in the UK from those amongst the Catholic powers that have predominated on the continent. Where continental historians would see the sixteenth-century revolt of the Netherlands as an unfortunate episode, pulling apart political and religious union on the continent, English historians see it as a rather bold and successful attempt to free part of the Low Countries from the grip of Spanish and Habsburg control. Where many on the continent see Charlemagne and subsequent Holy Roman Emperors and Empire as a forerunner of the European Union, Britain sees the rupturing of the Holy Roman Empire as an improvement, creating more balance and diversity on the continent. We need to remember that countries like Germany and Italy that now sit around the ministerial table as unified were fractured into warring states and cities throughout most of the last millennium.

The endless wars, twisting alliances and changes of fortune in the five hundred years that preceded our membership of the EU have been mirrored almost entirely in diplomatic and peaceful ways since we joined. The EU still maintains many of the old divisions of Europe around the ministerial table. Very often the Protestant countries find themselves in disagreement with the Catholic ones. A permanent disagreement between the southern Mediterranean countries and the northern countries is there for all to see. The smaller countries are often in disagreement with the larger countries, and on a fairly regular basis whether its prime minister is Harold Wilson, Jim Callaghan, Margaret Thatcher, John Major or Tony Blair, Britain ends up isolated and in disagreement with the lot. It will take a great deal of rewriting history, of changing the attitudes of British people towards freedom, democracy and self-determination, before this situation changes markedly.

Britain has drifted into its current position, perched precariously mid-Atlantic, subject to US commercial influences, on the one hand, and European political influences, on the other. It need not have been so. After winning the Second World War Britain was in a strong position to help fashion new alliances and a new architecture for Europe. Churchill set out his vision quite clearly in a series of important speeches. In Zurich, he thought the best solution was for France and Germany to merge. He wished them to join with the smaller countries and the defeated and crushed Western Europe to form a United States of Europe. He felt this was best for Franco-German security and likely to prevent future wars. He also made it very clear that he did not think the UK need or should join such a grouping. Churchill always saw Britain as one of the big powers of the world – after all, Britain had apparently been an equal partner with the US and the Soviet Union in waging the war in Europe and then in settling the peace. Although Britain had had to commit a far larger proportion of its people and resources to the war effort than the US did to the war in Europe, and although Britain had been stretched by the global operations necessary for an imperial power, it had nonetheless more than pulled its weight and had an important influence over the decisions of the Peace Treaty and beyond. We must now turn to look at how the military relationship between the victorious Anglo-Saxon allies in 1945 has developed.

Notes

The two important speeches by Sir Winston Churchill are 'The Sinews of Peace', Fulton, Missouri, 5 March 1946, and 'The Tragedy of Europe', Zurich, 19 September 1946.

Chancellor Kohl's thoughts are set out in 'Our Future in Europe', Edinburgh, 23 May 1991, 'The European Process is Irreversible', Munich, May 1992, and 'Speech on Receiving the Honorary Freedom of the City of London', 18 February 1998.

Jacques Chirac spoke in Berlin on 27 June 2000 in a speech called 'Our Europe'.

Churchill's four-volume *History of the English Speaking Peoples* (Cassell, 1957) is useful here and for other parts of the historical narrative.

6
The US, the UK and the UN: The Special Relationship Policing the World

After the Second World War, the victorious powers decided there had to be a new attempt to impose some world order on the warring nations around the globe. In the immediate aftermath of the First World War in 1918 there were high hopes that the League of Nations would provide the answer. The League soon broke down, unable to tackle the aggressive intents of the new fascist and communist tyrannies which emerged in that fateful generation. There was less enthusiasm and more realism amongst the victor powers in 1945. Nonetheless, the Charter of the United Nations set out with high resolve to establish a framework of international law. It aimed at a new world order based upon the principles that had formed the substance of the Atlantic Declaration uniting Britain and the US at the height of the struggle. The Atlantic Declaration was the best statement of war aims produced during the conflict.

The foundation of the UN

The Charter of the United Nations decided it needed to 'save succeeding generations from the scourge of war'. It reaffirmed 'faith in fundamental human rights, in the dignity and worth of the human person, in the equal rights of men and women and of nations large and small'. It set out to promote social progress and better standards of life and to ensure that nations respected obligations arising under treaties. It urged nations to live tolerantly in peace with one another, to employ international machinery for the promotion of the economic and social advancement of all peoples, and to accept the idea that armed force should only be used in the common interest.

The UN intended to be a kind of international police force. It decided that the organisation would be based on the principle of the sovereign equality of all its members. All members have to agree to refrain from using force or the threat of force against the territory of any other state. The UN is above all based upon the principle of the self-determination of nations and peoples, one of the leading principles for which the Allies fought the Second World War.

The founding principles were heavily influenced by US rather than by British ideals. Indeed, some US thinkers and politicians were rather embarrassed that Britain still had such a large empire in the 1940s. That is why, amongst other reasons, the Charter is laced with a strong stress on the individual rights and liberties of people in each state and upon the right of any nation to a separate existence. The Charter of the United Nations prevents its members from intervening in what are domestic matters within a nation but allows the organisation to intervene to save a small nation under pressure from an international aggressor, even where that aggressor believes that the small nation should rightly be absorbed into the larger whole.

The UN wrestled with the problem that it wished every country to be sovereign, to still have its own equal rights, but it also wished the new security architecture to be based upon the power reality of the modern world as it appeared after 1945. It hit upon the solution of every sovereign nation that so wished, to belong to the UN and meet in General Assembly, but with a special Security Council to deal with day-to-day matters and to make recommendations. The General Assembly of all the member nations can, under Article 10, 'discuss any questions or any matters within the scope of the present Charter ... and may make recommendations to the members of the United Nations or to the Security Council or to both on any such questions or matters'. The General Assembly is charged with the duty or the power to consider cooperation and the maintenance of international peace. The General Assembly receives annual special reports from the Security Council, including accounts of the measures the Security Council has decided upon or taken to maintain international peace and security. The General Assembly approves the budget of the organisation, whilst the expenses are defrayed under a system of apportionment by all the members. Each national member of the General Assembly has one vote. Important decisions are made by a two-thirds majority, including recommendations with respect to the maintenance of international peace and security, the election of non-permanent members of the Security

Council, election of members of the Economic and Social Council, the election of members to the Trusteeship Council, the admission of new members, the suspension of members, the expulsion of members and budgetary matters.

The UN Security Council

The Security Council is the main guiding hand of the UN. It consists of fifteen members. Five members are permanent members of the Council. China, France, USSR (now Russia), the UK and the US comprise the five permanent members. Each one of them has a veto over any matter coming before the Security Council. An additional ten members are elected by the General Assembly to represent the other nations. The idea was that the five most important military powers of the day would provide much of the military back-up to Security Council policy and therefore should have individually the right of veto over it. They can, however, be collectively out-voted by the ten other members who are elected from amongst the general body of the UN. The Security Council is required under the Articles to try to find a peaceful or negotiated answer to any problem before proceeding to the use of force. The Security Council can impose sanctions against countries breaking international law. Members of the UN are required through a separate agreement to make available agreed types of force should troops be needed. Before any member not represented on the Security Council has to provide armed forces for any Security Council proposal, that member may participate in the decisions of the Security Council concerning such deployment. In practice, countries remain in charge of whether or not their forces will be committed. Typical UN action is rather like summoning the Christian powers to a crusade. A general invitation is issued and volunteers are usually plentifully available.

The UN Economic and Social Council

In addition to its well known role as a world policeman, the UN was set up to promote higher standards of living, full employment, improved social, health, cultural and educational facilities, and universal respect for human rights. The Economic and Social Council consists of fifty-four members of the UN elected from the General Assembly. A number of ways of working are set out in general terms in the Articles. In practice, the UN has worked with a large number of governmental and non-governmental organisations in countries in need of assistance to improve health care and to promote economic progress and social justice.

Those countries who are signatories to the Treaty who retained colonies or dependent territories were guided under Articles 73 and 74 to develop self-government, to protect their subject peoples against abuse and to promote good neighbourliness. The UN also set up a trusteeship system to deal with states that had been held under mandate or had been detached from enemy states so-called, the countries which had lost the Second World War. The whole UN structure is backed up by the International Court of Justice (ICJ). Every member of the UN agrees to comply with any decisions of the ICJ and also provides its membership. The Court itself depends on fifteen judges who have to be independent and come from different countries. They are elected by the General Assembly of the UN. The judges have to remain independent and the Court was established at The Hague.

The UN in practice

This complicated structure was designed with the immediate post-war circumstances very much in mind. Germany and Japan were still called the enemy countries. They were not to be part of the structure in the first instance. The victor powers decided that they could work together to deal with unforeseen but possibly dangerous problems likely to arise around the world as the incredibly complicated task of fitting the world back together was undertaken after years of war, bloodshed, devastation, mass migration and death. Hunger, poverty, ignorance, squalor and disease stalked the world. Humankind, through its own barbarism, had brought itself to a low point through unleashing so much high explosive. What is surprising about the UN, launched as the creature of its times against an unprepossessing background, is that it has lasted so long and in some ways has done so well.

Throughout much of the second half of the twentieth century there were those who thought the UN impotent to deal with the most pressing problem of the day, the danger of the Cold War between the Soviet Union and the United States breaking out into hot war through the clash of a democratic free system in the West and the communist system in the East. There is some truth in the argument that the containment of the Cold War owed much more to the attitudes of the US and the USSR than it did to anything the UN could do. The UN by definition is best at tackling smaller or medium-sized conflicts when the five large powers of the world, as defined by the Security Council, are in broad agreement about what should be done. There were numerous occasions in the Cold War period when this role was interrupted as the communist states and the democratic ones found themselves on opposite sides of the divide in the scramble for influence and authority around the world between these two competing systems. With the collapse of communism in 1990, many felt the UN would then come of age. In a way they were right, and in a way they were wrong. There are now more occasions when there is commonality of agreement around the Security Council table, but there are now also occasions when the overriding power of US weaponry is sufficient for the US effectively to sideline the UN and lead a moral and military crusade of its own.

People in the US are rather ambivalent about the whole idea of the UN. Some see it as the necessary guarantor of a world order providing a framework of international law. They accept the constraint it places upon a free foreign policy for the world's only superpower and are in sympathy with the objectives set out almost sixty years ago by the victorious powers. Others in the US resent the infringement upon the sovereign liberties of the US. They believe there is a necessary coincidence of US action and a moral cause, and can become impatient with the need on occasions to persuade the Security Council and the General Assembly that the US and its friends should intervene in the interests of peace or a more just settlement.

The 2003 war in Iraq brought the tensions within the Security Council of the UN out into the open. President Bush used UN resolutions as part of the case for going to war. He also humoured his British ally by allowing the British Prime Minister the opportunity to gain a specific resolution from the UN endorsing military action. Unfortunately for both the British government and the UN such a resolution was not forthcoming, largely blocked by France organising countries hostile to the United States against the idea. This has led to very strong anti-French reaction in America and has strengthened the hand of those in the US, particularly on the Republican side, who have nothing but scorn for the UN and its pitiful lack of action against tyrannies around the world.

The US presidential election of 2004 was primarily fought over the issue of Iraq. The Democratic challenger to Bush, Senator Kerry, attempted to draw a veil over his support for the war in the Senate and became the anti-war candidate. At the same time he made much play of Bush's isolation within the UN and the wider international community, and argued that if he were elected President he would rebuild America's relationship with countries like France, with the EU, and with the UN. The more Kerry distanced himself from the Iraqi war and independent American action, the more he struggled to retain and gain support. In the end his defeat was much bigger than the pundits and pollsters had suggested, and showed that a very divided America nonetheless had a convincing majority in favour of unilateral American action, supported by winning members of the coalition America formed outside the UN itself.

To British eyes the amount of sovereignty surrendered by the US or Britain in the UN is modest compared with the sacrifice of sovereignty the UK has made in joining the EU. Whilst theoretically under the United Nations Charter a country can be required to field its forces where it is not fully persuaded of the cause, in practice this does not arise. It can never even arise theoretically for the UK or the US as both have a veto on any Security Council proposals. In practice, armies, navies and air forces being committed to Security Council adventures are committed willingly by the member states. Any member state of the UN can resign its membership at the drop of a hat. For this, if for no other reason, no member state has to commit forces against its will.

In contrast, membership of the EU implies going along with the majority view in many areas and facing court sanctions if a country refuses to do so. It is not practical politics to withdraw from the EU just because one decision is not to a country's liking. Nor can a country negotiate non-compliance with a proposal just because it doesn't suit it. This is very different from the position of the UN where in practice all the important decisions are voluntary ones for an individual member state and are definitely voluntary ones for any of the big five. It is true that UN policy-making in other areas is at times vexatious from the Anglo-Saxon viewpoint. There is a need to restrain some UN agencies from becoming a proxy government for different parts of the world, and from over-zealous regulation.

It is possible to be optimistic about war and peace after 1945. Viewed from the perspective of the victorious powers Britain, the US, Russia and, in the later stages of the war, France, things have been a lot easier since then. None of these four powers has faced invasion or serious threat to its home territory since 1945. This contrasts with France being overrun by German invaders in 1940, Britain facing a full-blown air and sea-borne invasion threat, and Russia having to fight off one of the biggest and deadliest threats to its territory from the German army. In another sense the world has remained very strife torn. All too many disagreements and conflicts in the regions of the world have flared up into intense and often very damaging wars. British and US forces have been called upon to fight in Korea. America made a huge military commitment to Vietnam. Britain had to fight to recapture the Falkland Islands; the US and British allies stood shoulder to shoulder to reclaim Kuwaiti independence from Iraq; a number of UN member countries and their forces have been committed to an endless series of disputes and wars in the Balkans, stretching from Croatia and Bosnia to Kosovo. The aim of the UN to sit everybody down and negotiate a settlement, has not proved possible in any of these cases. Nor has it been possible to bring countries and races to heel by applying sanctions. In each case UN member states have ended up as combatants trying to enforce a precarious peace on reluctant countries.

Similarly, since the horrendous terrorist attack upon the Twin Towers of the World Trade Center, the UN has proved unable to speak for the world and to tackle the terrorist problem in a way which satisfies the leading powers. The US decided to take action against Afghanistan and the Taliban regime which sponsored and harboured terrorists in conjunction with those allies that agreed. The invasion of Iraq followed which proved to be so divisive in the world community. The President of the United States of America, the world's dominant superpower, backed by a majority of the American people, believes that America has to rout out evil dictators and regimes that harbour terrorists, as it is clear to them both that the United Nations is not up to the task. In its turn, the UN believes that it has to proceed by consensus, that these are very divisive policies, and that the US is acting without proper moral or legal authority.

The world community has discovered that the simple distinction made in the United Nations Charter between military aggression against a sovereign state, on the one hand, and intervention in the home affairs of a sovereign state, on the other, has not been nearly as easy to make as they hoped. There are many more countries now than there were in 1945. One of the characteristics of the latter twentieth century was the splintering of former large countries as individual ethnic groups and sub-nations emerged, demanding their own autonomy and independence. This was something that the United Nations Charter was not really designed to tackle. The UN was born in a generation which saw the most likely threat as being the resurgence of military intentions by an aggressive major country wishing to invade its neighbours who were themselves clearly defined sovereign states. It is understandable that the French should have taken this view in the negotiations, as their sovereign nation had been several times invaded by their neighbours Germany. Instead, the most intractable problems in the world have been created by the ideological clash between communism and democracy, and more recently by racial tension. Each of these has posed problems that sometimes reach beyond the power of the UN to solve.

The muddle became very clear in the way the Western Allies approached the problems in Croatia, Bosnia and Kosovo. When the UN began its activities, the theory was that there would be humanitarian intervention only. Soldiers were sent out with white vehicles carrying the red cross insignia to convoy food and other necessary supplies to the affected populations, seeking free passage between the warring armies and guerrilla bands. As the conflict escalated, UN troops sometimes switched into full combat fatigues to maintain peace between the warring sides. On occasions they were attempting to keep a peace that had never been brokered. The soldiers were placed in a difficult position, often under orders to maintain a peace which the politicians, diplomats and negotiators had failed to establish. Occasionally, in desperation, the UN troops, often amounting to little more than NATO forces, were required to try to impose a military solution between two or more warring groups.

It has been discovered in these difficult situations that there can be no peace until the different peoples are prepared to live in the same community, or until the warring bands reach some kind of agreement or accommodation about some new set of frontiers and separate territories. We saw the pitiful sight of thousands of refugees on the roads of Eastern and central Europe as Serbian aggression was met by Muslim resistance. The UN has often had to look on powerless, relying primarily on the forces of NATO which in turn have rested predominantly on the forces of the US.

Similarly, the UN has found it difficult to take up settling the peace in Iraq following the successful ousting of Saddam Hussein's regime by US and UK forces. Even when faced with the tsunami disaster which engulfed Indonesia, Thailand, Sri Lanka, India and other countries abutting the Indian Ocean on 26 December 2004, the UN was hesitant and slow to respond and found it difficult to coordinate the relief effort. As a result, the United States immediately stepped into the breach and formed a small group of rich, interested countries, capable of making an immediate response. The UN was left on the diplomatic and media back foot, having then to instigate talks with the US to see how America could be brought within the UN fold. When faced with civil disasters as well with military problems, the UN looks bureaucratic and slow.

Pax Americana

Over the last fifty years we have seen the *Pax Americana*. In the tense years of the Cold War it was US diplomacy backed up by US technological superiority that created the balance of power with the communist world.

Hot wars in Korea and Vietnam caused endless difficulties. US policy specialists debated the notion that they had to confront and roll back the communist advance through Asia. Some in the US believed in the domino theory – that the communists were going to move from island to island; from country to country; crossing borders; infiltrating the countryside; training guerrilla bands; providing support, ammunition and weapons from Russia and from China. They believed that only by confronting these forces in the field, offering full battle and putting a stop to the seemingly endless march of the communist troops, would the rest of the world be safe for democracy and freedom. Others felt that there was little the US could or should do about the changing attitudes of many people in countries volunteering to go communist. Left-wing commentators felt that communism was an attractive doctrine in its own right, and that it was wrong to try to stop it by military means. Conservatives felt there was a great deal of duress, manipulation and military persuasion being used to spread the communist message and therefore felt that it was an appropriate use of American weapons to confront the communist menace. There was never any question of the United Nations seeking to prevent communist subversion of states. With two communist states on the Security Council no one ever thought it likely that the UN would take such action. The UN also saw that given the disagreement in senior Western circles over the extent to which the conversion to communism was a voluntary process, it would have been hazardous in the extreme to introduce any UN force into such a situation.

The Cold War tested US resolve and encouraged its presidents and a sometimes difficult Congress to spend extremely large sums of money on fashioning the US arsenal, keeping it in working order and improving the technology. The shock to the American psyche when the Soviet communists caught up with the atomic and hydrogen bombs was considerable. There was an even bigger shock to the psyche when Russia leapfrogged the US in the space race and put the first man into orbit. Defeat in Vietnam, despite the superiority of weaponry, caused great disputes within US politics. The US fought back. Where the late 1950s and early 1960s were tense, by the 1970s and 1980s the US lead was growing with surprising speed. Looking back at the technological race, it appears that the communist system was capable of matching heavy industry, basic atomic technology and the technology of the wireless resistor, cathode and electrical equipment. The communist world proved quite incapable of matching the supremacy of US technology based upon the silicon chip, the computer, new materials and stealth design. By the early 1990s, US weapons were supreme. Wherever they were tested in open warfare against Russian-supplied equipment, even where that Russian-supplied equipment was well backed up with technical support, the US arms triumphed easily.

It was partly the clear establishment of US supremacy reinforced by President Reagan's Star Wars programme, a missile protection system which would have completely changed the balance of terror, that led to the collapse of communism in the early 1990s. Far-sighted communists like President Gorbachev in the Soviet Union realised that the game was up. They realised that their economic and social system was failing to deliver the breakthroughs, the technical leaps, the more open working which enabled the US systems to excel. The collapse of communism in all parts of the world, save China and Cuba, led to but a short period of rejoicing in the West. Instead of removing the imminent threat of nuclear war, the lifting of the Iron Curtain in Europe and the breakdown of the communist bloc, opened up old wounds and divides between nations, races and ideologies. It led directly to the collapse of Yugoslavia, the separation of Czechoslovakia, old arguments about the true borders of Hungary and Poland, and an uneasy relationship between the Baltic States and the former Soviet Union.

Local wars characterised the experiences in Latin America, in Asia, in Africa and in the Middle East. The last fifty years have seen frequent flare-ups between the Arabs and the Israelis. Chile has fought Argentina, Iraq has made its bid for supremacy in the Arab world, China has threatened Taiwan, and Japan has had an uneasy relationship with its giant neighbour. At times, the US – acting through the UN or on its own – has been decisive in avoiding conflict. There have been several occasions when the US has imposed its will or its ships to ensure that Taiwan has not been invaded by China. US diplomacy and sometimes force of arms has been important in keeping an uneasy peace over many years in the Middle East. No one around the world is likely to make a move of any military significance without first asking the question, 'What might the US do if we did this?' More recently it is the United States of America that has used its own military might with a few allies to try and impose a new settlement on the Middle East. It has caused many ruffled feathers in the Arab world who think America is far too pro-Israel and pursuing a pro-Israeli agenda. The US had set out the roadmap to peace between Israel and Palestine but then became rather more preoccupied with regime change in those parts of the Arab world that it thought were harbouring terrorists. Now the US has set out a model of a freedom loving world full of vibrant democratic countries, making progress through free enterprise. The US is seeking to remodel the world in her own image, to extend the undoubted benefits of capitalism and political freedom to many more people.

It is perhaps easier for Britain to understand the awesome responsibilities and the feelings subsequently generated in the US because Britain was the world's previous superpower. In the nineteenth century it was the British Navy that was the force to be reckoned with. Larger than any other two navies that could be assembled against it, the British Navy straddled the world with bases and ports of arrival and departure on shores of the five continents. It was Britain who often took the lead in sorting out conflicts in the Middle East, in trying to force China into more Western ways, interfering in the futures of the fledgling Latin American republics, fighting in the Crimea against the Russians, or attempting to exercise its influence on the continent of Europe when tensions flared up between France, Germany and the other great powers. This experience lives on in the folk memory. It means the British people have more natural sympathy with the US dilemma of whether to intervene or to leave well alone, and more understanding of how the rest of the world can retaliate.

The global vocation of the US

Twentieth-century US policy has been characterised by many arguments. One of the most critical has been whether the US should withdraw into its continental frontiers or whether it should continue with any kind of world role. There have been periods when the isolationists have held sway. The US was very reluctant to commit forces in either the First or Second World War. The US did not enter the First World War until 1917, and then only when it thought Germany might foment trouble on the Mexican border. If Japan had not struck at Pearl Harbor in 1941, the US would not have entered the conflict as a combatant. If Germany had not declared war on the US it may have remained reluctant to declare war on Germany. Sitting in the Midwest or on the Californian seaboard, it is very easy for US citizens to say, 'What are those faraway conflicts in Europe to do with us?' Whilst many Americans can trace their descent to Italians or Spaniards, British or Irish, it does not necessarily mean that they share the views of the successive generations who have remained in the old countries who have yet again fallen out with each other. America is a great melting pot which has brought together these different races, languages and cultures and fashioned out of them one mighty country. Irish, British, Spanish and Italian Americans are more likely to see eye to eye in favouring non-intervention in a European war than they are to return to the old battles re-enacted over there. It has so often been events which have impelled the US to intervene in Europe, rather than any more elevated sense of duty.

In recent years the US has become impatient about the lack of progress to a more integrated Europe. Successive presidential teams have thought it would be convenient to have one Europe, one unified command, one larger country that they could do business with. Successive administrations have hoped that Germany would start to spend more on weaponry itself and take more of an interest in the wider world around. Many Americans have been urging Germany to overturn the *Grundgesetz* or basic law adopted by Germany at the end of the Second World War on the advice of the Allied powers. This constitutional document expressly forbade German troops to be deployed outside the country's own borders. Many have felt that the Germans and other European countries have been free-riding on the back of the US taxpayers' generosity, deliberately spending far less European national product on defence, safe in the knowledge that they were covered by the US nuclear and conventional weapons umbrella.

There has also been a strong revisionist strand, particularly in Republican thinking, as events have unfolded. The decision of the German government to do a deal with Russia about Russian troops in East Germany without first consulting the US properly caused considerable alarm in Washington after the rapid reunification of the two Germanys. The realisation that Germany was going to follow an *Ostpolitik* of its own, trying to bring Hungary, Poland, the Czech Republic and Slovakia into a European federation which could do business direct with Moscow, worried the US, which still sees Moscow as the most important second-power centre on the planet, and the one that needs to be viewed with the greatest suspicion. When this has been allied to a number of positions adopted by the EU which are seen by the US as unhelpful, maybe in restraint of trade, or against other US interests, it provides a reason for caution in US policy circles over the idea of a United Europe. The refusal of France and other leading European, continental countries to back the war on Iraq was a further jolt to those in America who favour dialling one number for Europe. The anti-French feeling it has unleashed has strengthened the hand of those in Washington who see the virtues of Euro-scepticism, at least for the United Kingdom.

Both Germany and France have tested the US's patience through their pro-Russia policies. They are now embarked on a desperate attempt to catch up with US military technologies through a major expansion of their interests in space and surveillance. France has launched her Helios IIA military satellite. Germany plans five military satellites, to be launched over a two and half year period up to the summer of 2007. Called SAR-

Lupe, it will enable German military commanders to send orders out on a global basis and to transmit high resolution radar images. Germany works with Russia on space launches. The French system only operates in clear skies. The German system has some capability through cloud and darkness. The two will be combined to form the core of an EU surveillance and command structure.

There is still studied ambiguity or an unresolved tension in American attitudes towards the evolving European Union. Many officials, even within a Republican administration that has had a bad experience of dealing with the main EU countries, still feel that it would make sense for Europe to get together and make a bigger contribution to its own defence. Others now see the growing threat to world stability that an emerging EU, hostile to the US, can pose. So how then is the *Pax Americana* likely to develop? We can make certain forecasts. For the foreseeable future, it is highly likely that US military dominance will survive. Indeed, such is the speed of the digital revolution in America, and such are the relative levels of defence spending, that we may witness a further increase in the lead as US technology and defence spending outstrips those of any other country or group of countries. It is inconceivable that Moscow could quickly regain first-power status, given the enfeebled state of the former Soviet economy and the growing internal problems within the rather ramshackle Russian Federation. It looks extremely unlikely that electorates and governments in the EU are going to make a sea-change in the amount they spend on defence. Many of the leading continental countries are also finding it difficult to keep up or catch up with the US lead in digital technology. The US defence industry simply outclasses the more disparate European one in terms of its capacity for innovation, long production runs and commercial success.

We are therefore going to continue to live in a world where the US will be able to call the shots. No country around the world is going to wish to push the US over the edge, to test the giant's patience too much, given the colossal superiority of its missile systems, its military planes, the size of its navy, and its capacity to mobilise huge numbers of well armed troops.

Life at the top can be tough

However, the giant also has a vulnerable side. We are going to live in a world where more and more countries have access to basic nuclear technology, and where many countries follow in the path of Iraq by developing the capability to engage in chemical and biological warfare.

Chemical, biological and nuclear warfare is difficult to counter for a democracy which does not wish to place the lives of its troops or its civilian population in jeopardy. The US has lived through a relatively long period when, with the exception of the Soviet Union, no one was able to threaten the mainland of the US. China, or Middle Eastern tyrannies, did not have rockets with sufficient range to target New York City or Washington, DC. No one felt that any country in Europe, the Middle East or Asia could unleash naval or air forces that were likely to survive the barrage of US firepower clustered offshore and in defensive locations throughout America. The Russians became petrified when America looked as if it was close to designing an anti-missile system which would have made redundant Russia's threat of striking from afar through unmanned rockets.

The world has also noticed that US democracy is particularly open, that its people are understandably reluctant to sacrifice any part of their luxurious lifestyle and will ask lots of questions before allowing their President, their Commander-in-Chief, to commit US troops to dangerous situations. The biggest threat to US power in the short to medium term is the actions of dedicated groups of terrorists, guerrilla bands and those who are prepared to use weapons that the West has banned to blackmail and terrorise others. This is why the US has been particularly keen to launch missile or bomb attacks on any recalcitrant tyrant who looks as if he is close to making usable quantities of biological or chemical weapons, or may be developing a nuclear capability of his own.

Looking beyond the short to medium term, we cannot take US superiority for granted. Whilst there is nothing yet to suggest that any country is about to challenge US technical superiority, there are several large countries around the world with much bigger populations which could provide a serious threat to democratic institutions and free societies, at least in their parts of the world, if they decided to use their considerable muscle power, conventional weapons or fledgling nuclear power with less concern for human life than is shown by the Western democracies. The first part of the twenty-first century is likely to continue to see the United States as a technical and economic giant backed by the most formidable arsenal of weapons the world has ever seen. As the twenty-first century advances, so people in the US and the other Western democracies will have to adjust to the idea that our societies have relatively small populations and that, in terms of economic power, other parts of the world are catching up or have surpassed us. Above all, we will look to the East as China emerges from a long period of relative poverty and introspection. The new China is modernising its armed forces, extending its diplomatic reach. A mark of its success in joining the elite nations is its successful bid to stage the Olympics for 2008 in Beijing. The world is braced for a massive statement that China has arrived on the world's stage and wishes to play an important role.

China has already threatened to invade democratic Taiwan if the island declares formal independence, and is vigorously pursuing claims to disputed islands in the South China Sea. It is a strong opponent of more democracy in Hong Kong, and has uneasy relationships with Japan. Recently China sent a nuclear powered submarine into Japanese waters.

China is close to persuading the European Union to end its arms embargo in order to speed up the modernisation of its military machinery. The Chinese government has been developing new friendly relationships with governments in Africa, the Middle East, Central Asia and Latin America, and pursuing its hunt for oil, gas, minerals and food that its growing prosperity will require to import.

To date the Bush regime has decided on the course of friendly cooperation. Bush has been pleased with China's support for the fight against Islamic terrorism. China is also trying to assist in resolving the crisis over North Korea's nuclear weapons programmes, which the US is most concerned about. America is determined to deal with the 'Axis of Evil' and knows it has to keep China sweet to allow it to do so. Colin Powell, the former US Secretary of State, in 2004 described US relations with China as excellent, 'perhaps the best in thirty years'. The Bush regime is following the traditional Republican pattern begun by President Nixon before his impeachment, of opening and maintaining friendly relations with the emerging giant.

It was Napoleon who said that China should be allowed to sleep, 'for when she awakes, she will shake the world'. The giant is now awakening. America will be friends with her and cooperate with her for the time being, but it is to China rather than the EU that America should look as she ponders the question, how much longer can American supremacy grow and survive?

The special relationship

More than half a century later, and we are still living in the long shadow cast by the Second World War. The only reason Germany and Japan are not today colossal nuclear and military powers is that they were deliberately disarmed by the Allies at the end of the Second World War and have been circumspect about the extent of their rearmament ever since. I remember visiting Berlin just before the Wall came down. I still have in my possession one of the last passes of the British military government for the British sector of Berlin, issued to a British visitor. Although it was only fifteen years ago, it could have been a different age. Berlin was partitioned. It remained under military government and people could only come out and go across the wall and between the sectors if they had the necessary paperwork. The fall of the Berlin Wall changed a great deal, but much of the rest of the post-war architecture has remained in place. Germany and Japan are not members of the UN Security Council. They are not nuclear powers. Their technical development in the latter part of the twentieth century has been much more heavily directed towards civil uses than military ones, leaving the field free for the United States and, to a lesser extent, Britain and France. At the end of the Second World War the US in particular attracted a great deal of the German technical and weapons-making talent to the great research laboratories in the western continent, and made good use of the expertise they had acquired. Whilst Europe was attempting to overcome the problems of poverty, mass migration and endless bomb sites, the US, safe in its continental redoubt, was getting on with the business of making sure it had the superpower weaponry for the second half of the twentieth century.

Why, then, given US superiority, has it been seemingly so keen to have Britain as an ally? When the war ended, Britain was a serious partner. It was after all the UK that had kept the conflict going in the dog days of 1940 and 1941 before the US entered the war and geared up to take it seriously. It was above all Churchill's voice and tones which rang in the ears of many Americans, making them realise that freedom was on the line, and that Britain was prepared to put in a super-human effort. Whilst the US could see that Britain had given a great deal, was poor, was overstretching its resources, and was going to be the junior partner in the final attack upon Hitler's continental fortress, it could also see that Britain was a critical partner, carrying more than its fair share of the burden of defending the West when compared with its means. This naturally earned Britain considerable respect, aided by the way Churchill determined to play the part of one of the big three wartime leaders in all the important conferences and meetings. It may have been a US general who led the victorious Allied forces into Germany, but no one doubted the role played by the RAF, by the British Army in Burma, by Montgomery in the desert, by the British Army that had fought its way up through Italy or by the excellent British forces which had landed on their own D-Day beaches and made their way to Berlin itself. The Union flag could proudly fly alongside the Stars and Stripes as a serious partner.

There is, however, little sentiment in relationships even between friends and allies in the international arena. The US clearly saw that by the end of the war it was its mighty industrial and war machine that had proved decisive. Looking ahead, America saw that it was going to be its money, the scientific base, its ability to use wandering German and even British talent, and its ability to extend its lead technically and economically that would make it the dominant power of the latter twentieth century. The British sometimes suffered from an inferiority complex which they concealed well to US minds who felt that Britain came across often as pompous and superior. The use of Britain as a wartime base camp for the US forces that were to invade the continent of Europe had not always helped relations. For every GI marriage, there were another two or three people who had formed bad impressions on both sides. The British resented the Americans' easy access to wealth and success. The Americans were somewhat scornful of a little, old, tired, dirty country, as they saw it, peeking out from behind the blackout sheets and muddling through with the ration books.

Successive British prime ministers decided that the best way of keeping Britain alive and sitting around the big table was to remain a special friend of the US. Churchill set it off with the ringing declarations of English-Speaking Union in his Fulton, Missouri, speech. It was continued, especially by Harold Macmillan, who was determined that Britain should have access to the best of US weapons technology; by Harold Wilson, who even flirted with the idea of a US union himself; by James Callaghan, and quintessentially by Margaret Thatcher with her very special political relationship with her friend Ronald Reagan. Tony Blair, when he signed up to Bush's 'War on Terror' in general and the invasion of Iraq in particular, was continuing a long tradition of special UK–US collaboration.

It was easy to see what the UK was getting out of this. Britain could enjoy some of the reflected strength and glory of the US position. Britain could gain from joint deals and the sharing of technology with the US defence industry. Britain could help America intervene well beyond Britain's own capacity to intervene separately and on its own. Even in the case of Iraq, Britain had some influence over the timing and the diplomatic processes which surrounded the hostilities. Britain got enormous goodwill in the US by backing such an unpopular war, and as news filtered across the Atlantic just how much political damage it was doing to the British Prime Minister at home, it strengthened the sympathy and support for him in the US.

The policy, however, did have its drawbacks from the British point of view. Perhaps the worst reversal came at the time of Suez. Britain still felt it had the power and authority to intervene with France in an area that affected one of its crucial interests. Britain had always been the titan of the Middle East. It was the British and French who had seen through the Suez Canal in the first place. It was British shipping lines more than any others which were thought to be at risk. The failure of the US to back the British action and the climb-down which followed caused resentments on this side of the Atlantic but also summed up the *realpolitik* of the power balance. From Suez onwards, Britain was unable to go it alone if the US disagreed with its actions.

More recently, Britain had to finesse the US relationship when it decided to intervene to recapture the Falklands. In the end, US intelligence and support behind the scenes was helpful, but there were some difficult times when the British government was not entirely sure that Washington would approve of all it was doing and was well aware that if Washington turned against the operation – at best hazardous – it would become impossible. It is never easy for a former imperial power that once bestrode the world like a colossus itself to accept the dominance of another nation, especially one that had spun off following an open rebellion against the mother country.

Above all, the decision to back President Bush's 'War on Terror' so wholeheartedly has done great damage to the Prime Minister's standing at home and has split the country, with a big majority against him. Indeed, so unpopular was Bush's war that it has caused more anti-American sentiment in Britain than is desirable for a country living by the special relationship with the US. It has damaged the framework and fabric of British diplomatic efforts elsewhere in the world. It also displayed two rather different styles of tackling the problem. The American army was clearly dominant and in the lead in winning the war, with its smart weapons and its battlefield information systems. The British Army came into its own in trying to win the peace when the hard lessons learned in Northern Ireland were put to good effect. The British Army understood from experience and intuition that it was a battle for hearts and minds on the ground that had to follow the ousting of the evil regime, whilst the Americans were continuing the battle and finding it difficult to work with the local population. It is true that Britain was given the easier areas but also true that the different styles of policing and military activity made life tougher for the American GIs.

But what was there in this relationship for the US? It is important not to underestimate the loneliness of the world's only superpower. Whilst the

US knows that it has the military might to do more or less what it wishes, being a democracy it also knows that it has to behave to high standards and that there are moral and political pressures constraining its action, as well as military ones. The US could successfully invade virtually any country on the planet and take the country over if it was so minded, and if it was prepared to accept the retaliation, the hatred and the loss of life that would entail. Because the US is a freedom-loving democracy which practises what it preaches on the self-determination of peoples, this has never crossed policy-makers' minds as an option in Washington. It is this type of consideration that has often meant to Washington that London has a use. It is good when advancing a strong case in the councils of the world for Washington to be able to say that it is not alone in taking this view. Britain, too, has considerable moral authority in the world. Whilst there are still those who resent some elements of colonial experience or who resent the side Britain may have taken in some long-forgotten war, there are many others around the world who have valued British involvement on the side of freedom and self-determination against the abuse of power or tyranny. There are many in former colonies who now, freed of British control, recognise that Britain did bequeath some good things from that colonial experience. There are traditions of democratic practice, fair play, sound administration and honest dealing which have served many a former colonial country rather better than some of the bad habits or traditions picked up in other parts of the world. So the US has been able to draw on that reservoir of contacts, goodwill, skill and diplomatic understanding that Britain at its best has been able to demonstrate.

There have been times when British military support has also been valuable. In the earlier part of the post-war period Britain still had a large number of important and well located bases which could add to the strength of the joint position. Although Britain now has very modest armaments in terms of numbers compared with the US, Britain's armaments are among some of the most modern and effective in the world, and the adjunct of British expertise, British ships, British aeroplanes or British missiles alongside US ones can be a useful addition. America may have the high-level Stealth bombers, but Britain, for example, has the Harrier jump jets. British know-how and military capability can also be valuable. Britain fought a different pattern of wars to the US in the twentieth century, whilst at the same time fighting many of the big ones alongside the US itself. Britain learned a great deal about jungle warfare in Burma, about amphibious landing capability in the Falklands theatre, about policing tense and difficult situations in Northern Ireland: these things are of use to the US and there has been some joint training and debriefing. Above all, Britain's moral and political support in Iraq was a godsend. It protected the President against some of the domestic criticism that he was going it alone and lacked any international support, and it gave the President some assistance when dealing with the UN and the powers most likely to be angry with the US over her action.

We should not underestimate the importance of the common language and the interests of the personalities involved. Many British prime ministers have enjoyed hobnobbing with US presidents. US presidents, often short of language skills themselves, have rather welcomed being able to meet largely friendly foreign leaders who speak their own language and enjoy some of the same pursuits. The common culture, language and history has often helped and has meant that it is very likely that a US president is going to get on better with a British prime minister, and vice versa, than with a prime minister from Japan or a chancellor from Germany. The common understanding inherited on both sides of the Atlantic can do wonders for the special relationship.

There are those who now fashionably say that the special relationship is dead. Those in Britain who scorn Britain and the British, who think that we are now already part of a much bigger European empire, try to play down our significance to the US and ridicule the idea that we will any longer be important enough in Washington to warrant that special status. There are those in Washington who still hanker after the big European scheme, who see the special relationship as a bygone relic of the former age. There are other isolationists in Washington who do not want a special relationship with anybody because it may bring with it trouble and the impulse to intervene in world events. There were times in the Thatcher–Reagan relationship when Thatcher was providing the lead as to where the two powers combined should seek to assert their influence. There was the famous moment in the Bush–Thatcher relationship when Thatcher told the President memorably not to wobble in prosecuting the war against Iraq.

It is my judgement that the special relationship will have its ups and downs and there will be times when indeed forces on either side of the Atlantic will conspire to suggest it is over. But it is also my judgement that it is not over, because the language, culture and common history still count for a certain amount; history is likely to throw up new pairs of presidents and prime ministers who actually like each other; and there is still logic on both sides to carry on trying to make something of the common defence arrangements. It is true that there are now strong pressures to have a common European defence industry in opposition to that of the US. There are those who would like to do in defence what Airbus has done in the civil aviation sphere, creating a rival to the US and encouraging some kind of trade and technical war between the two. It is true that there is now much more common European defence procurement and a British prime minister who has boasted of a special relationship with the President is at the same time busily trying to rush us into a special defence arrangement with our European partners.

The option remains for Britain to develop a special relationship across the Atlantic, to build a bigger common defence industry across the Atlantic, to pool more know-how and to make common cause.

The UK needs to send clear signals if she wishes to pursue this, as events are driving her closer to the Franco-German rivals to the US. Worry over the tensions caused by the war in Iraq will incline the UK's Labour government to move closer to the EU for a bit. It does so at a tense time in the transatlantic relationship, when the US is concerned that Franco-German flirtation with China and Russia make them dangerous allies to share intelligence with. The EU may well do enough in defence to shatter the NATO working relationship with US intelligence, without doing enough to have a comparable system that matches the US one. It does not make it a good choice for the UK, used in the last fifty years to a very close relationship with the US in defence.

Time is running out for the Anglo-American option in defence to be sustained and improved. The decisions now being taken over common defence procurement in Brussels, the early rows over the Galileo project, and the draft wording of the EU Treaty, all point in the direction of Britain gradually losing its special relationship with the United States of America in defence matters. If Britain wishes to preserve the special relationship, she will have to show in the weeks and months ahead that she is not committed to the European project. The two are going to be incompatible and we are fast approaching the decision point.

Notes

Nye and Morpurgo (1955) chart the way in which the US rebelled against the mother country and came of age.

The Fontana History of Europe examines Franco-British rivalry, especially in Rude (1965) and Grenville (1976).

Bullock's (1952) work remains a classic study of the racist and imperialist ambitions of German Nazism.

7
Doing Business the US Way: Selling US Enterprise and Technology

Over the last fifty years the links between the US and UK economy have grown ever stronger. Shared language, the aftermath of the Second World War, and the restless pursuit of European markets by Americans led naturally to a surge of US investment in Britain. What has been less noticed but has been equally pronounced has been the way British companies return the compliment. Indeed, British companies have invested more in the US than US companies have invested in Britain. We have now reached the point where half of all the foreign investment in Britain comes from America (Table 7.1). Two-fifths of all Britain's investments around the world are in the US. Only a quarter of foreign investment in Britain has come from our EU trading partners, and only a third of our outward investment has gone to other EU states.

When we look at Britain's wealth held overseas, it gives a very different picture of where our true interests lie compared with the crude trade figures showing that we export a large proportion of our manufactured goods to our near neighbours on the continent. Investment is a much more important and longer-lasting relationship than trade. Many British goods counted as exports to the European continent are in practice exports going through the large *entrepôts* of Rotterdam and Amsterdam, often destined for markets well beyond the shores of Europe itself. When we sell things like oil into the European market, we are selling a commodity product which will sell on price in dollars according to demand. Building investment relationships requires much more understanding, common working and friendship to make it succeed.

There are many reasons why the lure of the United States has been much bigger for British companies than the lure of the continent of

Europe. Most British businessmen have little or no understanding of French, Spanish, Italian and German. The language barrier is a very considerable one. They can go to New York or Washington, immediately make themselves understood, and establish friendships and investment relationships quite quickly. There is a common culture in the Anglo-Saxon business world drawing on the strength of the common language.

Table 7.1 Cumulative inward net investment to the UK 1993–98

		£ million	%
From	US	54,893	53
	Switzerland	16,206	16
	Netherlands	6,659	6
	Germany	4,980	5
	France	4,775	5
	Australia	3,304	3
	Irish Republic	2,274	2
	Belgium/Luxembourg	1,633	2
	Bermuda	1,630	2
	Norway	1,162	1
	Others		5
	(Main EU partners)		20

Source: *Hansard*, House of Lords, 14 February 2000, Answer to Lord Pearson.

Many British businesses have found it extremely difficult to make money on the European continent. Markets are more protected and cartelised. It is more difficult to gain entry into those markets and exceedingly difficult to convert that entry into profitability. Many great British retailers have sought their fortune on the continent, only to find that tastes, fashions and attitudes are rather different, limiting their scope for profitable expansion. British Airways has attempted to construct a global alliance, including important investments in France and Germany. Despite putting in a great deal of managerial effort and investment, the British Airways shareholders never saw a profit from Deutsche BA, Air Liberté, or TAT in France. They have encountered considerable regulatory difficulty in growing and developing the businesses in the way that they would like. The British corporate world is littered with the memories and corpses of great British businessmen who thought they could buck the trend and build a successful chain or profitable enterprise on the continent, only to discover that failure stared them in the face.

Proximity to the continental market also means there is no need for many British manufacturers to set up factories in France or Germany.

They have reasonable access to French and German markets already by sending another container across the Channel. They cannot face the high taxes, substantial regulation, complexities of working in another language, and the high cost of employing people, and above all the difficulty of removing people if they make a mistake. Most US and UK manufacturers would prefer to keep their factory in Britain open and use that as the offshore base for supplying the continental market. When Britain itself becomes too expensive, such manufacturers usually look to establish a plant either in Asia to supply lower value-added goods or important components, or to Eastern Europe where labour costs are still much below those of the Western EU members.

Technology is going the US way. The latest wave of investment is fuelled by the internet, computers and telecommunications. Everyone agrees that the US is several years ahead of all other parts of the world. All agree that the European continent has been held back by regulation, monopoly and a flight of talent to the more entrepreneurial culture in the US. Businesses looking for the latest technology to enable them to change and adapt would naturally look across the Atlantic rather than across the Channel.

The European continent has also suffered from believing in closed or protected markets. Any British entrepreneur can arrive in Wall Street and, after a few days' or weeks' work, can put together a takeover bid for a US quoted company. Most larger and many medium-sized US companies do have quotes on one or more of the successful US stock markets. Their shares are freely traded, and it is possible for a foreign business to mount a successful takeover bid. Until recently this has been quite impossible on the continent of Europe. Many medium-sized and even larger German and French companies are controlled by shareholders who have no intention of selling out to a foreign bidder. Many German companies are effectively owned by their bankers who wish to keep them as client companies in all senses. Many French and German companies have strong family shareholdings, or crossholdings from other companies in the same or a related industry. Again, these shareholders are usually reluctant to sell out, especially to a foreign bidder. The continent of Europe sees the contested takeover as an undesirable feature of Anglo-Saxon capitalism which it is reluctant to import.

At the beginning of 2000, a British company decided to challenge this orthodoxy in a very dramatic way. Vodaphone Air Touch wanted to buy Mannesmann, the German telecommunications company. It chose its target wisely. Mannesmann was a rare German company with a large number of foreign and independent shareholders open to persuasion if a good takeover bid came along. The German government panicked when it saw the scale and attractiveness of the bid. The Chancellor of Germany himself, Gerhard Schroeder, intervened, condemning the British raiders. Whereas the German government had been very happy to see BMW buy Rover, the British car company, and to see both Rolls-Royce and Bentley passed to German ownership, it felt very differently when there was a proposal that something should go the other way.

The pursuit of the Mannesmann bid was an important development in European markets. It was unlikely to herald a major restructuring of European business. The European bourses are not subject to the same creative and destructive waves of mergers and acquisitions that both the Wall Street and London markets create. There remains deep in continental culture a belief that unless there is general agreement over a takeover bid, it is unsporting to mount one. There still remains a wide nexus of relationships between banks, families, and other shareholders which makes it more difficult for a British or US company to acquire a French or German partner.

It is quite possible for a British or US company to proceed to invest in a greenfield operation, starting from scratch. However, the pace of change worldwide is now so great, and the power of brands so strong, that this is rarely as attractive an option to boards of directors of larger companies as the decision to buy market and market-share, brand and physical equipment through takeover bids. It is also difficult where a licence or other regulatory approval is needed, as continental governments are reluctant to grant permission to new UK competitors.

Post-war US investment

The wave of US investment in Britain began shortly after the war. It was a natural follow-on to the hospitality the US found when it used Britain as the base from which to launch its sea-borne invasion of occupied France and Germany, alongside British allies. The US was deeply involved in the rebuilding of Europe after the disaster of the Second World War. A great deal of American money was pumped into the continent, and US businesses saw the opportunity that US goodwill and cash support would obviously generate. The great names of the US consumer revolution were alert to the opportunity to base a factory in Britain, both to supply the growing British consumer market as prosperity picked up after 1945, and to use Britain as a base to export onto the continent.

In those early years, the political stability of Britain was an added advantage. The continental countries made investors more nervous.

They had, after all, only recently recovered from an extremely damaging war and several of the countries had only just established democratic institutions after a period of tyranny and dictatorship. It took Spain rather longer to emerge from its political troubles than Italy or Germany, where new institutions were set up by the victorious powers after 1945.

There was some comfort to the US investor in the ubiquitous English language: similar standards of accounting, a legal code they could understand – although they no longer shared it – and a general attitude towards the ways of conducting business in an open and honest manner that made sense to US corporate managers. The US brought to Britain its mighty motor industry. Ford made substantial investments to supply the growing British market with popular, sensibly priced cars. General Motors followed later, acquiring Vauxhall, Hillman and other well known British brands. US oil companies increased their presence as motoring took off. Exxon successfully built up the Esso brand in Britain. Mobil, Gulf and others followed suit, alongside homegrown British Petroleum and Anglo-Dutch Shell. Boeing gradually displaced the outclassed British civil airline manufacturing industry as the principal supplier of planes to British-based airlines. This led to important aerospace work for the British aerospace industry, including the successful twinning of Rolls-Royce Engines with Boeing Airframes. The US computer industry arrived in force in the 1970s and 1980s, spawning hi-tech revolution in Silicon Glen in Scotland, near Glasgow; in Silicon Valley along the Thames, and in several other British locations.

In each case the managements felt at home in Britain. They would have their disagreements and they kept some of their US ways, but it was relatively easy going as there was that common cultural understanding. British resentment of US power and success, so obvious during the war and in the immediate post-war period, dulled as British achievements built up and as the US showed its paces worldwide. Why knock its success when the fruits of it could be so enjoyable?

The British and US economies grew closer and closer together in many respects as the Thatcher and Reagan revolutions were unleashed in the 1980s. Both Britain and America developed mighty worldwide financial service and banking industries. Where Britain had led the world as principal banker and financial service provider in the nineteenth century, based on its success as an imperial and financial power, so the US emerged as a crucial provider of financial services and banking in the latter part of the twentieth century. The remarkable thing was the way in which London managed to increase its lead in some areas and remain an important competitor as well as a trading partner of Wall Street in the latter part of the twentieth century. There are still only three really large stock markets, foreign exchange markets and banking markets in the world. These are New York, London and Tokyo. Everyone agrees that those centres have gained pre-eminence within their respective time zones. There is a flood of global trading which starts as the sun rises in Tokyo, which passes through London and ends up in New York when Tokyo has long since gone to bed.

Both the US and Britain have been in the forefront of pioneering the global services revolution. They have seen that Anglo-Saxon accounting and legal skills can be developed and applied to world markets. They have been in the forefront of creating links around the world so that the same legal or accountancy firm can offer advice based on different national and continental systems on the five continents. Both the US and Britain have benefited from early and thoroughgoing liberalisation of their telecommunication systems. The US began with the decision to allow MCI and Sprint to compete against the Bell telephone monopoly. Subsequently they decided to split up the Bell company itself. This was consciously followed in the UK when the Conservative government of the 1980s chose privatisation and liberalisation. When I worked out those policies for the Thatcher government, I based much of them on the remarkable experience of new technology and dynamic growth in the US that had followed from the crucial decisions there.

The result of the different attitude towards services and the ability to project services on a global basis can be seen in the shapes of the different economies. By the late 1990s, manufacturing was down to only 16% of US employment and 18% of the UK's. Conversely, it still remained at 27% in Germany and 23% in Italy. The British and US service sectors were proportionately larger, showing that they had adjusted more rapidly to the global pressures which will shift more and more manufacturing to lower cost parts of the world.

The dominance of Britain and the US in financial service activity is quite startling. In 1998, the UK accounted for 32% of the market in foreign exchange. The US accounted for 18% whereas Germany only accounted for 5%. London's stock market capitalisation is almost double the capitalisation of the Frankfurt and Paris stock markets combined. The UK trades more overseas equity than the US and Japanese markets do together; and they in turn trade much more than the other European stock markets. There are 540 foreign banks with offices in London – more than double the number in Germany, and three times the number in France.

There has been considerable argument in the UK about whether it is right for us to follow the US model to such an extent. Critics of the

Americanisation of the British economy claim that the US encourages a much harsher climate for the poor and the unemployed than Germany or France. They claim that the continental system assures people of jobs and security and takes care of them in a much more compassionate way. This is not borne out by the income or unemployment figures. Europe's big problem is the massive increase in unemployment in recent years. The EU outside the UK has found it almost impossible to generate new jobs in the private sector. High levels of taxation and regulation have produced a hostile atmosphere for business. Most of the new jobs and new technologies have come via the US and Asia. Unemployment in France and Germany has in recent years been double the level we now see in the US and the UK. Income levels in the US are considerably higher than in continental countries. It is better to be on a low income in work in the US than out of work and on an even lower benefit income in the EU.

There has also been considerable criticism of the US way of allowing companies to mount takeovers of their competitors and to force change upon reluctant or sleepy managements. Of course, many businessmen would be comforted to think that government interference and regulation guaranteed them a job for life, freeing them from the constraint of having to perform in order to avoid takeover. Unfortunately for the EU, world economic development is not going to be like that. The US model is dominant. US companies have a long reach. US companies account for the ten leading brands in the world and show excellence and drive in a wide range of industrial and service activities. Because America is the modern colossus, it is inevitable that much of the US style will work its way round the world.

The different responses of Britain, on the one hand, and France and Germany, on the other, are instructive. Since the 1980s, when the UK has tried to copy more of the US model with lower taxes, lower government spending and less regulation than adopted on the continent, the British economy has performed much better and has caught up with the US to a greater extent than France and Germany. Britain is now the fourth largest economy in the world after only the US, Japan and Germany. After adjusting for the larger number of people in Germany, Britain is better off per head than Germany, and better off than most of the other EU countries. This has been achieved through huge changes in the UK economy. In the motor industry we have seen the decline and fall of all indigenous motor manufacturing. There are only a handful of companies left producing specialist vehicles in small numbers that are British-owned and British-managed. The UK has welcomed the wave of investment and management from the US and from Japan, more recently from France and Germany, to transform its car industry and rebuild it. BMW has found the task of owning and managing Rover too difficult, but Peugeot has been more successful making cars in the UK. The euro has been on a roller coaster. It was weak in the early days following its launch, much to consternation of its main continental proponents. In 2003–04 it has been much stronger, causing considerable difficulties for manufacturers seeking to export from a continental European platform. The pound has been more stable against the dollar, the world's dominant trading currency, which has made conditions a little easier for the UK manufacturing sector than for the continental.

The City revolution was triggered by the UK government decision to open the City of London up to much more foreign capital and competition. The City went through a rapid metamorphosis at the end of the 1980s which fuelled the phenomenal growth of the 1990s as the City stretched its lead over other European financial centres. In telecommunications, the UK went from being one of the laggards amongst the developed world into one of the world leaders. Britain has been at the forefront of developing mobile telephony and digital communication.

Exchange rates and economic performance

We can see the same convergence of the US and British economies in the performance of our currencies. At the end of the 1980s and in the early 1990s, the UK decided to hitch its fortunes more strongly to those on the continent. Before joining the Exchange Rate Mechanism (ERM) Britain tried to keep sterling in line with the Deutschmark. It led to interest rates too low for the UK and a substantial monetary expansion. For a while it created good times. There is always a delay before inflation takes off. We then entered the mechanism and had to keep sterling stable at DM2.95 until the markets forced us out in September 1992. The price of keeping our currency in line with the Deutschmark was colossal. In the late 1980s, when sterling had wanted to go up, it was held down only at the price of a monetary explosion. The government printed money to sell sterling on the market to try to keep it down. Interest rates were kept low to deter foreign deposits in the UK. In the early 1990s inflation picked up as a result. Then the process reversed. Sterling wanted to go down. Interest rates were sent sky-high and money policy tightened dramatically. Recession naturally followed.

If we take the performance of sterling from the beginning of 1993 when the impact of being in the ERM had worn off, and sterling could settle down to a new lower level against the Deutschmark, we can see that sterling has for a period of seven years been extremely stable against the dollar. Between 1993 and 2000, sterling never fell by more than 6% from its then dollar level, and never rose by more than 12% from its then rate. Conversely, sterling has been much less stable against the Deutschmark, rising from DM2.20 to DM3.40. During our time in the ERM, sterling was very unstable against the dollar, damaging our business with America. US tourists were priced out of London. All those dealing in dollar commodities and products were put under considerable pressure. Since 2000 there has been a little more variation with the downward drift in the dollar visible against all-comers.

The relative stability of the dollar–pound exchange rate can be accounted for by the strong two-way pulls across the Atlantic. With the US as the biggest overseas investor in the UK, and the UK in turn the biggest overseas investor in the US, it means that there are strong flows of investment monies, dividends and interest payments going both ways. The City of London transacts most of its business in dollars, and as one of the world's premier financial centres, alongside New York and Tokyo, the huge volume of London-based transactions is another important factor. Most of the UK's hi-tech exports – such as aerospace, wholesale pharmaceuticals, software, computers and microchips – are priced in dollars. The main commodity markets, including the metals, oil, gas and soft commodities, trade in dollars. The US is the UK's biggest single export market, accounting for more than Germany and France combined when taking visibles and invisibles together.

Many in manufacturing want a stable pound–dollar rate, and since we left the ERM, we enjoyed one in the early years but have suffered to some extent along with everyone else during the period of sharp dollar decline in 2003 and 2004. People do not always get what they want in business life. There was no particular reason why the pound should be stable against the dollar. The government wasn't trying to engineer such a controlled exchange rate. No government could marshal enough money to intervene to hold the exchange rate for any length of time, given the enormous flows going across the exchanges between sterling and dollars. The stability in the later 1990s shows that over this extended time period there were enough similarities in the trading pattern of the US and British economies and in the conduct of their respective monetary policies for the two rates to stay more or less in line. In 2003 and 2004 there was some divergence as the British monetary authorities followed a more restrictive policy than the US ones.

The dominance of Anglo-American capitalism is now everywhere to be seen. Whilst the US is clearly the senior partner, the UK has been no slouch in building global business and coat-tailing behind the US. A study for *Business Week* in July 1999 of the world's most valuable companies underlined this success. Whilst the US could account for 494 of the top 1,000 companies in the world by value of their shares, Britain was in second place with 108 companies worth US$2 trillion, just ahead of Japan's 120 slightly smaller companies, worth US$1.9 trillion. Germany, with 36 companies worth US$820 billion; France, with 45 companies worth US$756 billion; and Italy, with 23 companies worth US$380 billion, were between them smaller than Britain when measuring the global reach and market power of their companies. Indeed, it was interesting to see that Switzerland was ahead of Italy, proving that from a small mountain base not part of the EU itself, Switzerland was able to provide a good home for multinational companies operating in the five continents of the world, an exercise in considerable market power.

The other interesting thing about the *Business Week* table was that Britain, out of all the countries on the list, achieved the highest returns on capital. Some of the techniques of Anglo-American and now global capitalism have been pioneered first in Britain. Whilst in the 1960s and 1970s it was common for British people to apply American management styles and manuals to their businesses, in the 1980s and 1990s the United Kingdom added something of its own, which enabled it to some extent to return the management fire across the Atlantic. BP's acquisition of Sohio brought home to the US corporate world that British capitalism also had some claws.

The language of business

More important, perhaps, than the facts and figures of the great Anglo-Saxon markets and the global reach of their companies is the feeling in Britain that we are getting closer to the US than to the continent. The common language is a very important force which is drawing us closer together just as Churchill had forecast. Whilst Churchill honestly admitted that he could not foretell the final form the union of the English-speaking peoples would take, he would feel vindicated seeing how English is now the driving force behind many of the new connections and much of the new technology. English is the language of the internet. It is the language of computer software and intelligent systems. It is the language of business consultants, corporate advisers, management advisers and international managements worldwide.

English is also the cultural language of the dominant group on the planet. British television serves up a regular diet of US sitcoms, westerns,

US movies. The Hollywood influence is everywhere and frequent, on widescreen and narrow screen. British people welcome Hollywood stars into their living rooms, on television, in tabloid newspapers, and on the radio, as if they were long-lost friends. The fact that they talk the same language makes it easier to accept them as everyday parts of individuals' lives. The tabloid newspaper editor is always screaming to the staff to bring more stories on stars and royals. The Royal Family lives in that star-studded kingdom that mixes Hollywood with big business, with the top of government. Beneath the Star Spangled Banner there is a new global jet-set of stars and their allies. Others have stars in their eyes.

US cultural imperialism began as a good business proposition. The early successes of the US lay more in exporting the hardware of the American way of life. It has more recently evolved to export the ideas and the English language that go with it. The global giants in the inter-war period were the large US motor manufacturers, the oil companies, and the producers of exciting new products like Coca-Cola and Pepsi. The US brought to the world the hamburger, the drive-in, the movie, fast food and the supermarket in the post-war world. All of these things have become a regular part of British daily life. They slid effortlessly across the Atlantic and are no longer seen as raw imports or something exotic and foreign.

Cola and hamburgers: Britain in the diner

If people consciously choose to go out to an Italian or French restaurant, they have a sense of some ethnic differences in cuisine, strengthened by the different language spoken if the restaurant is authentic. Choosing to go to an Italian or French restaurant is rather like choosing to go to a Chinese or a Japanese restaurant. You go because you like the culture, you like its differences, and you expect it to feel foreign. You are consciously adventuring, trying something different. Conversely, when we go to McDonald's or to a Kentucky Fried Chicken outlet there is no similar sense of ethnic adventure. Many people would do so without realising it was a US import. The staff are self-consciously normal British kids with the mongrel mixture of accents you would expect depending on where in the country the restaurant is based. There is less shock and less sense of novelty than going to a restaurant themed to one of our continental partners.

Britain goes to Hollywood

The same is even truer of films, books and plays. Again, the language barrier is the prime difference. If you wish to go to see a good French or

Italian film, you will be wrestling with subtitles or your own grasp – or lack of it – of the language. A US film will have different accents, but usually as the film develops people suspend their disbelief and regard it as part of their cultural inheritance as well. The US and the UK share a language and a literature. Americans regard Shakespeare as their dramatist and often make pilgrimages to Stratford-upon-Avon to celebrate his success. British citizens are familiar with Huckleberry Finn, Tom Sawyer, westerns and Henry James. Whilst the British tradition is more maritime and the US more new frontier, both are literatures of adventure, of venturing against the odds, of battling with the mighty sea, or fighting with the Indians for control of the mighty plains. English boys will re-enact the cowboy struggles against the Indians as if it were their heritage. They are not so keen to be Napoleon or the Kaiser in war games.

The new wave of technology puts the US in the driving seat. As I sit writing my book on a modern word processor, I am told I have misspelt a word because I have followed the English rather than the US spelling. The computer games and databanks are in US English. We accept them. Most of us do not rant and rave against US success. We do not have the problem the French have of fighting to keep their language and culture going in a world which is anglicising rapidly.

There are British people who resent US success and would rather join a varied European culture, but they are in a minority. I find that those who are most fanatical about us joining a European political union usually betray with their own choice of words a feeling of otherness from the continent. They ask me how often I go to Europe, and are surprised when I say I am nearly always in Europe, for Europe is my continent. Many in Britain still talk about whether we join Europe, failing to see that geographically we are a series of offshore European islands, and that politically we joined part of the European scheme a long time ago. We are now a polyglot people living a varied cultural life. We watch US movies, are becoming more dependent on our cars, may soon be regularly driving to the gym to use the walking machines, and are happy to see the mushrooming of US corporations on the high street and in the industrial parks.

Indeed, after years of encouragement to become more European, the British public remains obstinately committed to the English-speaking world. A YouGov poll taken at the end of 2004 asked Britons where they would most like to live: 49% said the United Kingdom, 37% Australia, 28% Canada, 27% New Zealand, and 22% said the United States of America. No continental European country appeared in the top five. Australia, Ireland, the United Kingdom, the United States and Canada were also the top five countries when it came to evaluating the places with the friendliest people, whilst Canada, Australia, New Zealand and Britain were voted the safest countries by a substantial margin over fifth-place Sweden.

France and Germany topped the poll for having the least friendly people whilst Israel, India, Russia, China and Egypt were the countries where Britons would least like to live. Britons most wanted to take a holiday in Australia, Canada, New Zealand, the United States or Britain, and least wanted to visit Israel, Dubai, India, Russia and Egypt. China won the least democratic country award by a huge margin, with 43% seeing her as the least democratic, followed by Russia at 27% and Dubai at 24%. Britain won the most democratic country award with 48% of the votes, Australia came second with 38%, Canada third with 26%, and the United States fourth with 24%.

Drinking the odd cappuccino, liking continental as well as New World wines, going to Spain on holiday and admiring some European art and architecture, is a European attachment, but it is only part of our story. The English language, the ubiquitous cola and hamburgers, and the all-conquering might of US capital makes us mid-Atlantic. Most British people do not want to become Americans, but you are more likely to see them praising Hollywood than French culture, and more likely to see them sipping a rum and cola than downing a grappa. As the YouGov poll revealed, if British people were not able to live in Britain you would be likely to find them in New Zealand, Australia or Canada. The ubiquitous, English-speaking soaps on television reinforce the idyllic view of Australia to many British people. There is no enthusiasm to live in France or Germany despite the trips there to buy cheaper wine. The Atlantic is 3,000 miles narrow, and the Channel is 30 miles wide, thanks to the difference of language and customs.

Whilst the EU asks itself why the gap is widening in the US's favour in recent years of world economic growth, the Chinese whirlwind is taking over from both developed areas of the world in crucial industrial sectors. They should heed the low ranking of France in the Heritage Foundation and *Wall Street Journal*'s Index of Economic Freedom. The results of the 2004 index are shown in Table 7.2.

The combination of lower taxes and less regulation has helped power the US economy to a growing lead. The EU itself, in its 2002 Review of the EU economy, forecast that the EU's share (15 members) of world output will fall from 18% in 2000 to only 10% in 2050, whilst the US share will rise from 23 to 26% over the same half century. This may prove to be an optimistic forecast by the EU, given the United Nations estimate that the EU 15's working population will fall by almost a fifth in the first half of the twenty-first century. The Organisation for Economic Cooperation and Development (OECD) shows just how highly taxed Euroland is. The EU 15 paid an average 40.6% in tax in 2002, compared to the US paying just 26.4% of national income to the Revenue.

Table 7.2   Heritage Foundation and *Wall Street Journal*'s Index of Economic Freedom, 2004

	Rank	*Score*
Hong Kong	1	1.34
UK	7	1.79
US	10	1.85
France	44	2.63

Note: The lower the score the freer the economy.

Between 1995 and 2003 the US economy grew by almost one quarter, whereas the EU only managed one sixth. Table 7.3 shows that the US economy outpaced the EU in every year save 2001, the year of the hi-tech crash.

Table 7.3   EU 15 and US real GDP growth rates per annum (OECD figures)

Year	*US growth (%)*	*EU growth (%)*
1997	4.5	2.6
1998	4.2	3.0
1999	4.4	2.9
2000	3.6	3.6
2001	0.5	1.7
2002	2.2	1.1
2003	3.2	0.8

Even the Institut Français des Relations Internationales recognise that by 2050 the EU's share of world trade will be well down on its current level, whilst they envisage China surging, to account for almost a quarter of world trade by then. They, too, are likely to be underestimating the power of China's economic development, which is driven by specialisation in areas where China can export large quantities of manufactures to the West.

The UK will develop her links with China and India in the East, and will maintain her strong ties across the Atlantic. The EU will spend the next decade wrestling with the problems of relative decline. Her model will be tried and found wanting. Fast growth will be happening elsewhere in the world. Success still requires companies and individuals to carry on business the American way. The world runs on US computer platforms, harnessing US software, trading in English and often using dollars for exchange. It is not suddenly going to change, but we will see 'Made in China' on more and more products.

Notes

The Agreement Establishing the World Trade Organization is a long and complex document. There are annexes dealing with Intellectual Property, settlement of disputes, trade policy, government procurement and a series of sector agreements.

The founding agreement of the IMF was first drawn up in 1945 at a UN Monetary and Financial Conference.

The International Bank for Reconstruction and Development *Articles of Agreement*, 16 February 1989.

The Commonwealth's evolution can be traced through *The Declaration of Principles*, Singapore, 1971; *The Lusaka Declaration*, Zambia, 1979; *The Harare Commonwealth Declaration*, Zimbabwe, 1991; and *The Millbank Action Programme*, New Zealand, 1995.

These are all reproduced in the *Commonwealth Year Book* for 1998.

Bayne (1997), Howell (1998) and Marshall (1998) provide good articles on the Commonwealth.

NATO was established under *The North Atlantic Treaty*, Washington, DC, 4 April 1949.

The shifting patterns of world trade in favour of the English-speaking world are reported in *Eurofacts*, a Global Britain publication, 14 July 2000.

The impact of the US on the continent of Europe is illuminated in Lindemann (1995).

The North American Free Trade Agreement: *Eurofacts*, 10 September 1999, 'How to lose market share', charts how NAFTA's share of world trade has risen and the EU's has fallen, 1987–97.

Jamieson and Minford (1999) make a good statistical comparison between the US and the EU on trade, taxes and jobs.

8

The United States of America and the United States of Europe

The coming conflicts

The United States of Europe is being fashioned from anti-Americanism. The United States of America needs to prepare for the coming conflicts. Many great nations have been created or resurrected on the back of a defined antipathy. The US itself began by a passionate revolt against colonial government from the UK. France and Britain have often defined themselves by competing against each other for territory and glory or fighting over styles of government. China and Japan dislike each other, as only close neighbours can.

The danger of emerging European nationalism is that it will be born in this crude image. Many of the fathers and progenitors of the United States of Europe think its role is to challenge the world's current dominant superpower, the US.

There is an important distinction between aggressive nationalism and sensible cultural patriotism. I am very patriotic about my country. It means I am at ease with its history, its culture, its past and its future. It means that I do not wish to see my country run down. I support our teams in sporting competitions. I have a penchant for the music, the landscape, the literature and the traditions of my country. It does not mean that at the same time I have to run down the culture, language and legitimate ambitions of other countries. It means I believe Britain and other countries have a place in the world without conflict. We can enjoy each other's differences whilst resting secure in the knowledge that ours is right for us.

Narrow nationalists transmute their love for country into a hatred of others. They set ambitions for their country that involve treading on the toes of other nations. They do not know where to stop when supporting national teams. Aggressive nationalism can be allied to racism, to a sense of supremacy and right. It leads to verbal abuse and physical violence against others from different races or nations.

The danger, in the creation of a United States of Europe, rests in this fundamental paradox. I am quite sure that those who wish to create a United States of Europe hate narrow nationalism and racism at the level of the individual European country. They rightly perceive that nationalism, racism and fanaticism under the German Reich wrought great atrocities and barbarisms in the 1930s and 1940s. They rightly wish to put behind them an era when France competed for territory against Germany and the other Latin countries, when Spain set out on conquest, and a period when Germany wished to spread her borders east and west by violent means. They loathe Nazism and all its works and are understandably alarmed by the rise of new neo-Nazi groups on the continent. I entirely agree with them that an end to narrow, racial, aggressive competitive nationalism in Western Europe is good.

The irony is that they are in danger of replacing the petty nationalisms of the nations of Europe with an aggressive nationalism of their own at the European level. It is born of a sense of superiority of the European system to any other. It is based on the assumption that Europe needs to challenge the US for supremacy, it needs to get even with the US, and in some fields needs to surpass it. It is competitive and aggressive, but not yet racist or violent.

The idea of a United States of Europe, which looks so appealing to some French and German politicians, can look very threatening from other parts of the world. The common borders that Europe seeks are only common frontiers within part of the EU area. They will be allied to a restrictive immigration policy against all those seeking a better life from the Arab, African and Asian lands beyond. To struggling farmers in the third world, the sound of the gates clanking shut around Fortress Europe is not an attractive one. To the makers of industrial products from outside Europe who find themselves confronted with a range of non-tariff barriers to trade, the growing central power in Brussels is far from good. The country which should worry most about the emergence of a baby superstate in Europe is the US itself. The United States of Europe may as yet have few offensive intercontinental weapons and no military intention against the US, but it is growing rapidly in power and pretension.

The United States of Europe will have command of united armies of more than 2 million people in arms, and a substantial navy and air force. However, these forces will not have the technological expertise and intercontinental capability of the US forces, and there is no immediate sign that the continental governments are prepared to tax their people more to spend at anything like the level of US defence spending. There is every sign that European forces will remain strongest at home, without the ability to deploy rapidly on a big scale in other parts of the world. The EU and its armaments agency is well aware of the drawbacks. The advent of the European fighter programme is designed to improve EU airpower and there are now discussions about improving Europe's heavy lift capability, to enable it to project its power across greater distances and to take in the equipment to back up troops on the ground that would be required. The rapid development of aerial observation is designed to bring the EU a little closer to the US's global surveillance ability.

There is, however, clear indication that the European governments first wish to confront the US economically. One of the most cited reasons for creating a new currency, the euro, is that Europeans want to have a currency that rivals the US dollar. It is difficult to understand why this would be in the interests of the Western European peoples unless it is the intention to create an economic area and then a state which can rival the US.

The euro

In 1999, eleven countries agreed to go ahead and replace their own currencies with the euro. France, Germany, Belgium, the Netherlands, Austria, Finland and Luxembourg were always expected to be in. They were joined as founder members by Portugal, Spain, Ireland and Italy. These countries had more difficulty in meeting the requirements, but as the leading members had also found the criteria awkward, every country bar Greece, who wanted to join, was allowed in. This left four members of the EU outside the first grouping of Euroland. The UK and Denmark had opt-outs from the scheme and decided for the time being to say 'No'. Greece was not allowed in because its economy was so out of line with the rest. Subsequently, its main economic figures improved and it joined at the same time as the others. Sweden decided against immediate entry, even though under the Treaty it was meant to join with the others.

In 2002, notes and coin were issued in euros and the old currencies gradually phased out. From its launch as a trading currency on 1 January 1999, the new currency fell sharply against the dollar, yen and sterling in its first two years. Subsequently it has risen, recovering all of the lost ground. The European creators of the currency were extremely disappointed by its early refusal to rise against the almighty dollar. They had set themselves the task of displacing the dollar and wanted a strong currency as a symbol of resurgent European national economic success. The weakness of the currency disappointed them and reflected the poor performance of the European economy. Paradoxically, the creators of the currency have been even more alarmed by sharp rises in the currency in 2004, for this has not reflected a strengthening of the European economy. Instead, the weaker dollar has made it even more difficult for European exporters to compete, and has further highlighted the underlying structural weaknesses of the European Union economy itself.

At its launch at the beginning of 1999 extravagant claims were made for the euro. Many around the world took them quite seriously. European bankers and politicians claimed that the euro would soon build up to be of similar importance in world trade to the mighty dollar, and then in due course might surpass it. They painted a picture of millions of traders around the world having to buy euros to trade in, taking pleasure in helping build a rival to the US dollar. Things have not worked out quite as they envisaged, but it still remains their aim.

Over the years more countries will build up reserves in euros to complement their reserves in dollars, gold and other convertible currencies. Many countries are attracted to the euro all the time the European Central Bank runs a tight money policy leading to euro strength. However, it is difficult to see the euro displacing the dollar as the world's principal trading currency, given the relative sizes of the EU, US and dollar influenced economies around the world, and given the prevalence of dollar trading in the main commodity markets and in the markets for hi-tech products. Nor will it necessarily represent a great triumph for European policy should the euro be more widely adopted as a trading currency. What matters is the health and success of the European Union economy. So far the euro has failed to generate extra growth in jobs as promised. Indeed, the 'one size fits all' interest rate policy has caused inflationary difficulties in some peripheral countries like Ireland, and has worsened the slow growth or recession in the core countries like Germany.

EU governments seem to believe that if they can build a substantial currency which third parties wish to trade in, invest in, and hold in their bank accounts, they will have made their first important dent in the economic power of the US and the dollar. They are promoting many other forms of rivalry.

Airbus

The most intense has taken place in the field of civil aircraft manufacture. The huge costs of researching and developing new planes had led, ineluctably, to monopoly or cartel in the world market, dominated by a few large US corporations, and especially by Boeing. The EU decided that it, too, must create a big centre of civil aircraft manufacture to rival that of the US. In one sense this was public spirited from the world's point of view. There is no doubt that competition and choice is a good thing and the arrival of the Airbus has empowered airlines to compare deals across the Atlantic to create some pressure for lower prices. If this had been the only reason for the European adventure, I would have been happy to praise their benign nature.

Unfortunately, it is quite clear from reading their words and listening to their statements that the creators of Airbus had in mind a very traditional and old-fashioned type of commercial rivalry. They decided that whatever the cost in terms of public subsidy, government orders and encouragement, Europe would have its own civil aviation industry. In the big bidding competitions between Boeing and Airbus to win the business, some of the freer spirits in the European aviation world portrayed the battle as a titanic struggle between the good and the bad, the European and the US. The process of bitter commercial contest soon spilled over into government against government, lobbying and dispute.

The Americans claimed that in the early days Airbus attracted massive subsidy and in later days attracted easy-terms finance in the form of launch aid which would not have been available from the marketplace. They regarded this as unfair. The Europeans countered with their argument that Boeing received hidden subsidies, being generously rewarded for its defence contracts which the company had used to cross-subsidise civil aircraft manufacture. There may be some truth in both sets of allegations. The deliberate creation of a rival business to a large US combine which has close relationships with the US government has led directly to a festering trade dispute. The world airline passenger may be better off, and the airlines undoubtedly have more choice as a result, but Euro–US relations have taken a move for the worse as a result of this European attempt to pitch against US dominance in a given area. The two rivals have now decided to offer different visions of the future. Airbus has gone for a much larger plane, Boeing for faster quieter smaller jets to offer more regular services. With any luck the world will need both types of aircraft.

Agriculture

In the two big areas where the EU already has almost complete control over the policies of the nations of Western Europe, agriculture and trade, a number of disputes have blown up between the EU and the US. In the agricultural field, the EU has banned imports of US beef on the grounds that the US farmers use hormones to improve the quality and to make their farming more efficient. The EU claims that these hormones could be damaging to health, yet they have failed to produce any evidence to sustain this contention. The US could point to the fact that it has had no rash of illnesses or premature deaths amongst its people based on their beef-eating habits.

The EU can counter by saying that many people in the EU do not like the idea of hormone-based beef and that the European government is merely speaking for them. A fairer way of tackling the problem would be clear labelling, leaving the customers of Europe the same choice as the customers in the US as to whether they wished to buy hormone-based beef or not. If the hormone-based beef is a better quality for a given price, as the Americans claim, some will wish to purchase it in the marketplace. Others of a purer frame of mind might wish to buy organically reared beef at a higher price.

The obstinate refusal of the EU to allow customer choice in this field has naturally alienated US opinion. The US claims that it has many more efficient farmers and that it is being penalised in order to support less efficient European producers in their domestic market. The US has also been able to retaliate by pointing out that some of the beef reared in the EU has been reared in herds contaminated by BSE, which the EU itself has decided is extremely dangerous. The irony has not been lost on US commentators.

Trade wars

The beef war has been mirrored in several other areas of trade. A regular spectre at the feast is that of the banana wars. Several EU countries were imperial powers. Since shedding colonial responsibility they have nonetheless retained an affection and special links with a number of third world banana producers who like to sell their product into the European market. The UK, for example, has close links with the Windward and Leeward Islands, and Jamaica, who have traditionally supplied many of the bananas into the UK market.

The banana producers closest to the EU have enjoyed favoured arrangements to the exclusion of so-called dollar bananas coming from parts of Latin America where US influence is stronger. The US claims that the dollar bananas are bigger, better and cheaper than those produced in the Caribbean and sold on special terms into the EU. The US took its case to the World Trade Organisation, which found in favour of the US, and told the EU to remove the favoured protective arrangements that were in place. The EU has so far failed to comply with this requirement, and the US is angrily trying to get satisfaction through international legal means. It has also led to US retaliation. The US has announced categories of imports from the EU which will attract high tariffs as a warning against what the US sees as unfair trading.

We have also fallen into rum wars. Bacardi of Bermuda, and France's Pernod Ricard both seek the rights to the Havana Club trademark, a coveted brand in the rum world. The Havana Club rum factory was confiscated by Fidel Castro. France's Pernod Ricard acquired the rights from the Cuban business. Meanwhile, the US said that the rights belong to Bacardi, which bought the rights from the Cuban plant's original owners who owned them before the expropriation by Fidel Castro.

Once again there are rights on both sides, but the EU has failed to understand the true causes of US anger and the dispute is gaining a nasty political edge. To the US trade negotiators, the de facto recognition of Fidel Castro's expropriation of assets inherent in the French claim is unacceptable. The US has had a very fraught relationship with Cuba, not least during the period of the extremely dangerous Cuban missile crisis, and cannot easily forgive the expropriations by its arch-communist antagonist so close to its borders. The Europeans believe that Castro is the de facto leader of Cuba, and that he has established control over the assets expropriated from former owners. They believe the French company has acquired them in a legal and sensible manner and their claim ought to be upheld.

When it comes to international negotiations over freer trade, it is all too often the case that the US and Europe find themselves on different sides. US trade policy was directed by Charlene Barshefsky for President Clinton. Europe's was directed by the French socialist Pascal Lamy. These two were unlikely to agree. Lamy's socialism was one obstacle, and his belief that the world must be kept free from US domination was another. The socialist mindset of the European trade position is favourable to European protectionism. They see nothing wrong with subsidies, restraints on trade, tariff barriers and the like, as legitimate weapons in the war for economic supremacy around the world. More recent trade negotiators have continued to fall out, with each seeing the other's obstacles to trade as the only problem.

Both the US and Europe run protected and subsidised agricultural systems. Both engage in a macabre dance in world trade talks over whether any of this elaborate structure can be removed without an unreasonable political backlash in the farming heartlands of the US Midwest, or amongst the small and not very profitable farms of Germany and France in Europe. Despite this convergence of view on some agricultural matters, nearly everything sparks problems in the world trading system, producing a divergence of opinion between the US and the united Europe.

The question we need to answer is, 'How serious could this set of tensions and conflicts become?' The pattern so far is that as Europe gains control over an area, so it produces policies and attitudes of mind that are hostile to the US. The danger is that these trade disputes will escalate, and take on a wider significance with a more worrying political edge.

Europe goes it alone on foreign policy

Until recently, the US has not taken any of this very seriously. They have decided that dialling one number for Europe has all sorts of advantages and believe that the trade rows are just teething problems as the new European state attempts to position itself. Now that Europe is talking about creating a defence identity – in other words, having its own army, navy and air force – and a common foreign policy, the US policy establishment in Washington is having second thoughts. There is absolutely no reason to suppose that European foreign policy as it develops will be compatible with, or even friendly towards US foreign policy. The self-same people who have decided that the euro should topple the dollar, that Airbus should overwhelm Boeing, and that European farming methods will exclude the Midwest, are now out to design a foreign policy and a defence policy for their fledgling European state. US policy-makers are at last realising that this foreign policy will be designed in part by people who are distrustful of the US and would dearly love to see it removed from its position of world supremacy.

There have been three warning signs that have shaken US policy-makers so far. The first occurred shortly after German reunification. The US was an enthusiastic proponent of the greater Germany and thought that the greater Germany might lead on to the greater Europe. The first President Bush's administration, keen to foster it, was dismayed when Germany immediately opened negotiations with the Soviet Union and developed a special relationship with the emerging Russia. The US is still very worried about the stability and long-term intentions of Russia, and is not very keen on Germany's *Ostpolitik* extending to Moscow.

The second worry emerged when Germany recognised Croatia in 1995, dragging the rest of the EU into similar action at a time when the US judged that recognition of Croatia would intensify the simmering civil war in the Balkans. The EU's action was followed up by a lack of resolve and a lack of troops to sort out the problem. It ended in embarrassment with the Europeans unable to handle a crisis in their own backyard. The US flirted with the policy of allowing the Europeans to solve the crisis on their own, only to discover that European diplomacy was pointing in the wrong direction on many occasions, and was allied to a weakness in military resolve that proved fatal. The crisis took much longer and involved much more loss of life and many more complexities than the US would have liked. Many in the US policy establishment blame EU diplomatic and military leadership for the blunders which followed.

The third worry that has emerged under the second President Bush, as we have seen in the skirmishes so far concerning Galileo, is the gathering of military intelligence, and the role of China. If the EU continues its pro-Chinese policy in a worrying way, the US will conclude that an independent EU foreign policy is a very bad idea.

The emerging attitudes in Western Europe could lead to some strengthening of isolationism in the US. If the EU decides to provoke the US in an ever-wider range of areas, many more in the US will say, 'let them stew in their own juice'. The main thing which holds back the serious US policy establishment from saying this is the potential threat of Russia if it fell into the wrong hands, and the need for the US to have a first line of defence somewhere on the European continent. The British allies of the US have always understood this need. The UK helped the US with the installation of Cruise missiles as a line of defence on European soil at a time when some other countries in Western Europe were unhelpful or downright hostile to the endeavour. The same role may be needed on the part of friendly European countries in the latest US development of a missile shield and early warning system.

If all goes according to the plans of the progenitors of the European state, anti-American feeling will build up gradually and will spread to a whole range of policy areas. Europeans will be taught that US foodstuff is not fit to eat, that US planes are not as good as European ones, that the US is the evil force in the environmental world, doing more damage than any other country to the planet, that European foreign policy has to put European interests first and may not extend to being part of a US pan-Western defence system. Both France and Germany are much friendlier to Russia than the US has been in the last fifty years, and both would probably like to see an end to US troops in Europe. There is little doubt that a European government in Brussels will be anti-American, and will regard it as a sign of success if the relationship between the two deteriorates at a suitable pace.

This will be a tragedy in the making. It is not in the interests of either Europe or the US to allow more tensions to develop and the relationship to become strained. The US does have an interest in the defence of democracy and freedom around the world. The US does need some defence collaboration on the continent of Europe for its own interests, as well as for European interests. The EU for its part will have to accept that it is not prepared to put the effort, money and technology into a sufficient defence for Western Europe and is dependent upon the US alliance. The EU should understand that, given US technological superiority in so many fields, collaboration and friendly competition in the private sector is a much better route than head-to-head government confrontation and an attempt to close markets against each other's goods and services. It is important for people on both sides to understand the deep resentments that underlie the European strategy and for the US to turn to those allies within the EU and parts of the European continent that are friendly and understand the need for a good relationship.

The next steps in the conflict

The next steps in the conflict are also all too easy to forecast. Trade disputes will intensify as more and more items are found on both sides that irritate and annoy. We can expect to see a series of EU decisions designed to favour domestic European businesses at the expense of US ones in fields as wide-ranging as media, telephony, internet technology and transport. In the aviation field, those who wish to construct alliances amongst dominant European carriers normally find the going in Brussels easy, whereas those who wish to include a major US company in their alliance find it much more difficult. In media, there will be an attempt in the name of defending French and German culture to resist the growing global claims of the large US corporations. In the world of internet and telephony, there will be attempts to impose European standards that are not necessarily compatible with US ones and a battle over who has the right to settle these kind of issues. There will be many more agricultural disputes, and further rows over trading relationships with former colonies and countries in respective spheres of influence.

More worrying will be the widening of the foreign policy disputes to cover ever more areas. It will not consist solely of disputes about the Balkans that result from the growing confidence of the EU in a united

European foreign policy. There will be different attitudes towards the Middle East, towards the Arab world, and towards Asia. European defence evolution in itself is going to cause tensions within NATO and will alarm some Americans. The more independent the EU becomes, the less inclined the US will be to share technology, intelligence and information with its former European allies. We have already had a taster of this with the EU objecting to British involvement in intelligence-gathering with the Americans in a combined defence operation. The EU is now claiming that this has extended into the field of commercial espionage and shows that Britain is on the wrong side in the trade war.

Ideological adversaries

The EU adventure is hostile to many Anglo-American values. The leading English-speaking countries believe in free trade, democracy, free speech, liberty, freedom of association, religious tolerance, competition, enterprise and choice. The EU for its part has rather different beliefs. It values solidarity, cooperation, partnership, corporate solutions, European champions, some limitations upon the freedom of speech and the support of good order and consensus above liberty. There will undoubtedly be a clash as the years pass between the corporatist, bureaucratic virtues of the EU and the liberty-seeking outspokenness of the Anglo-Saxon countries. The EU is careless about democracy, usually preferring secretive bureaucracy.

The differences are very clear in the attitude towards democracy itself. The EU has decided to create a government before creating a strong parliament or congress. In the UK, a strong Parliament emerged to impose limitations on the power of the Crown, and more recently, upon the power of the elected executive government. In the US, the Congress was formed to defend people's liberties, to give voice to their worries and grievances, and to provide strong scrutiny over the actions of the president, who was in turn directly elected.

The European Parliament is almost an afterthought, a presentational device rather than a serious spanner in the works of executive government. The European Parliament has no power to tax, whereas the British Parliament and the US Senate and House of Representatives are based upon the power to grant or withhold tax revenues to the government. The European Parliament has modest influence over legislation with no direct entitlement to draft new laws itself. Conversely, both the British Parliament and the US representative houses can initiate legislation, and are solely responsible for deciding its fate.

The executive government of the EU, formed out of the Commission, is made up of unelected people. In Britain, most Ministers of the Crown are elected, and all have to be in one of the two chambers of Parliament subject to scrutiny. In the US, most senior office-holders go through an election before they gain their position, including judges as well as governors, and of course the President himself. In the EU, the most powerful people in the government, the Commissioners, are selected by member state governments and are not directly answerable to the European Parliament. They are never Members of the European Parliament, and when they go there they are not nearly as accountable as British Ministers in the House of Commons. People on the continent just do not believe that such strong scrutiny of the executive is a necessary or desirable part of good government. They have come to accept that government is often a matter of self-serving bureaucracies, that much of it is conducted behind closed doors, and that elections settle very little. Italy has become used to seeing administrations come and go, as the proportional representation system used there rarely delivers a decisive result at a general election. In Germany, the government has only changed once in the post-war period, as a result of votes cast in a general election when Chancellor Kohl was thrown out of office. On other occasions the government has changed as a result of decisions by politicians behind closed doors changing their allegiances and shifting coalitions.

In the US, one or other of the main parties wins the presidency, and has a four-year period to change the shape and direction of the country (and the president can only hold office for two consecutive terms). In the UK, majority governments are usually produced by the electors and held to account by the electors at a subsequent general election. This creates a very different relationship between the electors and the elected than in a proportional representation system where the important decisions are taken after the election, when the deal-making and coalition-building begins. On the continent, many ministers are not elected, heads of state and government are not subject to the same degree of press, parliamentary and congressional scrutiny, and political elites contain debate within narrow confines.

Could the EU be democratic?

Some European partners had hoped that the British involvement in the EU in general, and in the European Parliament in particular, would give more democratic incisiveness and legitimacy to the European government. They have been disappointed as, for a variety of reasons, successive British governments have been unwilling to see big powers passed to the European Parliament, whilst the Commission and the bureaucracy of Brussels have fought a usually successful action to make sure that they are not directly accountable to the European Parliament in the same way as a British Minister is to the UK Parliament. If Anglo-Americans were designing a new country called the United States of Europe, they would begin by trying to gain consent to the proposition through a public campaign followed by a general election to a much more powerful European Parliament. Out of that Parliament ministers would be chosen. Political debate would soon be organised in trans-European parties representing the different points of view on European issues, and ministers would be brought regularly to account before that Parliament. Alternatively, following the US model, the president of the European Commission would be directly elected by all the peoples of the member countries of the Union, and he or she in turn would be directly answerable to the media day to day and to the electorate at the presidential election. Europe has eschewed either model, reluctant to see so much prying into the affairs of the European government. This has created more mistrust in the Anglo-Saxon world than if a more democratic system had been adopted.

There are similar disagreements between the English-speaking approach and that of the continent when it comes to free speech. British and US democracy is based on the proposition that people should be free to say what they wish, to associate with whom they wish, to run for office and to form parties to make a lively democratic debate. Neither Britain nor the US has been troubled in the last century by either a strong fascist or a strong communist movement. There was a murky period in US history when suspected communists were purged from office, but most Americans now look on that era with a distaste that reflects their underlying belief in the right of individuals to express opinions and to fight for them in a democratic way.

In contrast, the European continent has been grossly disfigured by both communist and fascist activities over much of the last hundred years. The impact of Nazism and fascism in Italy and Spain on the political process has been very marked. Indeed, it would be surprising if it were not. It has meant that many in the governing elites in those countries are suspicious of giving people the right to free speech, fearing that baser instincts might prevail and extreme parties and attitudes re-emerge. The EU is adopting a high and mighty tone, seeking ways to determine whether parties are suitable to run for office or not, and seeking to outlaw certain political attitudes and choice of phrases from the political debate altogether.

The Anglo-American approach says that there should be a law of libel and a law to prevent racism and other undesirable traits. Under such a law a politician is governed by the same criminal law as the rest of the community. As long as he or she does not go over the criminal boundary in what he or she wishes to do or say, that person is then free to express his or her views and to debate them openly. The EU is not prepared to rely on the long shot of criminal action against those who are clearly beyond the pale, but is seeking to narrow the wide range of political views on the continent by those in power actually determining what is and is not a reasonable attitude for the political debate. The British find this all rather scary, as it gives undue power to those who are already in government to control the access to power of those who would challenge them.

Free trade

The English-speaking world strongly believes in freer trade. It is true that there have been imperfections in both the US and British approach to free trade, especially in the agricultural areas, but, as we will see in the next chapter, the general thrust of trade policy on both sides of the Atlantic, in the UK and the US, is towards the reduction or abolition of tariffs, the reduction or abolition of subsidies and state intervention, and the development of a healthy and competitive market. On the continent of Europe, attitudes are rather different. French policy in particular is driven by a wish to create French national champion companies. This is now being supplanted in the minds of both the French and Brussels by the wish to create Euro-champions capable of taking on the mighty US and Japanese corporations. There is not the same wish on the continent to create conditions in which small companies, entrepreneurs, and foreign competitors can challenge the existence of the mighty established corporations. In the US, whenever a large corporation becomes so successful that it has a dominant position in the marketplace, the politicians and government usually intervene to break it up. They successfully broke up the giant Rockefeller oil company earlier in the twentieth century, the Bell telephone company in the 1980s, and are now taking similar action against Microsoft at the beginning of the twenty-first century. If the Franco-German alliance had such a giant company, with such a strong position in world markets, they would be inclined to back it and help it, rather than break it up in the US way.

Continental economies have found it very difficult to create conditions in which entrepreneurs thrive, small businesses set up and a lively competitive challenge to existing corporations emerges. In contrast, the

US has been very good at this. In recent years the UK has moved nearer to the US than to the continental European experience. It comes down to the difference in cultures. The EU believes in a cosy relationship between government and the large corporations. The Anglo-Saxon world believes in a more sceptical and distant relationship where government intervenes only when it feels the corporations have gone too far, in order to protect the market or to restore competition.

Anglo-Saxons are very worried about any suggestion that government is corrupt, self-serving, or has too cosy a relationship with those who are being governed. European government is much happier with the idea of ease of access and frequent transition between the different members of the governing elites in business, academic life and government. The UK has been strongest in seeking to expose the graft, corruption and incompetence in much EU budgeting. Each year, the Court of Auditors produces a long list of mistakes and irregularities in the handling of large EU funds. Each year the Commission promises to do better and then regularly buries the report and fails to follow it up. The EU's attitude towards corruption is so lax that when a middle-ranking official, Paul van Buitenen, decided to blow the whistle on a big scandal, the EU retaliated by suspending him from his job rather than by taking action to tackle the underlying problem he had revealed. In the US and in the UK, politicians are much more hostile to the idea of corruption and incompetence. Senatorial inquiries, Select Committee inquiries in Britain, strong parliamentary debate, and an intrusive media on both sides of the Atlantic are regularly able to expose corruption, waste and incompetence as a means of encouraging all those in government to follow a straighter and narrower path than in the EU.

We can see a similar difference in attitudes in the approach to green issues. On both sides of the Atlantic in the Anglo-Saxon world, people want to look after the environment and value the forest and field, valley and mountain. They also believe, however, that a prosperous country needs to keep its people warm and needs to be mobile. People do not see motorists or users of central heating systems as criminals who should be banned or controlled. Conversely, on the continent, there is a much more entrenched green lobby. Proportional representation systems mean they often get people elected to their respective parliaments. There is a consensus view on the continent that all environmental protection measures are good and necessary, whatever impact they may have on the prosperity machine of business. It goes with the general view that the consensus should be sought, the politically fashionable should always be given strong support, and that dissenting views are undesirable. The

EU is less prepared to see technology as the answer to environmental pollution, ignoring the way the private sector, with some pressure from the regulators, has succeeded in cutting substantially the amount of pollution from the average family saloon car.

In the Anglo-American world, the man or woman with a different idea, with a better way of doing things, with the enterprising company, with the challenging theory, with the uncomfortable propensity to caricature or to criticise the powers that be, the satirist, the cartoonist, the witty columnist, are all revered and valued. Independence of mind and spirit is at a premium. This leads naturally to commercial success, to an outward-going approach, to trading in the five continents and oceans of the world, and to a belief in the diversity of political life and political debate. On the continent, there is a rather different view. People value belonging to elites, seeking consensus, confining disagreements behind closed doors, finding ways of smoothing the passage of large corporations, forging partnerships, confining disagreeable or outspoken debate and regarding those who challenge or think differently as a threat rather than a stimulus to a more prosperous future. This big cultural and attitudinal difference between the EU on the continent, and the Anglo-Saxon world, lies behind many of the disputes that it is now our task to chronicle. US policy, which for several years has felt it was a good idea to unite Europe, is coming to see that unification could be a mistake for US influence in the world, and for continuing good relations with the individual nations that now make up the European Union.

The development of tensions between the EU and the US will happen gradually over an ever-widening range of areas. We will see how disagreements in trade policy are now spreading to disagreements over defence, foreign policy, environmental policy and the whole gamut of governmental issues. The tensions will broaden, they will become more persistent, and they will come to infect every part of the relationship between the emerging European super-state, on the one hand, and the powerful US, on the other. US policy-makers will come to see that dialling one number for Europe may simply result in a whole series of disagreeable phone calls. Forcing the EU countries into a premature or unwanted unity may be bad not only for the European countries themselves, but also for the conduct of US foreign policy as well.

In particular, the US would be well advised to realise that the special relationship between the US and the UK has served both countries well in the post-war period, and still has a great deal to offer. The EU, without the UK as an important economic region is a much weaker body than the EU which has annexed and incorporated the UK within it. A world in which the UK is still free to speak its mind and to support the US when it sees fit is a better place for the US than a world in which the British voice has been silenced and has become part of a consensus view in Fortress Europe. There are not that many powerful national voices in the world that speak up for freedom of speech, democracy, enterprise and liberty. The UK is one of the most prominent after the US. It is in US interests that Britain's voice should not be silenced, just as much as it is in Britain's interest to keep that voice and to make sure it is heard loud and clear in the five continents of the world.

Notes

Eurofacts, Global Britain (1999) sets out the main figures on Britain's pattern of trade with EU and NAFTA countries.

British Management Data Foundation charts the progress of the pound and the dollar.

The early claims for the euro from 1 January 2000 onwards were detailed in the *Financial Times* during January 2000.

9
What's in an English-Speaking Union for the US?

Should the UK join NAFTA?

During the first weekend of July 2000, a group of US Republican senators arrived in the UK to talk about possible British membership of the North American Free Trade Agreement. A number of contacts had been made over the years between British Conservatives and US Republicans with this in mind. The quickening of the pace represented by the delegation led by Phil Gramm, a senior high-ranking senator, was doubly important. They came during the throes of a presidential election when Republicans confidently expected Governor George W. Bush to win as a Republican. They spoke for the majority of Republicans in the Senate and Congress. They shared a common vision with British Conservatives of the type of world they wished to create. It was doubly exciting for British Conservatives as it offered an alternative to the model of ever-increasing European integration, bigger and dearer government from Brussels, and less and less control over our own destiny that has been dominating British foreign policy for so long.

The North American free trade area has not been without its problems at birth, but it is now progressing well. When it was first constructed between the US and Canada, there were many in Canada who feared a US takeover. They have been pleasantly surprised. It has made trade and friendly contact between Canada and the US easier, but Canada is still a self-governing democracy capable of making its own decisions about foreign policy, taxation, and all the other important matters that constitute a political nation. There were even bigger fears amongst many in the US when NAFTA's doors were opened to the south, to Mexico. There had been long-running battles over the permeable southern US borders as more and more Mexicans migrated to the riches of their northern neighbour. But now many in the US would agree that offering Mexico the hand of friendship and more liberal trade was a good way to stimulate the Mexican economy. In the end, most Americans realised that the only thing which will slow the steady drift of economic migrants north from Mexico to the US is a more prosperous and successful Mexico. NAFTA represents the most positive way for the US to assist Mexico to greater prosperity and higher living standards.

The idea behind the North American Free Trade Agreement is very different from the way the EU idea has evolved. It is a free trade area, rather than a customs union. Its aim is not to create new barriers against the rest of the world in the way that the EU has done through its agricultural and commercial policies, but to reduce the barriers of trade between the members even more rapidly than the barriers to trade are being removed globally through the World Trade Organisation. It is an institution hostile to tariff and subsidy. It is based upon the proposition that no government impediment should be placed in the way of a fair and free trade between friendly peoples. It is demonstrating that trade and friendship are solvents of disagreement and political conflict. People are much more reluctant to row if they feel good business will be lost as a result.

The logic of a free trade area is to keep on expanding. It is not an aggressive, imperial operation. It is not a real threat to anyone, and the mood of the world is shifting to see that free trade is an offer and an opportunity rather than a damaging attack on people's way of life. Now that the US is more comfortable with its free trade area with its two nearest neighbours, Canada and Mexico, it is casting its eyes further afield to see who else might be suitable for membership of this exciting project. It has the advantage to Americans of being primarily a US idea. It is not so threatening to the US as it does not curtail its sovereignty in any way that matters to it. It gently expands the US sphere of influence, but mainly through improved contacts, private sector to private sector, which goes with the grain of much US thinking. It is an idea whose time has come, and an idea that the UK should take seriously.

The origins of US enthusiasm to extend free trade to selected countries are varied. The most important point in Washington to date and in US political psychology is the fear that the US has of too much control or intervention from supranational bodies. It may seem surprising to a British audience to learn that exactly the fears that many people legitimately have in Britain about control of their own destiny passing to unelected bureaucracies in Brussels are mirrored by debates in the US about some of the powers of the mighty and sovereign US passing to bureaucratic bodies like the UN, the World Bank, UNESCO and world environmental conferences. The US finds it particularly difficult to accept controls over its policy or freedom of action from others as in the twentieth century it became accustomed to being the most important power in the world, and was able on many occasions to have its own way. US concepts of liberty are bound up with being a successful country economically and politically. Many Americans take the view that the US is pumping out so much cash to support and help countries around the world, it is a bit rich if those same countries then seek to combine through world bodies to impose what to US eyes are unreasonable restrictions on US action.

The paradox is the greater because the US was a crucial founding member of most of the bodies it now has most trouble in dealing with. To British eyes, the constitutions of bodies like the UN, the World Bank and the IMF are carefully drawn as part of the post-war settlement to avoid making unreasonable incursions into the freedom of action of successful countries. The US and the UK were important architects and authors of the post-war supranational institutions, and they are very keen to defend the individual liberties and democracies of the member states that first constituted them. The veto was built in for Security Council members at the UN. No one has ever suggested that the US should have to accept a programme of economic policy laid down by the IMF or World Bank, as the US has never been in a position where it needed to beg favours from those organisations.

Nonetheless, there is a real and understandable worry in the US that transferring too much power to supranational bodies would bode ill for the successful conduct of US foreign policy and the successful upholding of the Anglo-American virtues of liberty, free trade and democracy. An important part of the background to the development of NAFTA is to find an international route forward which leaves countries free to make their own decisions and to place their own bets. Even so, some in the US bridle at the modest international requirements of a free trade area. The UN's equivocations over the war against Iraq reinforced US worries about the UN. American certainty and her decision to go to war led to the UN fearing it had been usurped by the world's most powerful country.

The second important point in the US background is the backlash against the world's largest power and the world's policeman. In the post-war period there has been a lot of resentment of US success in many parts of the globe. This resentment has intensified since the invasion of Iraq. There has been studied ambivalence on the part of many countries. They resent both the strength of US arms and the strength and depth of the US economy, but when in trouble they often call upon the US to intervene or assist. There have been calls from the Middle East for US mediation, US intervention and US military support during the various conflicts between the Arab states and Israel, and in the individual conflicts between different Arab states. In the Far East, Taiwan needs US support against the imperial ambitions of China. China and Japan compete for the attention and support of the US, whilst China from time to time expresses hostility about any US intervention in Asia. In South America, US money, influence and ideas are regularly sought as juntas and democracies jostle with each other and vie for supremacy. In Europe, many of the countries on the continent expect the US nuclear shield and the promise of US conventional forces in the event of problems to be ever-present, although many of those same continental countries are often damning in their comments on US policy and ideals.

The US was remarkably even-tempered prior to 9/11 as many Lilliputian dictatorships and unpleasant regimes around the world have tried to tie the giant down. In many parts of the political establishment in the US, there is an understanding that there can be some future as well as past meaning to the phrase 'the special relationship' between the UK and the US because of this shared experience of being a first power in the world.

Successive British governments after the Suez problems have responded to this by being sympathetic on the whole to the US cause, and offering substantial moral and political support to the US in its chosen courses of action. As we have seen, the special relationship still brings something to both parties. In the case of Iraq the British Prime Minister acted almost as Bush's Secretary of State, trying to gain worldwide support for the US action and acting as a special envoy in parts of the world where the UK had influence.

The idea of offering the UK potential membership of NAFTA was a sign of US Republicans recognising the importance of the special relationship and offering to British Conservatives something that could be very useful to us at a time of decision for the UK. Both believe that British membership of NAFTA would help Britain further to develop its prosperity and economic strength. Both, more importantly, see that it would be a very important gesture to the world, showing that the US and Britain have a lot in common. We should do more things together. It would reinforce the union we have achieved on defence and wider political matters through our joint stance at the UN and our membership of NATO, with an economic grouping based upon principles that together we hold dear.

Many Americans have anglophile leanings, or wish to learn and understand more of the English past. Whilst the US has been successful in creating a cohesive and distinctive culture and a sense of political union out of divergent peoples that came to settle in an important part of the North American continent, many of those peoples are conscious that they are comparatively recent arrivals in a relatively new nation. They do go in search of their origins and seek to understand how their history as an independent country grew directly out of the squabbles and tensions of European settlers and out of the fundamental disagreement between those European settlers and the old home country. Whilst there are now many Spanish-speaking, Italian and Middle European settlers in the US as well, who look to somewhat different cultural and political origins, they are all interested, to some extent, in their English and British background because it had such a decisive impact upon the form, structure, language and early history of the US.

Senator Gramm confirmed this in his speech on UK membership of NAFTA. Although his ancestors came from the continent of Europe, he is conscious of the English origin of his politics, language and the culture of his nation. He values and believes in the English legacy.

US tourists come in their millions to the shores of the UK. They do not come to see 'cool Britannia', or even to celebrate the Beatles. We are not likely to see many of them making the journey to see the new architecture of Docklands, or visiting Liverpool. They come to see the great heritage buildings of the UK. They wish to see the Palace of Westminster to understand the origins of their own democratic system and their own common law. St Paul's Cathedral is of more interest to them than Canary Wharf. They wish to see the castles and palaces and great cathedrals scattered around the country, and to marvel at how people lived before any white man settled in the US. For all US people, there is a historical purpose in coming to the UK. For those who are the direct descendants of the original English settlers, especially the direct descendants of the Puritan Fathers who founded New England, there is a pull on the heart strings as they look at the half-timbered houses, castles and old manor houses inhabited by people at the time that the Puritan rebels set sail on the *Mayflower*.

Similarly, they are fascinated to compare the remains of eighteenth-century London and the great eighteenth-century houses out in the country with what they can see for themselves of the colonial style of architecture developed to such perfection by the men who launched the American War of Independence. Washington and Jefferson were quintessentially English gentlemen abroad. They were educated along English lines, thought the same thoughts, and used the same language to great effect. They were born of the same legal and political tradition.

It was their vision of how the colonies needed representation and freedom as much as the home country that led to the ringing words of the Declaration of Independence and the development of a federal constitution for an unruly emerging country.

This shared history is important in creating a climate in which many in the US would like to reinforce rather than diminish the links between the two countries. The War of Independence produced surprisingly little bitterness, as it was out of character with the relationship that has come to dominate in the last 150 years. The UK soon got over the loss of the colonies, recognising the US's right to self-government, and marvelling at the achievements of the US people as they explored and traversed the great continent and then settled it, turning it into an economic empire. On the US side, there could be forgiveness because it won and went on to make such a success of its independence. The American War of Independence is now the subject of the occasional joke when British people meet Americans. There is none of the awkwardness and difficulty that still characterises some meetings of British people with representatives of countries on the European continent who have been at war with us in more recent times.

The traditional reason why modern US politicians are interested in developing the British alliance through NAFTA lies in their understanding of the need to win over hearts and minds around the world, rather than simply trying to assert US power. In the post-war period the most searing experience on the US political psyche was that of Vietnam. Many Americans felt that, given the colossal economic strength of the United States and its preparedness to spend a large amount of effort, money and men on the battle against communism, it was only a matter of time before they succeeded in Vietnam. It came as a huge shock to the US that, despite the depressing run of body bags coming home, it was unable to defeat North Vietnam in open battle or guerrilla warfare. It came as an even bigger shock when it was finally forced out of South Vietnam altogether, defeated by what on paper looked to be a rather small and unimportant power with a backward economy. As the US mulled over the consequences of the defeat and tried to learn lessons from what had happened, many concluded that the way to beat communism was through a battle of ideas rather than a military exchange on the ground.

Subsequent events proved them right. The great democracies defeated communism without a shot being fired at the end of the 1980s. People in the communist world came to see for themselves that they were falling further and further behind the West in quality of life and prosperity. They at last also grasped that if enough of them wanted the collapse of the evil empires, then the evil empires would be no more. Winning hearts and minds has become more important to many thinkers in the US than winning military battles or deploying the fifth, sixth or seventh fleet in the right part of the world. NAFTA is more than a free trade area. It represents a coherent set of ideas on how government, people and economic life should be organised, which is to be exported by the soft sell to more and more countries around the world. The cardinal idea behind the whole operation is that free trade cements friendship and encourages common working, whilst individual trading blocs or nations that follow protectionist agendas are more likely to generate conflict and disagreement with one another.

UK interest in joining NAFTA has of course been reinforced by the way peoples and companies have been operating on both sides of the Atlantic for many years. We have seen elsewhere what a surge there has been in mutual investment in each other's countries and how much common action there now is across the Atlantic through mega-mergers and enterprising links. As this is something that US and British people wish to do, taking advantage of shared language and common enthusiasm for technology, it is something which politicians could belatedly catch up with by agreeing joint membership of a trade association.

US foreign policy towards the EEC, now the EU, is often argued as a reason against developing the NAFTA idea any further. It is true that on a fairly consistent basis, both Republican and Democratic presidents have seemed to favour the idea of closer European integration. The bureaucratic mind thinks it would be much tidier in trying to reach agreement on common action, or a united political stance, if they only had to ring the office of the president of Europe from the office of the US President, and sort it out in a few minutes over the phone. Instead, at the moment, the US President has to consult a series of leading allies, including Britain, France and Germany, on every major issue on which he wishes to progress. Whilst Ronald Reagan was sympathetic to Margaret Thatcher, and seemed to understand some of her difficulties with deeper European integration, George Bush was more guided by the policy establishment at the State Department and often applied subtle pressure on Britain to move closer to our European partners. This pressure was intensified by President Clinton, probably encouraged by the British Prime Minister, Tony Blair, in the hope that the British people will be swayed to more European integration if we think our US neighbours, friends and relatives are of a similar view. Under the second President Bush the experience of Iraq has changed things somewhat. Whilst there are still numerous Foreign Office advisers in the United States who favour European integration, the events that surrounded the invasion of Iraq have led the President to appreciate the importance of a special link with the United Kingdom in general, and his special friend the British Prime Minister, Tony Blair, in particular. Tony Blair would doubtless like US help to sell the EU to a reluctant British public, but now he sees the way French attitudes towards the war have soured US opinions of the EU.

The US comes across the EU most often and most actively in the area of trade. It now has a formidable range of cases to prove that the EU is often obstructive, protectionist and combative. The EU would say the same of the US.

Dial one number for Europe?

What America would really like is to be able to dial one number for Europe and to find at the other end of the phone a US voice agreeing with US philosophy and policies. US politicians and policy-makers are at last realising that this is the one thing that cannot be achieved. Some had naively hoped that if Britain plunged in more wholeheartedly to European union, it would mysteriously influence policy in a pro-American direction, and all would be well in the end. These people are now coming to see that European union is driven by Franco-German ideas and political weight, and that if Britain went along with it, it would be unlikely to be able to drag it back to belief in NATO and free trade along the lines that the US seeks. Others now see that having a Britain capable of forming an independent foreign and defence policy, and still in charge of most of its own economic affairs, gives the US a better chance. Geographically, the UK is several steps out into the Atlantic. Morally, politically and philosophically, it is probably mid-Atlantic, with European and US influences and leanings. There have been times in the past when Britain has acted as an honest broker between US and EU views. Many US strategists would now be reluctant to lose this helpful intermediation and are coming to understand that asking Britain to submerge itself in a centralised European union would break that link and remove that opportunity.

The US has not been very impressed by the foreign policy actions of the EU to date. It has seen how EU recognition of Croatia made the problems of a simmering Yugoslavia boil over. The US is learning by bitter experience that the EU is neither ready nor capable of making a decisive difference on the international stage. It is also learning that the slumbering giant of the EU is quite capable of putting its foot in it, but then does not have the capability to rescue or redeem the position.

American ambivalence to a military role for the EU has really been settled in US minds in favour of asking European states to make a bigger contribution to and through NATO, but being hostile to an independent military position by the emerging super-state. If the US had been serious about wanting European countries to take on their own defence without US support, they would, at the end of the Cold War, have issued a timetable or ultimatum for the full withdrawal of US troops, back-up and support, giving perhaps the European countries a ten-year period to recruit and equip sufficiently to take on the task for themselves. Many of us are very glad that the US did not take this view, although we would have understood it, given the hostility expressed – particularly in France – towards many US ideas and much US support. Those of us who favour a stronger and deeper US alliance believe that NATO is a model of how it can be achieved, and we are enthusiastic to keep NATO in being and grateful to the US for the military capability and technology it supplies to guarantee the freedom of the European countries. There is common ground across the Atlantic as US policy has fallen short of insisting that the Europeans spend more and take on more responsibility for themselves. It is important that we do not allow the EU to drive a wedge between the important NATO partners, the UK and the US, as the world would be a less safe place if it did so.

All these things in the US psyche impel many in the US to see the need for closer links with countries like the UK. The idea of extending NAFTA is not just to create an English-speaking alliance, although that will have the most impact when it extends beyond trade and commerce to foreign policy and defence. The idea of the economic alliance through NAFTA is to extend it as an opportunity to any country that wishes to join, and can meet the qualifying requirements. Unlike the EU, where once you have joined you are then put under more and more pressure to mend your ways and change your laws as the EU goes through a period of continuous revolution, in the case of joining NAFTA, once you have met the qualifying requirements no additional requirements will be imposed upon the member states. In the case of the EU, there is no clause in the treaty enabling a member state to leave if it has changed its mind, whereas in the case of NAFTA, countries are free to join and leave as they see fit. It is a voluntary association of like-minded states that have shown their like-mindedness by the policies they have followed.

In practice, British governments have failed to implement the policy or respond favourably to the offer of possible membership of NAFTA. The idea of joining NAFTA was adopted as official government policy when the Conservative Prime Minister, John Major, was in office in the

1990s. Under Tony Blair, the Labour Prime Minister first elected in 1997, there was no willingness to pursue this. The administration doubtless recognised the complexity of the negotiations with the EU, and saw it as yet another problem likely to cause tension with the European partners. Paradoxically, following the strengthening of the special relationship with the United States of America as a result of the joint invasion of Iraq, the British government has now moved in a more pro-European direction to try an offset some of the damage it did to the European relationships by joining America in an unpopular war. This makes it a very bad time for the United Kingdom to open up negotiations to join NAFTA in the government's view.

NAFTA

The overarching idea behind NAFTA is to promote the freest possible trade between those countries that believe in free trade. Belief in free trade extends to belief in keeping the demands of government to a modest level. It means that to qualify, countries have to show that they have law codes and tax regimes that leave people and companies as free as possible. In Washington they draw up an index of economic liberalism. Countries like Chile and the UK score rather well, as a result of the exciting market-oriented policies followed in both countries in the 1980s and 1990s. The idea is to use NAFTA as a magnet to attract countries to its prosperity and success and to encourage them, by that success, to understand the economic and commercial policies that underpin it.

The US–Canada agreement

The US and Canada entered a free trade agreement in 1989. The full North American Free Trade Agreement was signed by Canadian, Mexican and US representatives in December 1992, and the area came into effect on 1 January 1994. The objectives of the Agreement were stated clearly at the beginning of the document:

(a)   eliminate barriers to trade in, and facilitate the cross-border movement of, goods and services between the territories of the parties;
(b)   promote conditions of fair competition in the free trade area;
(c)   increase substantially investment opportunities in the territories of the parties;
(d)   provide adequate and effective protection and enforcement of intellectual property rights in each party's territory;

(e) create effective procedures for the implementation and application of this agreement, for its joint administration and for the resolution of disputes; and

(f) establish a framework for further trilateral, regional and multilateral cooperation to expand and enhance the benefits of this Agreement.

The general provisions entailed the reduction of tariffs over a fifteen-year period, with the exact timetable varying from sector to sector. Investment restrictions were lifted in most sectors, allowing companies in one country to invest in another with the exception of oil in Mexico, culture in Canada, and airline and radio communications in the US. Any of the signatory countries can leave the treaty with six months' notice, and the treaty allows for the inclusion of new members. Government procurement is opened up over a period of ten years, gradually eliminating the areas where a country like Mexico reserves contracts for Mexican competitors only. Panels of independent arbitrators were established to resolve disagreements arising out of the treaty.

Two side agreements were included at the insistence of President Clinton, who needed them to gain acceptance of the provisions of the treaty in the US. The first is on the environment, and the second is to guarantee minimum standards of treatment of employees in the labour market. From the year 2000, North American trucks can drive anywhere in the three countries without economic restriction. Mexico is gradually opening its financial sector to US and Canadian investment, eliminating all the barriers by 2007. Tariffs on cars are removed over a five-year period where any car for which local content exceeds 62.5% is free from tariffs. The US and Mexico set up a North American Development Bank to help finance the clean-up of the US–Mexican border. The treaty itself is very detailed, tackling third-country dumping, rules of origin, customs procedures, import and export restrictions, export taxes, technical barriers to trade, government procurement, investment services and related matters, telecommunications, competition policy, financial services, intellectual property, and all other relevant issues governing a complex trade in goods, services, investment and intellectual property between three sophisticated trading economies.

How NAFTA works

NAFTA is run by a commission and secretariat. Commissioners are empowered to call on technical advisers, to create working groups or expert groups as they see fit. Individual complainants can also request an arbitral panel. The three countries concerned maintain a roster of up to thirty individuals who are willing and able to serve as panellists. The roster members are appointed by consensus for terms of three years and may be reappointed. When there are two parties to a dispute, a panel is established of five members; two chosen by each side and a chairman selected by agreement. The two panellists chosen have to be citizens of the other country. After hearing evidence and going through the proper procedures, the panel presents a final report which the disputing parties are expected to accept and to comply with.

NAFTA is run by a series of committees. There is a committee on trade in goods, a committee on trade in worn clothing, a committee on agricultural trade, a committee on sanitary and phytosanitary measures, a committee on standards-related measures, a committee on small business, a financial services committee and an advisory committee on private commercial disputes. Article 2202 makes it quite clear that any country or group of countries may accede to the NAFTA agreement subject to satisfactory negotiations with NAFTA.

NAFTA is an example of a fairly open voluntary agreement. Members consent to an enforcement procedure to make sure that the agreement is seen through, but there is no supranational apparatus with a law court asserting itself above the individual member states as there is in the EU. Whereas the EU is a customs union, with substantial government apparatus on top, NAFTA is a genuinely free trade area whose main purpose is to lower tariff and non-tariff barriers to trade. If Britain were to join NAFTA, there would be no problem for the other NAFTA members, but Britain would have to secure from its EU partners agreement to cease levying the common external tariff on US, Canadian and Mexican products that would still be levied in the other member states of the EU. The difficulty some people have with the concept of dual membership of the EU and NAFTA for the UK shows how different a free market like NAFTA is from a constrained and protected market like the EU. Many people in Britain wrongly think that the single market, or common market, is also a free market, whereas it has more of the characteristics of a customs union with a number of laws and interventions by the European government to control the market and to keep out foreign competition.

Looking around the world, it is often the English-speaking countries that would find it easiest to qualify under the NAFTA rules. Countries like New Zealand and Australia, in common with the UK, have law codes and tax regimes that are friendlier to business activity than many of the more restrictive and higher tax regimes that we see on the continent of Europe. It is easier for English-speaking countries to be influenced by US culture, media and success, and in turn to wish to follow some US policies which underpin that success.

Belonging to NAFTA does not prevent people belonging to other alliances and bodies in the world. It does not produce any conflict with membership of the Security Council of the United Nations, nor, for that matter, with membership of the EU all the time that that, too, is wedded to removing barriers to trade within the EU area. The question most in debate in the UK is whether it is feasible for the UK to join NAFTA at the same time as belonging to the EU itself. There are four different positions argued by the protagonists in this debate.

1. First of all there is the position taken by the Labour government and many of its supporters that membership of NAFTA is impossible and undesirable. They have a fear of belonging to a body with so much US influence, and they are not philosophically well disposed towards the underlying principles which state clearly that you do not attempt to protect ailing businesses and failing industries, and you do believe that keeping the burdens of government light is the best way to create jobs and prosperity. Whilst many of these Labour supporters will accept clauses in the EU treaty, banning industrial subsidy and that type of protection within the European area, their conversion to these beliefs is at best skin-deep, as they do not wish to apply them more generally through the NAFTA area. Some in the Foreign Office believe that under the Treaty of Rome and subsequent amendments, the UK has no power or right to negotiate its own trade relationships with countries outside the EU. Asking the EU to do it for us, in the Foreign Office's view, is not likely to be successful or productive.

2. The second position is that adopted by some Conservatives, that we should try to persuade the EU as a whole to join NAFTA. There are obvious advantages in this. If it makes sense to have a free trade area extending over the North American continent, and if it makes sense to have a single market extending over much of the European continent, surely it would make sense to put the two together? There are two problems to be overcome. The first is that many of our European partners would allow their anti-American prejudices to come to the fore, and would not be enthusiastic about this proposal. It is likely that France would organise a resistance to any suggestion that the whole of the European single market should be joined with the North American free trade area in a large free trade system. The second

problem is that many of the European countries would be hard-pushed to fulfil the letter and spirit of the NAFTA rules, as they still maintain substantial protectionist elements in their individual and common policies through the EU Common Agricultural Policy (CAP) and the EU's rather selective approach to controlling industrial subsidy and intervention. It would be worth a try – and, were it possible to pull off this diplomatic coup, then of course the rules of NAFTA would become some kind of restraint on the wrong kind of policies being followed by some EU states. There is no direct conflict between the ideas of NAFTA and the free market strands in the European treaties. The problem rests in the selective interpretation and enforcement of the European treaties, meaning that in many parts of the Union there are still unacceptable protectionist measures which are not being properly controlled by Brussels or the European Court. The terms of the EU/Mexico Trade Agreement in March 2000 show that progress can be made in this field by the whole EU.

3. The third position is that it would be better for Britain to belong to NAFTA than to the EU, and that we should choose between the two. Given that NAFTA is a looser kind of association without a massive joining fee and subscription – one has to pay to belong to the EU – and given that NAFTA is based on the principles of allowing sovereign countries to make their own decisions, there is a growing body of opinion in Britain which thinks that this would be more compatible with the attitudes and genius of the British people than with the EU as it is evolving. Those who favour strengthening our links with Europe see this as the only honest position with respect to NAFTA. They are deliberately trying to make it an either–or choice as part of their political strategy of branding anyone who wants a different kind of European Union from the French and German model as being someone who in practice wants us to leave altogether.

4. The fourth position is that we should use the very considerable negotiating power we have during a period of renegotiating the treaties to get ourselves the opportunity to join NAFTA, even if the others do not wish to do so. I see nothing incompatible for Britain in belonging both to NAFTA and to the single market of Europe. I think it would be quite possible to negotiate that, as I have never taken the view that our partners really want to get rid of us from the whole operation. They would be extremely foolish to want to forgo the substantial British financial contribution, and they would at once appreciate that as they sell us so much more than we sell them, they have a lot more at risk. Of course, it would require considerable

political will and diplomatic skill on Britain's part to do this. There would be interesting problems with the CAP, but as we are committed to reform of the agricultural policy anyway, that, too, could be a proper matter for negotiation on both sides of the Atlantic. It could be that such a negotiation proves the trigger for tackling the rather intractable problems of agricultural protection on both sides of the Atlantic at the same time. It is certainly the case that we would be able to join NAFTA despite belonging to the CAP, given the very different way agriculture is treated in all of the jurisdictions concerned. We would need our partners' agreement to lowering the EU tariff on US goods into the UK. The EU negotiation of a Free Trade Agreement with Mexico shows that there are ways forward in bringing the two blocs closer together. Its success should give heart to British negotiators seeking a new relationship with NAFTA.

A Britain which was allowed by our partners to join NAFTA as well would also be a Britain that had decided to opt out of the further round of centralisation and integration on the continent of Europe. It would be a Britain much happier with itself, feeling that its instincts and ambitions had been better understood on both sides of the Atlantic. We would be in Europe but not run by it, in the words of the Conservative slogan. We would be a full part of the single market and a strong voice for its growing liberalisation, whilst at the same time being a leading member of NAFTA, wishing to take the NAFTA message to other parts of the world. Whilst countries like Chile may well join NAFTA and add a strong Spanish-speaking element to the Mexican contingent already in the organisation, the most likely future candidates of NAFTA are English-speaking countries. Churchill's vision of an ultimate English-speaking union would be one step nearer in the economic sphere if Britain joined NAFTA and was followed by other leading English-speaking countries.

The US has a lot to gain from this strategy. The world is changing a lot. The dot.com revolution is creating a world of networks and informal links. People in the US are getting tired of the heavy, bureaucratic, centralised institutions set up in the immediate post-war world, and are becoming frustrated at the way in which bringing in so many countries to these organisations for good reasons can slow down their decision-making, or alter their decision-making in a way that is not compatible with US aims and ideals. When you get to such a position, the best course of action is to do something new, something exciting and invigorating. NAFTA is an idea whose time has come. It would give a new impetus to economic progress, it would tie in with the spirit of the internet age, and it would bring English-speaking peoples closer together in a wholly desirable way.

The loneliness of the long-distance great power would be eased somewhat by having more friends and allies in an economic linking with the US, to supplement and complement the strength of the alliance on defence and foreign policy through NATO. The US has not always been well served by some of its NATO partners, but the structure of NATO has held because it does not force countries to do things they do not wish to do. NAFTA is a similarly strong but flexible structure which is more exciting, and more likely to survive, than the highly centralised structure which France and Germany wish to superimpose upon the EU.

The US will not, for the foreseeable future, be able to dial one number for Europe and get a European president on the end of the phone who can speak for all countries. It will certainly never be able to dial one number for Europe and get a European president on the phone who agrees with it. One of the least desirable characteristics of continental debate is the virulent brand of anti-Americanism which we see emerging at certain times over certain issues. Britain joining NAFTA would mean that we could continue our pivotal role in acting as a bridge across the Atlantic, an interpreter of the US to the continent, and the continent to the US. It does not mean we would become a US poodle any more than we would wish to be the poodle of the Franco-German alliance. Britain is a sizeable and important independent country still, whose weight could be important on commercial matters through NAFTA and on some single market matters through the EU.

The US and Britain intuitively understand that in this fast-moving, technologically driven internet-based world, the peoples and countries that will do best are the ones that control the demands of government, keep their law codes flexible and light, and keep their taxes down. Not all of our partners on the European continent have understood this, and those who have understood it find it difficult or impossible to practise it. That is why it would be good for Britain and good for the United States to make a blow for freedom by linking our trading patterns through NAFTA to supplement our current system of networks and alliances.

Notes

Thomson (1972) gives a view of twentieth-century UK foreign policy.

Clark (1998) offers a distinctive historical view, being especially interesting on the military history of the period.

10
What Kind of Renegotiation with the EU does Britain Want?

How feasible is renegotiation?

The UK has been an unhappy partner in the EU. Many on the continent have seen us as an anchor, pulling the ship of European integration backwards, or trying to slow it down as often as possible. Some people in Britain have grown impatient with the government's indecision over Europe because they wish to join more wholeheartedly in the schemes of European union and integration. Many others have grown despondent, seeing successive administrations claiming that all we want is a glorified free trade area, but being dragged ineluctably into something much bigger and deeper.

The EU is in a state of perpetual flux or renegotiation. In the current British debate there is a polarised and unenlightening argument between those who say that we need to renegotiate our entry and those who claim that all renegotiation is tantamount to saying we wish to leave the Union in its entirety. Any independent analysis of the current state of the EU would conclude that it is always possible to renegotiate. Most of the partners most of the time, led by the Commission, are constantly striving to renegotiate the founding treaties. There is very rarely a pause of longer than a year between one treaty and another. The ink is not normally dry on one treaty before people are talking about what should be in the next one. Like a regular bus service, if you miss the first bus there will be another along quickly.

Perhaps what people have in mind when they say that renegotiation is either impossible or tantamount to exit is their belief that the aims of many in Britain who wish to renegotiate the treaty more in our own image are unrealistic compared to the views of our other partners. The very same people who argue that Europe is going our way are the ones who claim that if we try to confirm it is going our way by putting the relevant clauses in the treaty, we are somehow upping sticks, taking our bat away and ceasing to play the game. Indeed, some of those who are keenest on more European integration seem to hold the dimmest view of our European partners. Those of us who wish to renegotiate a better deal for Britain are constantly told that if we try to do so they will stop trading with us, impose sanctions on us, or even throw us out of the club. There is no legal power under the treaty to do any of these things. Our trading ability is protected by international law as well as European law. The other European countries sell us rather more than we sell them giving them every reason to keep us in their single market. Europhiles in the UK believe that if Britain provokes the Community too far by seeking something different from the other members, we will be turned from pariah to former member quite quickly.

The Constitution for the European Union presents Britain with a stark choice and a unique opportunity. For those who want us to go along with the European scheme the choice is simple. They say join the Constitution or run the risk of being thrown into the outer darkness by our partners: sign up to the Constitution or run the risk of ending up completely outside the club. They point out that the club is moving on, adopting a new legal structure. The present British government has negotiated in good faith and consented to that legal structure, so it is now up to the British people to endorse what their politicians have done.

In practice, the British people do not think their government has negotiated a good deal for Britain and are extremely unhappy about what has been done in their name. They are very likely to vote down the Constitution. By doing so, they create a unique opportunity for the UK to negotiate a new, better and different relationship with the continental countries than that offered by the Constitution itself. Our partners will have to sit down to negotiate with us, as a British government will be unable to continue the relationship under the legal form of the Constitution which will become the Union. Some say if we vote 'No' the Constitution will be abandoned. I do not think this likely, given the political will on the continent to see it through. The other members and the Commission will welcome a renegotiation by the UK to solve the British problem once and for all, and to allow the rest of the Union to proceed in the way it wishes.

What might Britain seek in a renegotiation?

Given the big erosion of powers of the UK people and Parliament through successive treaties from Rome, the single European Act, Maastricht, Amsterdam, Nice, and now the European Constitution, we need to go back to the basic idea that the British electorate approved in a referendum in 1975. The debate prior to that referendum, and the referendum question itself were quite clear. The British people were asked to vote for a common market. Indeed the words 'common market' appeared in the referendum question. No one in favour of our remaining in the Common Market in that campaign said that we were joining a club about to evolve into an economic, monetary and political union. Speakers in the 'Yes' campaign fell over backwards to assure us that very little power would transfer, that we would remain a sovereign nation with a lively democratic Parliament in charge of most things. They were keen to scotch any rumours of a United States of Europe emerging with an army, a common economic policy, a common foreign policy, common policing, and its own criminal law code. Nothing was further from the minds of those who advocated 'Yes', and nothing was further from the minds of the British people when, by a big majority, they voted 'Yes' to remain in that Common Market.

Any renegotiation should take it as a given that the British people knowingly voted for a common market and, judging by recent opinion polls, would do so again if a simple common market were on offer without all the other trappings of a super-state being attached. In order to recreate this state of grace the British negotiators would need to set out the following propositions.

We should state that Britain wishes to remain a parliamentary democracy. Power resides with the British people and is leased for a period of up to five years to a Parliament trusted to undertake open and free democratic debate. The electorate is then in a position to judge the actions of the majority and minority in that Parliament at a subsequent general election and to endorse them for a further period, or to change the balance in the way that they would like. British people have not consented to a big extension of judge-made law from the European Court of Justice (ECJ), nor have they openly voted for a system of administration and decision-making on crucial issues behind closed doors in Brussels under the influence of, and in response to, the drafts of unelected Commissioners.

The first task must therefore be to restore British parliamentary democratic sovereignty in the name of the British people. To do this the legal structure for Britain needs to be clarified. The supremacy of Parliamentary law over ECJ decision-making can easily be reasserted with the agreement of our partners and the modification of the 1972 European Communities Act. We should remember that the EU on one definition of the current legal position only has legal powers in Britain because of that founding Act of Parliament and the treaty that underlies it. Countries can modify or change their views on treaties, and one Parliament can modify or change an Act of Parliament passed by another. If we accept that there has been an absolute change in our position with sovereignty passing from Parliament and statute and therefore from the British people to ECJ decisions, and if we accept that treaties can never be modified or changed, then we have ceased to be a sovereign country.

The revised European Communities Act could also include a list of reserve powers where the UK people and Parliament will regard it as their right to make all of the important decisions. Remaining in the Community we would need to accept that certain areas of law like competition, trade, and commerce are carried out on a joint basis with our European partners, and we would need to accept that the European courts have to have some rights over these matters. Once we have made clear, again, that Parliament could overturn or veto in extremis, we then need to play fair and to show that it would not normally do this. Parliament should expect to have complete control in areas of considerable national importance like defence, foreign policy and taxation. Successive British governments have always said that they have preserved the veto on taxation matters. In practice, Britain's power to settle its own tax affairs has been subtly eroded over the years, especially in the fields of excise duties and VAT. The Commission and many of our partners are determined that this erosion should now become a landslide. They are desperate to raise more money on a Community-wide basis, and keen to deal with what they see as unfair tax competition in jurisdictions like the UK and the Republic of Ireland which keep their tax rates lower than elsewhere. The Community is keen on taxing savings, environmental taxes and higher overall rates of corporate tax levied on a standard basis. The British Parliament and people need to preserve their right to independent taxation.

The British Parliament grew up through a series of bruising battles with the Crown over this very issue. It was the wish of those who paid the taxes to be represented in Parliament and to see some redress of their grievances that led to the massive extension of the English and of the British Parliament's powers from the Parliament of Simon de Montfort through the English Civil War. It was the same issue that led to the revolt of the American Colonies who felt it was unfair, being well educated in

British constitutional practice, that they should be required to pay taxes levied by the British Crown and Parliament when they had no direct representation in that body.

These matters can be put right by an amended 1972 European Communities Act. Britain should say, as indeed the German constitution does, that the ultimate source of authority in the UK is not the ECJ but the national Parliament. The Act should go on to say that Parliament has by treaty agreed to grant the ECJ powers in defined fields related to the single market we have joined and support. The Act should establish that in crucial areas like taxation, foreign policy, and big domestic policy areas like health and education, no power has been granted to the ECJ to interfere against our will.

The second thing British negotiators should seek to achieve in the renegotiation is a better deal in areas where the EU already has control and is the dominant shaping force. The sorest area for Britain in its thirty-year membership of the EC so far has been the area of fishing. Settled almost as an afterthought in the original accession negotiations, the British government gave away too much in allowing a common fisheries policy for the North Sea. It is one of the ironies of the situation that large fleets of Spanish trawlers may arrive in the North Sea to take our fish, but there is no similar common fishing policy in the Mediterranean allowing us to reciprocate. Indeed, the North Sea and the western approaches around Ireland and the west coast of Great Britain are the only maritime area subject to a common fishing policy at all. The Baltic, like the Mediterranean, is similarly free of any such encumbrance.

Fishing

The UK should seek to repatriate fishing matters. We should say that we want to harmonise the practices in the Mediterranean Sea, the Baltic Sea and the North Sea. We wish to have the same national control over our coastline and coastal waters as is enjoyed by Mediterranean countries. Whilst it is too late to save many of the great trawler fleets that have bitten the dust, particularly on the east coast of England and Scotland, it is possible to improve the position in the future. The UK should take its own view of what is a reasonable rate of extraction of fish from the sea in the interests of conservation, and could make sure that a bigger proportion of the permitted catch goes to British vessels rather than to foreign-flagged vessels. We would become the licensing and policy controlling authority. At the moment we have the rotten job of policing the policy without very much influence over drafting the policy itself.

Those countries, like Iceland and Norway, that have kept control of their own fisheries have been much more successful in dealing with the problems of over-fishing than the EU. The British fishing grounds have been pillaged by the combination of long distance, deep water Spanish trawlers and the Danish industrial trawlers. Their net sizes have been too small, catching too many young fish. Their trawling methods have done considerable damage to the environment of the seabed as well as our seas, causing great stresses and strains in our fishery. Domestic control could end the absurd practice of ordering fishermen to throw dead fish back into the sea when they have caught the wrong sort of fish, and could insist on appropriate net sizes to give young fish a chance.

Agriculture

Britain also needs to gain a bigger say and more control is the area of agriculture. One of the disappointing features of the EU is that where it has almost total control, it has adopted a common policy which does great damage to the consumers, considerable damage to the poorer countries of the world, and yet still doesn't manage to keep the producers happy. The CAP burdens the average British family with an extra £20 per week on their food bill because it keeps prices well above world market levels. At the same time it combines this with a protectionist system which keeps out the cheaper product from many third world countries who would dearly love the opportunity to sell into the rich markets of Britain, France and Germany but are prevented by physical restrictions. Talk to any British farmers about the CAP at the moment and, despite the high level of subsidy and protection, they do not have a good word to say about it. It is EU regulation that has helped wipe out most of the British beef industry through what is seen by farmers as a particularly heavy-handed response to BSE whilst failing to protect the health of people and animals. There is also a feeling that it was not an even-handed response, as British herds were not the only herds to be infected by BSE, but it was the UK that faced the full brunt of EU anger about the problems that had developed. Similarly, in the dairy sector, the UK was uniquely badly served by the original allocation of quotas. The quota system imposed by the EU means that British dairy farmers cannot expand their milk output even though their milk output is considerably below the amount of milk consumed in the UK. Other countries like France were given quotas in excess of their domestic requirements.

A new system for agriculture would require careful construction. Whilst it should be possible to create a better regulatory framework for farmers in Britain by making more sensible decisions about milk output, beef herd control and similar issues, any new system of domestic subsidy to replace the current price control and EU subsidy system would need clearance through the General Agreement on Tariffs and Trade (GATT) to avoid another bruising trade row. Trade rows are common in GATT on agricultural matters.

The World Trade Organisation (WTO) is understandably very critical of both the EU and the US for their complicated and expensive agricultural protection systems. The British government would have to enter discussions with the WTO, arguing that a domestic system of subsidy and protection would be less damaging than the EU one from which we were disengaging. It should be possible to reach an agreement, but it will require detailed analysis to satisfy the custodians of the GATT that our main aim in coming out of the CAP is not to increase the overall level of quota restriction, but to make a decisive shift in regulation in favour of British as opposed to continental farmers. Indeed, there may be allies and friends in the WTO who would see a Britain freed of most or all of the restrictions of CAP as a more useful ally in ensuing rounds of world trade talks designed to free the market in agricultural products more generally. Britain may well like to develop a system of agricultural support which concentrates on using the money freed from the break-up of the CAP to offer direct cash support to farmers whilst moving closer towards world pricing and a more open market in agricultural products.

The important thing is that in this area we would be out to assert more control and therefore more decision-making in Britain. There would be lively debate between consumer interests, in favour of a much more open market and lower prices, and producer interests in favour of protection geared to the specific interests of British farmers. Both groups would agree with any government move designed to halt the unfortunate intervention of EU policy-makers and administrators into the British farming scene, where the regulation both damages the customer whilst also favouring farmers outside the UK at the expense of those inside.

Regulation

The European Union has increased its power over the years by legislating more and more. It does not require a new treaty or even a new constitution for the EU to extend its power. Every year it puts through around 3,000 new laws. Many of these establish powers for the European Union. Each time a new area of activity comes under EU regulation the power of the Union is strengthened. Each time the Union regulates something new, the powers of the member states are proportionately reduced. This is made even more explicit in the draft Constitution, introducing the idea of shared competence for most fields of government endeavour. A shared competence is one where if the Union has legislated that takes priority, leaving the member states the right only to work around the edges of the European legislation. They can never repeal, amend or ignore the European regulation once made unless they can get the consent of the other member states to do so.

The volume of European legislation is now so immense that it is the prime way in which business in the European Union is regulated. The Union itself has recognised the regulations are very costly and burdensome. They are also enforced and implemented in a patchy manner across the Union, depending on the enthusiasm in EU member states to obey the law and to implement these matters thoroughly. The United Kingdom has always been a very keen implementer of EU legislation, living in a largely law-abiding community, where it is felt important and necessary to implement fully anything which has been agreed with the European partners.

The result of all this is to create a strong feeling of injustice amongst the British business community, and a growing feeling of concern in the wider EU business community about the excessive complication and cost of all the laws imposed. Any British renegotiation must include a commitment to deregulate. If we wish to keep jobs in the UK it is important to lower the costs imposed on business by government. As most of the regulatory costs now come from Brussels we must sort this out during the course of the renegotiation. If other Union members are sensible, they will recognise the need to agree with us on a general deregulation for the Union as a whole. If they are not then the UK must gain exemptions from the most onerous of these requirements, and put in place some mechanism to prevent us having to implement regulatory burdens in future that we cannot accept.

There are many examples of regulations that are undesirable or over the top. The EU has decided to regulate food supplements and alternative remedies. This has done considerable damage to a flourishing industry operating through many small companies, and small wholesale and retail outlets. The costs of regulation are too great for many of them to combat, requiring a costly approval structure for alternative remedies as if they were pharmaceuticals. Similarly, some in the City of London are concerned about the Transparency Directive and the Prospectus Directive. They feel that it gives the edge to the United States of America with its less prescriptive system. Many feel that the costs of raising money through the corporate bond market will be raised unnecessarily, and that more business will gravitate offshore from the EU as a whole. Similarly, the EU's regulation of working hours and conditions runs the risk of driving more and more jobs offshore. Whilst we would all like to live in a world in which the highest standards of employment dominated in the EU, some are left wondering whether this is a good idea to do it through a Europe-wide law. The result of such legislation seems to be high unemployment in many parts of the continent and a continuing manufacturing job haemorrhage from the UK as well as from Germany and France.

Overseas aid

The British government may also like to renegotiate existing EU policies is in the area of overseas aid. It is this area which has attracted most criticism from within and without the Commission and the other European institutions. It was allegations of fraud and malpractice in the overseas aid budget that led directly to the downfall of the Commission in 1999 in general, and the Overseas Aid Commissioner, Madame Cresson, in particular. There is the general feeling that European aid is not well targeted, that the programmes are not well run, and that more audit work would reveal more irregularities. Overseas aid can be a very important part of building and supporting a foreign policy. As one of the aims of the renegotiation would be to make clear that Britain still intends to have an independent foreign policy, with a set of views that may be the same or may be different from our European partners on international issues, so it is important to back that up with the direct payment of more British money for good causes abroad which should be done at the expense of making such a big contribution through the EU.

Budget contribution

The final issue which needs to be resolved in the renegotiation is the issue of our budget contribution. As Britain has in mind participation in a common market rather than a common government, it is only fair that Britain should make a smaller financial contribution to the costs of running the whole than those partners who wish to create a United States of Europe and a strong central government in Brussels. Margaret Thatcher attempted to resolve this dilemma in the 1980s. Her successful renegotiation then produced a British rebate which dealt with the immediate problems that our contribution was out of all proportion to our then wealth or our then involvement with the EEC. If we press ahead with repatriating fishing, parts of agriculture and overseas aid, we clearly need a new settlement on the budget. If we make clear that we wish to be members of the common market but not of the wider common government it is only reasonable that we should only make a contribution towards the common costs of running and policing that common market and not to the wider common costs of a growing bureaucratic European government. It is not possible to carry out the renegotiation without also looking at the question of the money.

The UK and the EU

Readers who believe that a stronger European government is inevitable and that Britain should go along with it will by now be saying to themselves that all these demands or requests from the UK are fanciful. They will argue that there is absolutely no way that they can be achieved in the real world. Similarly, my critics on the edges of the Euro-sceptic coalition will be saying that none of these things can be achieved unless Britain threatens to withdraw. Would it not be better to withdraw to get rid of the many adverse features of the European Union as it is developing?, they will ask. We must now turn to what powers and pressures the United Kingdom could bring to bear in order to achieve some or all of these negotiating objectives.

The first thing to understand is that the UK has a wide-ranging weaponry in European discussion which it can deploy. It is a negotiation or a debate between member states. For those who wish to see it as warfare by another means, the analogy would be that withdrawal from the Community is the nuclear weapon, whereas there are many other conventional weapons that could be deployed to good effect. Since 1945, the UK and the US have unfortunately regularly had to take up arms to settle a number of major and minor problems around the world. Never once have these two nuclear powers used their nuclear weapons, as they understand that the point of a nuclear weapon is to act as a deterrent.

So it would be with these negotiations to keep us in a common market. The first conventional weapon that the UK has at its disposal is the veto on any further treaty changes. Under the constitutional framework of the EU, it requires the consent of every member state before any change can be made in the founding treaties. The French and German governments and the Commission are well known to want substantial further changes to the treaties. All of these changes will still require the consent of the British government. The French and German governments wish to press on with an inner core of countries to much deeper entanglement in a

European government. Again, this procedure requires the consent of the UK.

Britain can therefore say in any treaty negotiation that it is not prepared to allow the others to go ahead in the way they wish unless its legitimate concerns are also taken into account. We should not agree to any single treaty modification, however desirable or undesirable, unless and until our requests for a different constitutional settlement for ourselves are taken seriously and moves are made to accommodate them.

This power to veto treaty changes is especially strong at the moment when the EU wishes us to ratify the Constitution. The UK's refusal to ratify the Constitution will either force a general renegotiation of the Constitution, or a separate negotiation for the UK so the rest can go ahead with that plan anyway.

The second power we have is the power to delay or impede existing business of the Union under the existing treaties. British parliamentarians are well used to the daily guerrilla warfare in the House of Commons. One of the main weapons the Opposition has at its disposal in Parliament is the weapon of time. Legitimate scrutiny, sensible questions, lengthy but relevant debate, are all tried and tested ways of delaying the government of the day. Scope for doing this in the EU is considerably greater. Many of the other players in the game are not used to British parliamentary tactics or ways. Given the large corpus of treaty law, ECJ judgments and procedural precedents, it is quite possible to delay business for very lengthy periods by astute coalition-building, by use of the rather ramshackle procedures of the EU, and by constant recourse to the courts where necessary. As the EU lives by the law courts, so it could be made to suffer by those same courts.

The third weapon at Britain's command is the weapon of money. Britain is the second largest net contributor to the EU. The cheques Britain sends on a regular basis are substantial and are important to paying the wage bills of officials in Brussels as well as paying for the expensive programmes of agriculture, overseas aid and regional aid that the Commission disburses. If the EU is totally unwilling to cooperate by examining Britain's agenda for a different kind of relationship to some of the others, then Britain could start to query why it is paying so much and could easily find legal reasons related to the lack of performance, fraud or incompetent administration of programmes in the EU as to why Britain should go slow or hold up payments to the Commission.

I am not recommending that we should do any of these things. Indeed, I think it is quite obvious that Britain would not have to behave like this as soon as it showed considerable political will in wishing to have a renegotiation. An honest British prime minister should go to Brussels immediately after winning an election on a platform of renegotiation and explain our position.

That British prime minister should say that we are sorry that there has been such a wide range of misunderstandings between successive UK governments and our partners over many years. We should say that British politicians have consistently told the British people that we are joining a common market where we can also make progress on some other common policies on areas like environment and transport where it makes sense for us as well as for them. British politicians have never set out, in the way that French and German politicians have set out, the full vision of a properly integrated federal or centralised Europe. Because the British people have not been readied for this and have not been persuaded that they want in, we are now in the position where many British people wish to be in the trading arrangements but do not wish to proceed towards political, monetary and judicial union. The British prime minister should say that the fault is probably more that of Britain than of our partners.

No one can deny that our partners have in recent years been crystal clear about what they are trying to achieve. It has been the mistakes of British politicians who have wished to keep their heads in the sand over the true intentions of our partners because they know the British people will not go along with them that has done more of the damage, rather than the attitudes of our partners themselves. This has been especially the case in the way the British government, led by Tony Blair, handled the negotiations for the Constitution. At home in the United Kingdom he made out that the British aim was to preserve a 'series of red lines' as he called them, designed to reassure the British people that no new powers were passing to the Union. When he then failed to secure some of the 'red lines' he changed his mind on them, as in the case of criminal and civil justice and asylum and common borders. He told the British people that the Constitution represented a triumph for Euro-scepticism and a strengthening of the role of member states. No one sensible on the continent believes this is true. A new British prime minister should apologise for his predecessor for the way in which he had misled people at home and abroad.

The British prime minister should continue by saying that the British people genuinely want to make a success of the common market we joined and we believe we still have a lot to offer when it comes to helping fashion a policy of low tariffs, less regulation, less intervention and common business law codes across the Community. We wish to remain full members of the single market and wish to contribute to its development. We would be quite happy to attend other meetings on other subjects as a country with a veto to see if we can reach agreement with our partners on items of foreign policy, social policy, whatever. What we cannot do is accept an ever-tightening, more centralised Community with less and less control over what happens in Britain as a result.

The prime minister should continue by saying that we are quite happy to continue making a financial contribution towards the administration and success of the single market. We accept that we will be net contributors, but we believe that our contribution should be related to the number of policy areas that we wish to be designed and policed from Brussels. Clearly, our net contribution per head should be lower than that of Germany or France, who wish to have a much bigger government of Western Europe.

In return for granting Britain membership of the common market but not of the common government, the UK would then remove any remaining obstacles in the way of all those who wish Europe to proceed at whatever pace they choose towards a more heavily integrated system. We will not be joining the euro, but we wish it well. As a big trading partner just offshore from Euroland and as one of the big financial markets of the world, we wish to see the euro's success and we will take any domestic action that Euroland would like and we agree is necessary in order to help create the conditions for the stability of the euro. Similarly, if France and Germany wish to proceed rapidly as they seem to do with creating a common army, navy and air force, we would be very happy to work alongside that defence force through NATO when we have common cause. However, we would not wish to commit our own forces to a separate European defence force that operated outside the framework of NATO, and we would certainly not wish to commit our forces to any military adventure which did not have the consent of the British people and government.

If Britain were allowed a relationship that made most of the people in Britain feel much happier, then many of the continuing running sores would go away. Britain would be kept advised of what the EU was trying to do next in all the areas that were reserved to the UK Parliament, and Britain could volunteer to join in whenever it saw fit. We might find that Britain wanted to join in with rather more than has been the case to date where there has been an element of coercion through qualified majority voting, legal actions and Commission pressure.

The problem of the UK has not been settled for some forty years. In the 1950s, the UK itself was rather dismissive of the *Club des Battus* forming on the continent and decided it wasn't going to be significant. In the 1960s, the UK changed its view, only to be met with resistance from de Gaulle, who rightly perceived that the UK would be a destabilising influence on what he saw even in those faraway days as an emerging European Union. In the 1970s, Britain was admitted to the club, only to find that from the day of its admission onwards, it was always being asked to deliver rather more to the central power of Brussels than it wished. Early rows under Labour and the Conservatives over the financial contribution were soon replaced by endless rows over how much power the Brussels government should have, and how many more things were going to be transferred from British parliamentary control to EU bureaucratic decision.

The UK has to gain confidence in its own position. There is a tug of love and hate in Britain about the EU itself. Whilst a big majority of people do not want more government from Brussels, and are certainly against Brussels taxation, the single currency, and the idea of sending our troops into a war where we have lost the vote, there is a reluctance amongst the majority to favour withdrawal completely. Most people would like to stay trading with our partners and to be friends with them wherever possible. It is this mood which would be captured by the renegotiation set out above.

Of course, there will be critics who say that none of this can be achieved and that our partners would not wish Britain to have the benefits of trade in the common market without more of the costs and problems of the common government. This attitude takes a very mean-minded approach to our European partners, and it also implies that all the other things they are trying to do are unhelpful, which is even more reason why we should not be involved with them. To those who say that by narrowing our interests to the single or common market we are doing ourselves a disfavour, the answer is easy. Under the model I have sketched any British government could opt into any part of what the EU was doing at any time, and I am sure this would be welcomed. Our partners would clearly like us to agree with them more often than we do at present. But what we would have achieved by the renegotiation is the preservation of the ultimate power of the British people and, through them, their Parliament to change our minds over individual policies and areas when we see fit. Britain is a country that does not like being coerced. If we are left free to do things we may be more agreeable partners.

France and Germany have a lot to gain from this proposal. They must be heartily sick of the UK problem. Every time they wish to develop their club in the way they have set out, they find that they have Britain trying to organise the awkward squad in the EU to slow them down or prevent them. Germany wants to stop its citizens putting deposits in Luxembourg and escaping German tax. Without British intervention Germany may have been able to use the EU institutions to impose a withholding tax it favours. With Britain's intervention, so far this has proved impossible. Of course, there would be haggling over what was a fair contribution to reflect those parts of the EU we wish to join, but we would be building on the variable geometry European approach which is emerging as the norm. We already have different types of member of the European Union.

The neutral countries in the EU have made clear they want no part of the emerging defence policy. Greece and the UK originally opted out of the common frontiers, or the Schengen Agreement, because Greece and the main island of the UK do not have common land borders with the other members of the Community. Three countries including the UK have opted out of the single currency so far. And France has from time to time opted out of NATO, which was been the most effective means of defending Western Europe in the post-war period.

Britain does not, however, want a two-speed Europe. The idea of a two-speed Europe implies that we are all going to the same place, it's just that some of us are dilatory about getting there. Looking at the lack of success of British foreign policy in general and the Eurocentric foreign policy in particular in the post-war period, I can see why many of the critics of Britain do see the issue in terms of two-speed rather than variable geometry. In all previous cases where Britain has offered dogged resistance to a set of policies for months or even years, Britain has usually caved in in the end. Britain tried to get a better deal on fishing before joining the Community, but gave in in order to complete the entry negotiations. Britain has long said that it wants a reformed CAP but it has never managed to pull it off. Britain said for many years that it wanted nothing to do with the Social Chapter, but has now, under a different government, signed up to it. Britain made clear that it needed an opt-out from the single currency because it had many doubts and problems with it, but now has a government which says in principle they wish to join it when the conditions are right. The expectation on the continent is always that a reluctant Britain will be dragged kicking and screaming, but will eventually end up at the same destination as the rest.

This is why we need a new British government which will clearly set out the mood of the British people and get our partners to understand that we are serious in saying we want a different kind of friendly relationship with them from those of the core countries who wish to complete a political, economic and monetary union. It will take time to persuade them of the seriousness of this point, but any EU witness of the present British debate must begin to see that this is the way the mood of the British people is developing. If the EU and the Commission wish to see more favourable press about themselves in our tabloid newspapers, they should understand that the best way of achieving this is to admit a renegotiation along the lines outlined above. Any such renegotiation should then be put to the British people so they can decide whether it's a deal they would like to take up.

Some in this debate believe that the only real answer is for Britain to pull out of the EU altogether. This is not the view of the Conservative Party and, judging by recent polls and opinion surveys, it is not the majority view of the British people. However, now that well over 40% of the British people regularly tell pollsters that they themselves would like to pull out of the EU altogether, it is worth examining what the consequences of this would be and how it would differ from renegotiation.

A policy of withdrawal would be seen as very different from renegotiation by our EU partners. However, a decision to withdraw would inevitably entail a substantial renegotiation of its own. The difference between the two policies is that withdrawal is entirely negative, likely to engender a hostile and stubborn reluctance to meet our wishes on the part of our partners, whereas renegotiation could be more successful. If you begin a negotiation for a better set of arrangements with your partners by saying 'we dislike you so much that we intend to end all our current relationships', it does not put them in a good mood for agreeing those things that need to be agreed. The approach for renegotiation is based upon a certain honesty and humility with our partners, offering them solutions to the British problem that has annoyed them for so long. Withdrawal is more likely to anger them and result in delays in achieving the outcome we would like.

Withdrawal from the EU is perfectly feasible for the simple reason that the EU does not yet have a standing army or standing police force in Britain to prevent us taking charge of our own affairs again. Indeed, there is a clear precedent for withdrawal from the EU in English history. The Reformation took place by decision of the executive government, in this case the king, endorsed by a series of parliamentary statutes. It was a unilateral action carried out against the wishes of the papal authorities who had legal jurisdiction and power in Britain but who had no standing army or police force in the country to enforce their powers. The crucial statute, the Statute of Appeals in 1533, asserted British sovereignty and struck away with a flourish of the legislative pen all papal legal jurisdiction in England and Wales. It led on to sweeping changes in English and Welsh society with a massive transfer of property represented by the dissolution of the monasteries, the pillaging of churches, the re-education of the clergy and the assertion of the King's control over all ecclesiastical matters as the supreme head and governor of the Church.

The reaction of our European friends and allies to this was, not surprisingly, one of considerable anger. Catholic powers, who were the dominant powers on the continent at the time, threatened Britain in all sorts of ways. The full moral and political wrath of the papacy was hurled down on England and there were threats of foreign armies backing up the assertion of papal power. The row was still going on as late as 1588, when the Spanish Armada arrived, a potent force designed to reassert Catholic authority and the supremacy of the Pope in England some fifty-five years after the crucial statute had removed all vestiges of papal power from these shores. It was only the defeat of the Armada and the subsequent successful pursuit of the Spanish War that confirmed England's right to self-determination.

No one is suggesting that withdrawal from the EU would result in a similar attempt by the continental forces to reassert control in Britain by military means. However, in EU terms, unilateral withdrawal of Britain and renunciation of the treaty would be a hostile and an illegal act. The EU might try to assert by legal means its rights to jurisdiction over the UK, but this would undoubtedly peter out, given their predicted unwillingness to back up the legal requests with any force. The important point about all this is that relationships would have been damaged by unscripted and unilateral withdrawal and it might take some time to rebuild friendships and alliances after such a big event. We could not expect any cooperation by our European partners as we tried to disentangle all the many things that have been muddled up with the continent as a result of our almost thirty years' membership of the EU to date. We have to accept that a lot of our law codes, especially in the areas of competition, business and industrial policy, have been built in common with our European partners. We have to accept that the European court system is part of the enforcement mechanism, and the words of the treaty are important in the way businesses conduct themselves in the UK as well as on the continent. Those advocating withdrawal would have to decide how much they wished to keep and how much of it would need revisiting or reasserting once the European court and legal system had been swept aside from the UK. As far as I can see, all of it would need re-basing in British statute law and businesses would need reassuring that the important parts of the law codes would remain in place and would remain compatible with those on the continent.

Advocates of immediate withdrawal point out that there would be many offsetting benefits. It is clearly true that if we withdrew unilaterally from the Community tomorrow, we would save a lot of money. The £12 billion gross contribution we make to the Community would no longer be payable. We would be able to decide how much of that we wished to spend on agriculture, regional aid and overseas aid, the principal uses of the funds through the EU, and how much of it we wished to give back to taxpayers by means of a tax cut or rebate. It is also true that as the EU countries sell us more than we sell them, it is difficult to believe that they would seek a trade confrontation by imposing penal tariffs upon our exports. They would get into immediate difficulties with the WTO if they did, and they would be vulnerable to retaliation.

The more likely worry of businesses and many people who do not advocate immediate withdrawal is the subtle pressures that could be exerted. Our experiences with the British beef crisis have shown what an impact bad relations can have on trade. Because relations between Britain, on the one hand, and France in particular, on the other, were inflamed through the EU, French customers boycotted English products and French farmers took retaliatory illegal action against British farm products on the move through France. If Britain handles its relationships with the EU clumsily, it could have a further impact on unfavourable consumer attitudes towards various British products. More importantly, if we alienate the administrations of France and Germany more than we have done so far by our dilatory and unhelpful EU policy, it would be quite possible for those jurisdictions to produce bureaucratic obstacles to a fair and free trade, as they have done during the period of our membership.

Those who favour withdrawal can say that it is a more honest policy than the one that we have at the moment. It would clearly signal the growing impatience of many in Britain with decisions coming from the EU and with the intentions of the EU's founders. It would save us a lot of money, and it would send a clear message to British business that the world is our oyster, not just the European market. The Labour and Liberal parties, the Confederation of British Industry and others would be implacably opposed. Handled badly, it would make a damaging impact upon our relations with the leading continental countries and it would give many British people a feeling that they had burned their boats and were rather isolated. Because the British people voted so conclusively in 1975 to stay in a common market, I think it preferable that a new British prime minister open friendly but clear negotiations with our European partners to produce a new kind of relationship that makes sense for us and them, rather than announcing a unilateral intention to withdraw at a specified date.

The policy of renegotiation is more likely to secure advances for Britain than unilateral withdrawal. Whether or not Britain would need to use some or all of the conventional weapons outlined in this chapter remains to be seen. Armed with a strong, decisive 'No' vote against the Constitution, a British prime minister would be in a very strong bargaining position. Those in the know in the corridors of power in Brussels have already indicated to me privately that getting control of our fishing industry back would not be difficult, should such a prime minister seek it armed with such strong backing from the British people. If we can get back fishing we could get back a great deal else as well.

One of the advantages about developing a new relationship is that it enables us to think globally rather than in narrower European terms. Many of the problems confronting European government in the business area are better solved on a global basis. The EU is working out mezzanine regulation of banking, financial services, telecommunications, transport and the like. Yet all of these things should now be looked at globally. If there are to be transnational standards for telecommunications, if there is to be transnational law on intercepting messages and cracking fraud, if there is to be transnational regulation to ensure honest bank deposits or successful international flights, this should be done on a worldwide basis by the consent of the important countries involved, rather than by creating an unnecessary regional set of regulations on top of the national ones and the evolving global ones. Britain's new settlement with Europe would enable us to be in the vanguard with the US, Japan and others in negotiating these global standards which could drive forward the emerging global market.

The alternative European vision

A minority of people in Britain do think that France and Germany are right. They believe that the EU has made a singular contribution to the development of post-war Europe. They believe that in some mysterious way the European Union has been the creator of peace and prosperity. Those of us who disagree say that the peace has been kept in Western Europe by the massive presence of US firepower and by the creation of stable democracies in Western Europe who no longer wish to fight each other. Prosperity has come about through successive GATT rounds, now under the guidance of the WTO, and by the development of a sophisticated global trading pattern which has enabled more and more national and local specialisation.

Nonetheless, it is a sincerely held view that European integration is good for Europe, it is inevitable, it is strongly wanted by our partners and therefore we should go along with it. It is therefore important to ask ourselves what would the world look like if we did accept that France and Germany were right and willingly joined in their schemes.

Were we to do so, we would first of all have to make an important creative leap. We would have to accept that whilst we would remain British linguistically and culturally, we would become citizens of the new Europe and should look to the European institutions for government, for foreign and economic policy and for general guidance. We should transfer our political loyalties to the EU whilst keeping our cultural loyalties closer to home. The UK is to a united EU as Wales is to the UK. Our national songs, sports teams and language would be no less powerfully supported because we had accepted government from a more distant capital, but we would have to accept that we were no longer a self-governing, independent democracy.

Britain might be able to make an important contribution to the development of such a United States of Europe. The obvious thing for Britain to do would be to say that one of the most disagreeable features of the way in which the EU is emerging is the concentration of power in the hands of unelected Commissioners and, to a lesser extent, in the hands of secretive ministers from national parliaments. If we truly wanted to be part of the great European project, it should be Britain that took upon itself the task of turning the European Parliament into a proper parliament, with powers to tax and to legislate. The government of Europe should emerge from that parliament and that government should be tried and tested through all the usual opposition guiles. Of course, it would require transnational parties, campaigning on transnational tickets and the creation of a whole series of issues which were seen as European issues rather than national issues handled in Brussels. The Commission would have to be scaled back to an active civil service, and the front men and women would have to emerge from the elected in the parliament itself. This would create a more democratic culture than we currently see in the emerging EU and would deal with some of the problems that people have identified in terms of lack of accountability and the democratic deficit.

Britain might be surprised to find that it could actually influence some of that, if at the same time it wanted to create a powerful state based around such a parliament with its own armies, currency, court system, legal codes and control of business. In the absence of any British leadership the terms available for British entry into the system are not good. We would become a province of the new European empire. We would be an important part of it, making a substantial contribution from our taxes to support the central government, but, as life has shown in recent years, we would have very little influence over what the government of that super-state did. The course is fully set out already by the French and German governments, and Britain is rather late to the game in trying to influence it. For my own part, I do not think it can work as I do not believe that the peoples of Western Europe are ready for such a revolution yet. Europe is designed to remain a bickering Tower of Babel, not a uniform and purposeful single country. There are no advantages for Britain in joining the present Franco-German scheme for a bigger government in Brussels. I doubt if we could make the EU genuinely democratic – we have left it too late. I do not think a country with so many languages, different histories and interests could come together and be at peace with itself. It is better not to try than to bring about decades of unrest and unease over the project itself. We do not want a United Europe full of Basque and Irish struggles against the central power.

Notes

Any study of the UK's relationship with the EU should begin with HMSO (1970); the Prime Minister's speech recommending membership, 28 October 1971, *Hansard*, cols 2197–2212; and *European Communities White Paper*, July 1971, London.

The European Central Bank has set out its views on the new euro currency in Duisenberg (1999).

The British government discusses the draft Treaty of Nice in *IGC: Reform for Enlargement* (2000).

Howe (1999) examines the issues which would need to be negotiated with the EU partners.

Brussels' ambitions to tax member states were set out in *Towards Tax Co-ordination in the European Union: A Package to Tackle Harmful Tax Competition*, Brussels, 1 October 1997.

The UK business case against more European integration is recorded in European Research Group (1998).

The background on the evolution of Europe is traced in Hill (1997), Booker and North (1994), Jamieson (1994), Hilton (1997) and Stevens (1997).

Leach (2004) is a good beginner's guide to the institutions viewed from a sceptical vantage point.

11
Conclusions

When I wrote *Stars and Strife* in the year 2001 I wrote:

> This book has demonstrated that the mighty project to create a United States of Europe is proceeding apace, but is unlikely to make the world a safer or better place. Instead, it is likely to lead to a trial of strength between two cultural and governing systems: the US democratic free trade one, and the Europe bureaucratic and regulated one. The 1950s and 1960s were dominated by a conflict between the communist and capitalist models, which was finally won without a shot being fired in anger between the two main protagonists, the US and the USSR, when the Western model proved so much more capable of delivering economic success. The next 20 years are likely to be dominated by a contest between the Europeans who think that governments can make societies better, and the North Americans who think free enterprise makes a bigger contribution to health and riches.
>
> The beginnings of the conflict are there for all to see, in the escalating trade disputes and the outlines of a row over independent European forces and foreign policy. US policy-makers will have to pull back from their enthusiasm for this emerging super-state and take stock of their position. They will find that what they may gain in a simpler command structure in Europe as one government displaces many, they will lose in terms of influence and friendship as that government sets out to rival the US. (pp. 182–3)

In the intervening three years the European Union has made further rapid progress towards asserting itself at home and abroad. It has taken more powers from the member states through the implementation of the Nice and Amsterdam Treaties; through the process of enlargement, bringing in ten countries to the east of the continent; and through the many steps it is taking in preparation for the ratification of the European Constitution. We have seen how an EU-led foreign policy took the EU into sharp dispute with the United States of America over how to handle the Middle East in general, and the problem of Iraq in particular. Trade disputes have continued to escalate and the European Union continues to press the case of EU champions against US rivals. Perhaps the most serious is the development of the Galileo communications and surveillance system, which has already led to threatening noises from the US about the danger for Europe and the world of the EU going it alone with military surveillance.

The new world of the Web, a global capital, of footloose businesses and of rapid technical change is teeming with opportunity. Although the internet revolution received a modest check to its ambitions in the early years of the twenty-first century, reflecting the over-expansion and euphoria at the end of the old century, growth has now resumed. The ability to route messages around the world opens up considerable scope for cross-border service sector trading. At the same time, the integration of the world market in manufacturers proceeds at a pace. All of this is making national and even continental politics look dated and insignificant. New technology will drive the changes in the way we work, shop and play. New technology will determine which people stay in jobs and which do not, which national and regional economies rise and which fall. The relentless movement of the global market is giving ever more scope to the English-speaking world to sell its computers, its information, its culture and its entertainment. The global market speaks English and transacts business primarily in dollars.

In the East the conditions are ripe for exploiting the opportunities globalisation creates. It is one of those ironies of the lobbies for greater fairness in incomes around the world, that often the same people arguing for more development in the poor world are also lobbying strongly against the export of jobs to that world from the West. Both India and China in recent years have shown that with Western capital and technology they can make rapid strides in improving their position. As the 1.3 billion Chinese and the 1.2 billion Indians raise their living standards and engage more fully in global trade, the consequences are felt in all four corners of the globe.

In 2004 we saw the first signs of the impact Chinese and Indian buying can have on the oil price, on the steel price, and on a number of other raw materials. Prices surged as Chinese and Indian manufacturing businesses bid them up in the marketplace. We should expect more of the same over the years ahead. Whilst there may be checks, reversals and disappointments in both Chinese and Indian growth, the trend is very clearly established. The Chinese and the Indians are determined to have better living standards. They will import the ideas, people and capital they need to achieve this. They will want a much bigger share of the world's natural resources as they industrialise and mechanise. By the time of the Beijing Olympic Games in 2008, we should expect China to be the third largest economy of the world when measured at market exchange rates, and the second largest economy in the world when measured taking into account relative costs of living. Even if the critics of China are right, and current growth levels cannot be sustained, the Chinese dragon has awakened and the direction of her progress is established. A banking crisis or political difficulties could slow her speedy progress, but are unlikely to put the Chinese economy into reverse for very long.

The US is keen to expand its influence and the geographical reach of its ideas. It will do so by expanding NAFTA, offering membership to some South American countries, and to other members of the Anglosphere. The US will also spread its belief in democracy through its foreign policy and sometimes by military interventions. The world is still moving towards democratic solutions for governments in most parts of the globe, although there is a danger to democracy in Russia and considerable difficulty in getting democracy to work well in many African states.

The fulcrum of world affairs for the foreseeable future is the Middle East. The explosive politics of the Arab-Israeli conflict, combined with the presence of substantial oil reserves, makes this of central interest to the United States. The US is hoping that by spreading democracies into the Arab world beyond the borders of Israel greater peace and prosperity will be achieved. Meanwhile the US is finding it difficult to retain the support of moderate Arab opinion following the military incursion into Iraq.

The US does not wish to end up friendless in the world. It was able to carry forward the Iraqi project on the back of British and old Commonwealth support. The Anglosphere rallied where the EU opposed and the Arab world expressed anger. If Britain throws in her lot with a common foreign and security policy in the EU the special relationship and the British alliance will no longer be a viable option for the US should it wish to embark on similar conflicts with other authoritarian or rogue states.

The US will be wary of picking a fight with China. Ever since President Nixon opened up friendlier lines of communication with the Chinese the US has been careful not to precipitate conflict. It is likely that American foreign policy will watch and manage the relationship as best it can, backing away from confrontation as China pursues her economic miracle. The US is posed with a huge dilemma as China succeeds in growing her economic strength. The US will try and prevent advanced military countries sharing weapons technology with China but will probably fail as the French, and through them the EU, seem very keen to offer military olive branches to China as she gets better at making plough shares. Only if China made a precipitant and foolish move against Taiwan would the wrath of America be aroused fully.

In the meantime the United States also has to manage its fractious relationship with the emerging European Union. All policymakers in Washington under the second George Bush are likely to conclude that dialling one number for Europe is not a good idea if there are French attitudes at the end of the phone line. Germany's flirtation with Russia, France's flirtation with China, and the whole EU's interest in creating a rival system and policy to the United States of America is beginning to ring alarm bells in the Pentagon and the White House. George Bush has built an unlikely special relationship with the Labour Prime Minister of the United Kingdom, Tony Blair. He has found Tony Blair to be a remarkably staunch ally, staying with the United States' President even when the domestic going was rough in the United Kingdom as a result. US policymakers will have to understand that such an option will not be possible in the future if the UK became a willing member of the European Union Constitution and the implied political union that goes with it.

The US has increased its lead over all the other countries of the world in the last ten years. Fashionable opinion in Japan in the late 1980s thought that America was tired and finished. The Japanese came to regret such hubris for it is the Japanese economy that plunged into difficult times from 1990 onwards. Many people in the EU in the run-up to the launch of the euro felt that they were close to toppling the mighty dollar, and to reducing or removing the gap between American income and productivity levels and European. Instead they too have been confounded, only to see the US outperform the EU in practically every year in the last decade, and to see the American lead grow rather than diminish.

It seems likely that American military, foreign policy and economic dominance will continue for the next decade. It seems very unlikely that the EU can change its attitudes and its policies sufficiently to reverse the relative decline. The EU is beginning to experience the problems of falling population. Over the fifty-year period from 2000 to 2050 the working age population of the fifteen original Western states in the EU is expected to fall, according to the United Nations' forecasts, by almost one-fifth compared with a rise of 31% in the projected US working age population. The decline is expected to be worst in Italy at 41%, followed by Spain at 35%, Greece 32%, Austria 29% and Germany 21%. Only Ireland and the United Kingdom out of the EU 15 are expected to see an increase in their working age populations.

The French Institut Français des Relations Internationales expects the EU's share of world trade to collapse from 22% in 2002 to only 12% in 2050, mirroring a similar decline in the relative importance of the national outputs of the EU compared with the rest of the world. This is likely to continue the trend of the last decade. Between 1995 and 2003 the United States' total output grew by one quarter whilst the EU's only grew by 16.8%. A combination of lower growth and a less successful application of technology to economic activity, and the big differences in population change, will mean that the US lead will continue to grow. The European Commission itself in its 2002 review believed that the EU 15 share of world output would only amount to 10% in 2050. Since it made that forecast, things have deteriorated relatively for the EU compared with Asia and America.

The United States of America will soon realise this fundamental truth about the huge change in world economic power currently under way. The US is likely to take the view that, although the EU can be a nuisance to it as it will often disagree with the Americans' view on environmental matters, trade matters, foreign policy and military affairs, the EU will not have the power to do anything about it. Over the next two decades, the EU will be increasingly confronted with the reality of its economic weakness and the relative decline in its importance in the world economy. Over-borrowed countries that are already taxing their citizens and businesses too much will not be able to raise substantial new sums of money to catch up with, let alone surpass, American military technology and military capability. As the EU thrashes around trying to buy in the technology necessary for surveillance control and communications, it discovers just how expensive and difficult it all is, given the length of the American lead.

The American view is that it is an internal European Union matter as to whether the EU is going to speak with one voice or many, and whether it is going to complete its political union or not. The official administration position is that the EU must make up its own mind and they will not seek to influence it. The one thing the United States will not tolerate is the idea that EU countries like Britain and France should maintain a seat on the Security Council of the United Nations and other international fora, if at the same time the EU demands or gains a seat on the UN Security Council in its own name. It is up to the member states to decide.

For the foreseeable future, the main American preoccupation is going to be how the mighty superpower protects herself, not against the economic and military challenges of the major countries and regional blocs of the world, but against terrorism, rogue states and military pressure groups. The United States will redouble her expenditure and efforts on intelligence and surveillance, recognising that only superior intelligence, knowing in advance the likely moves and intentions of terrorist groups and difficult regimes, can give the superpower any comfort and protection. The US will continue to see the Middle East as the most important part of the world where the dramas are acted out.

It seems clear that looking at the world in thirty to forty years' time, the EU will not have overtaken the US and will be massively smaller than the US, owing to poorer relative economic performance and population decline. Instead, on that time horizon, we will be living in a bipolar world where the riches and technological might of the United States of America has to take seriously the sheer scale of China emerging as the world's biggest economy, with by far and away the biggest military machine in terms of number of people in the armed services.

The United Kingdom has important decisions to make in the next couple of years. Once the British people have voted down the European Constitution, as they are likely to do, the British government has no choice but to negotiate a different kind of relationship between Britain and the continent. The UK has been waylaid too often by European squabbles when she should pursue her interests as a maritime and world trading nation. The best future for Britain is as an independent country, friendly to the continent and friendly with the United States. Our best hope is to keep a strong defence alliance going with the US, just as we have done since 1941 and the entry of the US into the Second World War. Britain will recognise that an increasing volume of her trade and investment activities will be with Asia and America as the numbers stack up against the continent of Europe.

It will not be an easy world for the superpower to police. We seem a long way distant from an independent Palestine living peacefully alongside an independent Israel, although it is an important first step on that long journey that the US and Israel have now recognised the need for an independent Palestine. There could be a number of flare-ups about access to natural resources around the world as Chinese and Indian demand becomes more and more influential in world markets. The West will have to get smarter and find ways of doing things that require less energy and less raw material input.

The new manufactory of the world is going to be in Asia. The West needs to innovate, to train and to grow its service economy. It is a sobering thought that the UK's manufacturing sector today only represents 13% of our total activity, and that remains vulnerable to the incessant pressures for change.

The Spanish Prime Minister's plaintive statement 'Europe must believe that it can be in 20 years the most important world power' will prove wide of the mark. It is difficult to know how much relative economic failure and lack of clout the member states will put up with over the years ahead. Today the direction of travel is still remorselessly in favour of the federal state and the centralising tendency. There are still Europeans dreaming dreams of a United States of Europe having the same kind of clout and influence in the world that the United States of America enjoys. The next twenty years will be a bitter time for such visionaries as they come to see that the EU lacks the wealth, the technology and the drive to become that world power they ache to be again. The truth is that the sun has long since set on the Spanish Empire, the French Empire and the British Empire. They cannot and should not be recreated in a different guise through the European Union. The United States has created a different kind of world. It is not one where the US wishes to occupy huge swathes of the globe with military force but it is one dominated by American multinationals, American ideas and American technology. The US wants the world to know it can see undesirable military activity anywhere on the planet and has the rapid and mobile means to intervene with force to block military action or destroy military force wherever it is deployed.

Governments that wish to succeed in this new environment must understand that there are many limits to their power. If they try to restrict individuals and businesses too much they will simply move away. The American and Soviet systems went head to head and the American one won by a mile because it backed freedom and enterprise more, and state planning and control less. Those who wish to succeed in the twenty-first century should learn that fundamental lesson of the twentieth.

We have seen how the UK and the US have worked together in the post-war world to create peace and stability, to defend threatened smaller nations and to advance the cause of democracy worldwide. The book sets out why it makes more sense to strengthen these ties for both sides than for the UK to become an important region in the new European state. Some US commentators ask, 'Why can't Britain be like Texas in the US union and accept the euro just as Texas accepts the dollar?' The answer is simple. Britain is not playing Texas to Germany's California. The correct analogy is between the national members of NAFTA and the position of Britain in Europe. No one in the US thinks that the US should surrender its dollar to join a new single currency system with Mexico and Canada, so why should Britain do that on the other side of the Atlantic?

The institutions that made up the post-1945 settlement are by and large still capable of adaptation to the emerging new conditions. Institutions like the Commonwealth are flexible, not too intrusive. They come together when there is a problem or a purpose. The WTO makes good progress in spreading free trade ever more widely. It is organisations that try to become alternative governments that threaten the spirit of the age, and threaten to burden participating countries beyond their patience.

The size and power of the new United States of Europe is quite considerable, but it is lopsided. It has a powerful potential army, but lacks capacity to operate beyond its own continent. It would be better if the European countries remained faithful members of NATO and the UN, not complicating matters by creating a new level of military organisation and bureaucracy. The economic strength is considerable, but the economies of the continent are inward-looking and the forces of protectionism are latent. The EU begins to look like an old organisation, developed from ideas that are now fifty years out of date. It is born of an era where coal and steel were the crucial industries, where agriculture was the dominant activity and where keeping France and Germany together was the most important issue. Today the problems are very different. There is no likelihood of modern Germany invading France, but a very cumbersome structure has been established just in case.

This book shows that the US has plenty of options, but should be careful about the EU. It also shows that the UK has plenty of choices, but needs to make up its mind soon on which way it is to go. The UK's decision on how much European integration to accept is awaited with baited breath on the continent of Europe. It should also be of great interest to Washington. If the UK chooses more freedom and democracy, it will mean a stronger transatlantic alliance and give a great boost to the forces of freedom everywhere. If the UK chooses further continental entanglements, it will be a dark day for freedom and free trade and will usher in a long period of international tension. Two systems will have to battle it out, with much more even forces on both sides. It will make for many conflicts, as European peoples wrestle against the new imperial power from within and the US comes to terms with it from without.

Meanwhile the trial of strength between the US and those rogue states and terrorist movements that have a very different world view is still in its infancy. The US will find it does not have all the cards on its side. Some religious movements will claim more loyalty than Western consumerism in some societies. Some newly created democracies will elect governments the US does not like, or even vote to be less democratic than the US thinks necessary. In some places the power of US ideas will overthrow tiresome regimes, in other places the force of US arms will do the job. However successful the war on terror, the US will come to recognise there are limits to the number of such regimes even the US can tackle, and there will remain movements, groups even whole nations who reject the US model. Some terrorist movements will not be curbed until the underlying injustices that generated them are solved. Others will continue whatever the justice of the US position.

The single most important thing to watch in the years ahead is the changing pace of demographic movements. Although the Anglosphere will continue to grow, mainly by allowing inward migration, the rise of Asia and the growth of Islamic populations will be far greater than the growth of the English-speaking peoples in their homelands. If for no other reason, the US as well as the UK has to understand that we share a world with these new peoples and we need to work out a way of living together in peace and mutual understanding.

Bibliography

Ashley, M. (1965) *England in the Seventeenth Century*. London: Penguin.

Bayne, N. (1997) 'Globalization and the Commonwealth', *The Round Table*, vol. 344.

Bogdanor, V. (1999) *Devolution in the United Kingdom*. Oxford: Oxford University Press.

Booker, C. and North, R. (1994) *The Mad Officials*. London: Constable.

British Management Data Foundation (1999) *Currency Volatility: The Steadiness of the £ sterling against the US Dollar*. Sheepscombe, Gloucestershire: BMDF.

British Management Data Foundation (2004) *The European Constitution in Perspective*. Sheepscombe, Gloucestershire: BMDF.

Bullock, A. (1952) *Hitler: A Study in Tyranny*. London: Penguin.

Chirac, J. (2000) 'Our Europe'. Speech at Berlin, 27 June.

Churchill, W. (1946) 'The Sinews of Peace'. Speech at Fulton, Missouri, 5 March.

Churchill, W. (1946) 'The Tragedy of Europe'. Speech at Zurich, 19 September.

Churchill, W. (1957) *History of the English Speaking Peoples*. London: Cassell.

Clark, A. (1998) *The Tories: Conservatives and the Nation State*. London: Weidenfeld and Nicolson.

Clark, J.C.D. (2003) *Our Shadowed Present: Modernism, Postmodernism and History*. London: Atlantic Books.

Commonwealth Yearbook (1998) *The Declaration of Principles*, Singapore, 1971; *The Lusaka Declaration*, Zambia, 1979; *The Harare Commonwealth Declaration*, Zimbabwe, 1991; *The Millbank Action Programme*, New Zealand, 1995.

Connolly, B. (1995) *The Rotten Heart of Europe*, London: Faber and Faber.

Davies, N. (1996) *Europe: A History*. Oxford: Oxford University Press.

Davis, S. and Meyer, C. (eds) (1998) *Blur*. Oxford: Capstone.

Duisenberg, W. (1999) 'A Stable Euro', *European Quarterly*, Autumn.

Elton, G.R. (1997) *England Under the Tudors*. London: Folio Society.

EU Competitiveness survey (2004) Brussels, November.

European Communities White Paper, July 1971.

Eurofacts (1999) Global Britain, 'How to Lose Market Share', 10 September. London.

Eurofacts (1999) *UK Trade in 1998 and Growth 1992–1998*. London.

Eurofacts (2000) Reports on shifting patterns of world trade in favour of the English-speaking world, 14 July, London.

European Research Group (1998) *Business Agenda for a Free Europe*. London: ERG (March).

Financial Times (2000) 'Early claims for the Euro', January.

Foreign Office (2000) *IGC: Reform for Enlargement*. London, February.

Gertz, Bill. (2004) *Treachery. How America's Friends and Foes are Secretly Arming our Enemies*. New York: Random House.

Gidoomal, R., Mahtani, D. and Porter, D. (2001) *The British and How to Deal with Them*. Middlesex University Press.

Gillingham, J. (2003) *European Integration 1950–2003*. New York and Cambridge: Cambridge University Press.

Global Britain (1999) *UK Trade in 1998 and Growth 1992–1998*. London.

Gough, R. (ed.) (2003) *Regime Change: It's Been Done Before*. London: Policy Exchange.

Grenville, J.A.S. (1976) *Europe Reshaped 1848–1878*, Fontana History of Europe. London: Fontana.

Hansard, Official Report of Parliamentary debates, 7 July 1971, cols 1338–1341; 28 October 1971, cols 2197–2212.

HMSO (1970) *Britain and the European Communities: An Economic Assessment*. London: HMSO.

HMSO (2004) *Provisional Text of the Constitutional Treaty for the EU*. London: HMSO, July.

HM Treasury (2004) *Long Term Global Economic Opportunities for the UK*. December.

Heffer, S. (1999) *Nor Shall My Sword*. London: Weidenfeld and Nicolson.

Hill, S. (ed.) (1997) *Visions of Europe*. London: Gerald Duckworth.

Hilton, A. (1997) *The Principality and Power of Europe*. Hertfordshire: Dorchester House.

Hitchens, P. (1999) *The Abolition of Britain*. London: Quartet Books.

House of Commons Foreign Affairs Select Committee, *The Future Role of the Commonwealth* House of Commons Paper 45, 1995–6 Session.

Howe, M. (1999) *Could the UK Join a Global Free Trade Association?* London: IEA.

Howell, D. (1998) 'The Place of the Commonwealth in the International Order', *The Round Table*, vol. 345.

IBRD (1989) *Articles of Agreement*, 16 February.

IMF (1945) Founding Agreement. Bretton Woods: IMF.

Index of Economic Freedom 2004. Washington and New York.

Jamieson, B. (1994) *Britain beyond Europe*. London: Gerald Duckworth.

Jamieson, B. and Minford, P. (1999) *Britain and Europe: Choices for Change*. London: Politico.

Jenkins, S. (1995) *Accountable to None*. London: Hamish Hamilton.

Kohl, H. (1991) 'Our Future in Europe'. Speech at Edinburgh, 23 May.

Kohl, H. (1992) 'The European Process in Irreversible'. Speech at Munich, May.

Kohl, H. (1998) 'Speech on Receiving the Honorary Freedom of the City of London'. 18 February.

Leach, R. (2004) *Europe: A Concise Encyclopaedia*. 4th edn. London: Profile Books.

Lindemann, B. (ed.) (1995) *America Within Us*. Mainz: Hase and Koehler Verlag.

Marr, A. (2000) *The Day Britain Died*. London: Profile Books.

Marshall, P. (1998) 'The United Kingdom, the Commonwealth and the EU', *The Round Table*, vol. 347.

Mortimer, E. (ed.) (1999) *People, Nations and State: The Meaning of Ethnicity and Nationalism*. London: I.B. Tauris.

NATO (1949) *The North Atlantic Treaty*, Washington, DC, 4 April.

Nye, R.B. and Morpurgo, J.E. (1955) *A History of the United States*. London: Penguin.

Official Journal of the European Communities 30.6.2000 Decision No. 2/2000 of the EC–Mexico Joint Council of 23 March 2000 (the EU/Mexico Trade Agreement).

Redwood, J. (1999) *The Death of Britain?* Basingstoke: Macmillan.

Redwood, J. (2001) *Just Say No*. London: Politico's.

Redwood, J. (2001) *Stars and Strife*. Basingstoke: Palgrave Macmillan.

Rosenbaum, M. (ed.) (2001) *Britain and Europe: The Choices We Face*. Oxford: Oxford University Press.

Rude, G. (1965) *Revolutionary Europe 1783–1815*, Fontana History of Europe. London: Fontana.

Sampson, A. (1965) *Anatomy of Britain*. London: Hodder and Stoughton.

Sampson, A. (1982) *The Changing Anatomy of Britain*. London: Hodder and Stoughton.

Stevens, R. (1997) *About Europe*. London: Bluebell Press.

Thomson, D. (1972) *Europe since Napoleon*. London: Penguin.

Towards Tax Co-ordination in the European Union: A Package to Tackle Harmful Tax Competition (1997) Brussels, 1 October.

van Buitenen, P. (2000) *Blowing the Whistle*. London: Politico's.

Walker, P. Gordon (1970) *The Cabinet*. London: Fontana.

World Trade Organisation, Agreement establishing the World Trade Organisation. Marrakesh, 15 April 1994.

Index